Foreign Policy Analysis

Classic and Contemporary Theory

Valerie M. Hudson

ROWMAN & LITTLEFIELD PUBLISHERS, INC.
Lanham • Boulder • New York • Toronto • Plymouth, UK

ROWMAN & LITTLEFIELD PUBLISHERS, INC.

Published in the United States of America
by Rowman & Littlefield Publishers, Inc.
A wholly owned subsidiary of The Rowman & Littlefield Publishing Group, Inc.
4501 Forbes Boulevard, Suite 200, Lanham, Maryland 20706
www.rowmanlittlefield.com

Estover Road, Plymouth PL6 7PY, United Kingdom

British Library Cataloguing in Publication Information Available

Library of Congress Cataloging-in-Publication Data

Hudson, Valerie M., 1958–
  Foreign policy analysis : classic and contemporary theory / Valerie M. Hudson.
    p. cm.
  Includes bibliographical references and index.
  ISBN-13: 978-0-7425-1688-5 (cloth : alk. paper)
  ISBN-10: 0-7425-1688-1 (cloth : alk. paper)
  ISBN-13: 978-0-7425-1689-2 (pbk. : alk. paper)
  ISBN-10: 0-7425-1689-X (pbk. : alk. paper)
    1. International relations—Decision making.   2. International relations—
Psychological aspects.   I. Title.
JZ1253.H83   2006
327.101—dc22

                                                                    2006018732

Printed in the United States of America

♾ ™The paper used in this publication meets the minimum requirements of
American National Standard for Information Sciences—Permanence of Paper for
Printed Library Materials, ANSI/NISO Z39.48-1992.

Foreign Policy Analysis

Contents

Acknowledgments   vii

Part I: Overview and Evolution of Foreign Policy Analysis

1   Introduction: The Situation and Evolution of Foreign Policy Analysis: A Road Map   3

Part II: Levels of Analysis

2   The Individual Decisionmaker: The Political Psychology of World Leaders   37

3   Group Decisionmaking: Small Group Dynamics, Organizational Process, and Bureaucratic Politics   65

4   Culture and National Identity   103

5   Domestic Politics and Opposition   125

6   The Levels of National Attributes and International System: Effects on Foreign Policy   143

Part III: Putting It All Together, or Not

7   Theoretical Integration in Foreign Policy Analysis: Promise and Frustration   165

8   The Future of Foreign Policy Analysis—and You   185

Bibliography   195

Index   217

About the Author   225

Acknowledgments

This book has taken many long years to complete, and I would be remiss if I did not thank all of those who helped and supported me along the way. First, to Jennifer Knerr for having faith in my vision of a Foreign Policy Analysis textbook. Second, to Renee Legatt and Susan McEachern for so seamlessly picking up where Jennifer left off. Third, to Douglas Van Belle, for his helpful suggestions on one of the early chapters, and to Rose McDermott for friendship and good suggestions. Fourth, I would like to thank my old mentors in Foreign Policy Analysis, such as Donald Sylvan, Chuck Hermann, and Peg Hermann, for the excellent education they provided and the passion for Foreign Policy Analysis they inspired in me. Fifth, I would like to thank my research assistant, S. Matthew Stearmer, for all of his help, especially with the ins and outs of graphics inserted into text files. Sixth, I would like to thank those publishers who graciously granted me permission to use some of my writings previously published with them, including Palgrave, Blackwell, and Lynne Rienner. Seventh, I would like to thank my Foreign Policy Analysis students, past, present, and future, for all that they have taught me in years past and will teach me in the years to come. Last, but certainly not least, I would like to thank my family—my husband David and my children Joseph, John, Thomas, and Jamison—for their unflagging support. I wish to dedicate this volume to my dear daughter, Ariel, who died as I was finishing it. We will be together in the eternities, Ariel, and if you wish it, I will tell you all about Foreign Policy Analysis then.

I

OVERVIEW AND EVOLUTION OF FOREIGN POLICY ANALYSIS

1

Introduction: The Situation and Evolution of Foreign Policy Analysis: A Road Map

Every theoretical discipline has a ground. A "ground" means the conceptualization of the fundamental or foundational level at which phenomena in the field of study occur. So, for example, the ground of physics is now that of matter and antimatter particles. Economists often use the ground of firms or households. It is upon such ground that theories are built, modified, and even discarded. Sometimes just the knowledge that the ground exists frees the researcher from having to anchor his or her work in it, permitting greater heights of abstraction to be reached. A physicist can work on problems related to black holes, and economists can speak of trends in world markets without having to begin each new research effort by going over the ground of their respective disciplines.

International Relations (IR) as a field of study has a ground, as well. All that occurs between nations and across nations is grounded in human decisionmakers acting singly or in groups. In a sense, the ground of IR is thus the same ground of all the social sciences. Understanding how humans perceive and react to the world around them, and how humans shape and are shaped by the world around them, is central to the inquiry of social scientists, even those in IR.

However, your previous training in IR probably gave you the impression that states are the ground of International Relations. Or, in slightly alternative language, that whatever decision-making unit is involved, be it a state or a human being or a group of humans, that that unit can be modeled as a unitary rational actor and therefore be made equivalent to the state. Sometimes this approach is referred to as "black-boxing" the state, or as a "billiard ball model" of state interaction. You may have even been taught that IR is *not* the study of foreign policymaking.

Alas, dear students, you have been taught amiss.

If you are taking this course, then someone in your department feels that the ground of IR is human decisionmakers who are not best approximated as strictly unitary rational actors, and who are not equivalent to the state. And, furthermore, that "the state" is a metaphysical abstraction that is useful as a shorthand for IR's ground, but cannot be a realistic conceptualization of it. In this course, you are entering a realm of IR theory that you may have never been exposed to otherwise; remember to thank your professor for this opportunity.

HALLMARKS OF FOREIGN
POLICY ANALYSIS THEORY

If the ground of IR is human decisionmakers acting singly or in groups, several other theoretical hallmarks follow naturally and serve to characterize Foreign Policy Analysis (FPA).

Explanandum: That Which Is to Be Explained in FPA

The explanandum, or that which is to be explained or understood, will be decisions taken by human decisionmakers with reference to or having known consequences for entities external to their nation-state. Such decisions may include inaction and indecision. Usually such decisions directly target external entities in the form of influence attempts, but may include decisions that target domestic entities but have ramifications for external entities. One may be examining not a single decision, but a constellation of decisions taken with reference to a particular situation. Furthermore, decisions may be modified over time, requiring an examination of sequences of decisions. Also, the stages of decisionmaking may be the focus of inquiry, from problem recognition, framing, and perception to more advanced stages of goal prioritization, contingency planning, and option assessment. Last, FPA traditionally finds itself most interested in decisions taken by human decisionmakers in positions of authority to commit the resources of the nation-state, though it is quite possible to analyze decisionmakers who do not hold such positions.

Indeed, the only things not examined are likely to be accidents or mistakes, or decisions that cannot be conceptualized as having an international component. In the first case, the action was not purposeful. It is difficult to explain nonpurposeful action. In the second case, the decision can be analyzed, but probably would not be analyzed by foreign policy analysts, but rather domestic policy analysts. However, the same conceptual and methodological tools used in FPA may still be useful in examining non-foreign policy decisions. That is, what you learn in FPA may help you to analyze human decisionmaking regardless of substantive focus.

In the world of foreign policy, however, the actual decisions (or indecisions) made may not be immediately observable to the analyst. Indeed, they may be secret, and may remain so for decades due to national security concerns. In many cases, this means the analyst is working with historical data, or contemporary data insofar as public sources provide that information (which may be incomplete or even false). Though these are by far the most common approaches, another approach is to use artifacts of decisions—the traces that decisions leave in newspapers or chronologies. These are termed "events," and the data produced by accumulating them are called "events data." We will examine events data in more detail in a following section of this chapter.

Explanans: That Which Will Provide Explanation in FPA

The explanans of FPA are those factors that influence foreign policy decisionmaking and foreign policy decisionmakers. The totality of such influence factors is overwhelming: for example, some studies have shown decisionmaking to be affected by the color of the room in which the decision is made! From its inception, critiques of FPA have centered around the impossibility of tracing all influences on a given decision, or even on decisionmaking in the abstract. Here, for example, is a critique from over forty years ago, which seems as contemporary today as when it was written:

> The inordinate complexity of [FPA] as it has so far been outlined is unquestionably its greatest shortcoming, one which in the end many prove its undoing. . . . A research design that requires an investigator to collect detailed information about such diverse matters as the social system, the economy, the foreign situation, the actors, the perceptions, the motivations, the values, the goals, the communication problems, the personality—in short, that asks him to account for a decision making event virtually *in its totality*—places a backbreaking burden upon him, one that he could never adequately accomplish even if he were willing to invest an exorbitant effort. If the mere magnitude of the task does not frighten him off, he is likely to be discouraged by the unrewarding prospect of having to collect data about a great number of variables whose relative importance he can only guess at and whose influence he cannot easily measure in any event (McClosky, 1962, 201).

Such criticism has been used to justify the move to use the nation-state or other abstractions as the principal actor in the study of IR. After all, if FPA research is too difficult, alternative traditions of theorizing must come to the fore. It has also been used as a reason to marginalize scholarship that retains use of the human decisionmaker as its theoretical focus. If most IR scholarship treats the nation-state or similar abstractions as the ground, then most IR scholarship will feel incommensurable with FPA scholarship.

However, such conclusions are not necessary, for the original critique of FPA's complexity is not completely accurate. It is true that two of the hallmarks of FPA scholarship are that it views the explanation of foreign policy decisionmaking as **multifactorial**, with the desideratum of examining variables from more than one level of analysis (**multilevel**). Explanatory variables from all levels of analysis, from the most micro to the most macro, are of interest to the analyst to the extent that they affect the decisionmaking process. As a result, insights from many intellectual disciplines, such as psychology, sociology, organizational behavior, anthropology, economics, and so forth, will be useful for the foreign policy analyst in efforts to explain foreign policy decisionmaking, making **multi-/interdisciplinarity** a third hallmark of FPA. Thus, of all subfields of IR, FPA is the most radically **integrative** theoretical enterprise, which is its fourth hallmark, for it integrates a variety of information across levels of analysis and spanning numerous disciplines of human knowledge.

It is also true that the ground of the human decisionmaker leads us toward an emphasis on **agent-oriented** theory, this being a fifth hallmark of FPA. States are not agents because states are abstractions and thus have no agency. Only human beings can be true agents. Going further, FPA theory is also profoundly **actor-specific** in its orientation (to use a term coined by Alexander George [1993]), unwilling to "black box" the human decisionmakers under study. The humans involved in the Cuban missile crisis, for example, were not interchangeable generic rational utility maximizers and were not equivalent to the states that they served. Not just general and abstract information, but specific and concrete information about the decisionmakers in all three countries (the Soviet Union, the United States, and Cuba) would be necessary to explain that crisis. Actor specificity, then, is FPA's sixth hallmark. The perspective of FPA is that the source of all international politics and all change in international politics is specific human beings using their agency and acting individually or in groups.

It is not true that FPA is impossible as a theoretical task. And it is not true that state-centered IR theory and FPA theory are incommensurable. In fact, I will argue that FPA cannot be impossible, for one of the consequences of this would be that IR could not exist as a field of social science scholarship. And if FPA is integral to the IR endeavor, then state-centered IR theory and FPA theory cannot be incommensurable. Furthermore, FPA offers a real grounding of IR theory, which provides real value in IR theorizing, as we shall explore.

FPA IS POSSIBLE AND VALUABLE TO IR (AND COMPARATIVE AND POLICY STUDIES)

The single most important contribution of FPA to IR theory is to identify the point of theoretical intersection between the most important determinants of state behavior: material and ideational factors. The point of intersection is *not* the state, it is human decisionmakers.

If our IR theories contain no human beings, they will erroneously paint for us a world of no change, no creativity, no persuasion, no accountability. And yet virtually none of our mainstream IR theories over the decades of the Cold War placed human beings in the theoretical mix. Adding human decisionmakers as the key theoretical intersection confers some advantages generally lacking in IR theory. Let us explore each in turn.

First, theories at different levels of analysis can finally be integrated in a meaningful fashion. As Snyder, Bruck, and Sapin put it over forty years ago,

> The central concept of decision-making may provide a basis for linking a group of theories which hitherto have been applicable only to a segment of international politics or have not been susceptible of application at all. . . . By emphasizing decision-making as a central focus, we have provided a way of organizing the determinants of action around those officials who act for the political society, Decision makers are viewed as operating in dual-aspect setting so that apparently unrelated internal and external factors become related in the actions of the decision-makers (1962, 74 and 85).

In IR, there are quite a number of well-developed theoretical threads, studying such phenomena as institutions, systems, group dynamics, domestic politics, and so forth. Often we refer to the "two-level" game that state decisionmakers must play: the simultaneous play of the game of domestic politics and the game of international politics (Putnam, 1988). The formidable task of weaving these threads together has been stymied by the insistence on retaining the state as a "metaphysical" actor. If one replaces metaphysics with a more realistic conceptualization of "actor," the weaving becomes feasible, though certainly still complex.

In addition, other types of theory that have not been well developed in IR, such as a theory of how cultural factors and social constructions within a culture affect state behavior, can now be attempted with a greater probability of success. It was not until the 1990s that serious work on this subject by IR scholars became more accepted as informing the major theoretical questions of the discipline (e.g., Katzenstein, 1996; Lapid and Kratochwil, 1996; Hudson, 1997). Only a move toward placing human decisionmakers at the center of the theoretical matrix would allow the theorist to link to the social constructions present in a culture.

The engine of theoretical integration in IR, then, is the definition of the situation created by the human decisionmakers.

The second major advantage conferred is the possibility of incorporating a more robust concept of agency into IR theory. Scholars in IR have struggled with the "agent-structure" problematique for some time now. Though no final resolution will ever be accepted, as this is a perennial philosophical conundrum, what is accepted is that IR theory currently provides much more insight into structure than agency. This is a severe theoretical handicap, for to lack a robust concept of the "agent" in IR means to be at a disadvantage when trying to explain or project significant change and noteworthy creativity. In FPA, we often speak of the concept of "foreign policy substitutability" (Most and Starr, 1986); that is to say, for any possible combination of material and structural conditions, there will still be variability in resulting foreign policy. FPA's agent-oriented and actor-specific theory is what is required in attempting to explain that variability. Furthermore, it is very difficult to grapple with the issue of accountability in international affairs if the theoretical language cannot, in a realistic fashion, link acts of human agency in that realm to the consequences thereof. That a standing international court to try individuals for crimes against humanity now exists suggests that the broader world community hungers after ideational frameworks that manifest the agency embedded in international affairs. Work in FPA empowers IR scholars to make an appreciated contribution in that regard.

The third major advantage is to move beyond description or postulation of natural lawlike generalizations of state behavior to a fuller and more satisfying explanation for state behavior that requires an account of the contributions of human beings. Again, as it was put decades ago by some of the founding fathers of FPA,

> We believe that the phenomena normally studied in the field of international politics can be interpreted and meaningfully related by means of [the decision-making approach] as we shall present it. It should be clearly understood that this is *not* to say that *all* useful work in the field must or can be done within the decision-making framework. . . . However, and the qualification is crucial, if one wishes to probe the "why" questions underlying the events, conditions, and interaction patterns which rest upon state action, then decision-making analysis is certainly necessary. We would go so far as to say *that the "why" questions cannot be answered without analysis of decision making* (Snyder, Bruck, and Sapin, 1962, 33).

Social science is unlike the physical sciences in that what is analyzed possesses agency. Neither description of an act of agency, nor assertion that natural law was operative in a particular case of the use of agency, can fully satisfy, for we know that agency means the agent could have acted otherwise. What is required is almost an anthropology of IR that delves into such agency-oriented concepts as motivation, emotion, and problem representation. Indeed, much of the early empirical work in FPA (see, for example, Snyder and Paige, 1958) does resemble a more anthropological or "verstehen" approach. (It may be for this reason that more bridges have been built between FPA and constructivist schools of IR than, say, between FPA and neorealist schools.)

Again, some would argue that this methodological approach proves unworkable for IR scholars. It might be true that if such research cannot be performed, then the state of current IR theory makes sense: abstractions are of necessity at the heart of our theories, agency vanishes, and to the extent that we speak of the power of ideational forces, we can only speak of them in a vague way, as if they were elusive mists that float through the theoretical landscape. But a rebuttal could be as follows: even if only a few IR scholars are willing to undertake FPA work, it salvages the entire enterprise of IR theorizing from irrelevance and vacuity. One can justify using shorthand if there is a full language underlying that use. We can justify theoretical shorthand in IR (e.g., using the metaphysical state as an actor) if we understand what spelling our sentences out in the underlying language would look like and what the meaning of those sentences would be in that fuller language. If *someone* is willing to write in the full language, we can still translate the shorthand. It is only if the shorthand completely replaces the fuller language that we are truly impoverished in a theoretical sense in IR. It is when we stop wincing slightly when the abstraction of the state is used as a theoretical actor, when we feel fully comfortable with the omission of the real human actors behind the abstraction, that we have lost something profoundly important in IR.

The fourth major benefit derived from FPA research is that it is often a natural bridge from IR to other fields, such as comparative politics and public policy. FPA's ability to speak to domestic political constraints and contexts provides a common language between FPA and comparative politics. Indeed, some of the most interesting FPA work in recent years has featured teams of FPA theorists and country or regional experts collaborating on specific theoretical projects (*International Studies Review*, special issue Summer 2001). Similarly, FPA research also shares a common language with public policy researchers. FPA's focus on decisionmaking allows for a fairly free exchange, but one that needs more explicit emphasis (George, 1993).

In sum, then, the existence of FPA scholarship provides several important benefits to the field of IR, many of which are only now beginning to become apparent to more mainstream IR researchers.

An Example: Waltz, Wendt, and FPA

An example using IR theorists with whose work most IR students are familiar might be useful here. Let's examine the debate between the neorealist work of Kenneth Waltz (1979) and the social constructionist work of Alexander Wendt (1999). In Waltz's neorealism, states are very much the archetypal black boxes, whose preferences are shaped primarily by power distributions within the system of states. Wendt contends ideas construct preferences and interests; that is, the material world is what the ideal world makes of it. Of course, it is not "ideas all the way down," for there is a material reality ruling out certain ideas somewhere: for example, land-locked Malawi is never going to be a naval power. Barring an examination of that material bedrock, then, a focus on ideational social constructs at the system level, with their production and reproduction, should explain everything neorealism and neoliberalism can explain, and more that they cannot, according to Wendt. In some specified situations, neorealism and neoliberalism can be used as more parsimonious shortcuts, but you could not know what those situations would be in advance of a constructivist analysis.

The beauty of Wendt's approach is twofold: first, you can have a system change without a material change (the system change would be based on ideational change: very important to have in IR theory since the end of the Cold War!), and second, arguably materially dissimilar states can act similarly, and arguably materially similar states can act dissimilarly, depending on their ideationally constructed identities within the state system (also helpful in this era of almost two hundred state entities with a dizzying variety of intelligible behavior). Between Waltz and Wendt, the agent–structure debate concerns whether structures, defined objectively, are primary shapers of system behavior (Waltz), or whether state actors help shape the structures and resultant behavior through their intersubjective understandings (Wendt). It is to Wendt's credit that he pointed out that the new clothes have no emperor (i.e., that structuralist IR theories have a woefully inadequate conception of the role of ideational social constructs), and that he helped initiate this version of the agent–structure debate in IR theory.

But there is an FPA critique that applies not only to the billiard ball world of Waltz's states but also to Wendt's world of ideational forces, as well. That FPA critique is simple: only human beings have ideas. Only human beings can create identities, only human beings can change identities, only human beings can act on the basis of identity. Only humans can be socialized or socialize others. Only humans are agents in international relations. It isn't "ideas all the way down," it is *human agents* all the way down, standing on the material bedrock noted above, sprouting ideas, persuading each other of the value of those ideas and attempting to transmit them forward in time through processes such as institutionalization. When you drop those humans out, you are left with a machine. Waltz dropped both humans and their ideas out of the mix, and he is left with a deterministic machine that cannot change without material change. Wendt only dropped humans, but not ideas, from his mix: curiously, he, too, is left with a machine—a machine that trumpets the possibility of change while being incapable of it. And FPA critique would suggest that Wendt and Waltz *have no adequate conceptualization of agency at all.*

In a way, this is more of a problem for Wendt than it is for Waltz, for Wendt claims to have developed a theory of how agents and structures co-construct one another, whereas Waltz is only interested in structure's causal effects on patterns of behavior in the system. Waltz never wanted agents; Wendt says he has them, but doesn't.

Why is this a problem? It is only a problem in relation to your explanatory ends. For Waltz, it is a problem for all the reasons Wendt says it is. Waltz simply cannot explain the range of behavior that Wendt can. As Rose succinctly put it, "Realism . . . is a theoretical hedgehog: it knows one big thing, that systemic forces and relative material power shape state behavior. . . . Yet people who cannot move beyond the system will have difficulty explaining most of what happens in international relations" (1998, 165). And as Vasquez maintains, the deductive inferences from neorealism come to resemble a vast definitional tautology in which everything—and nothing—can be explained (1997). In terms of the aims of explanation in any field, though neorealism might give us some small satisfaction for the first aim (how am I to understand what is going on?), it offers very little for the second (what's going to happen in the future?), and nothing for the third (what can I, or any of us, do to influence international relations in a desired direction?). Eventually, when you leave out both humans and their ideas in social science—and insist on theoretical autonomy from theories that leave them in—you end up with theory that cannot inform practice, theory fit only for the intellectual jousts of academic journals. This is theory that measures the size of the cage you are trapped in.

For Wendt, the problem is more nuanced. By leaving in ideas, but omitting true agency, he leaves ideas in the realm of the untouchable zeitgeist. (Indeed, it is interesting to think of Wendt playing Hegel to Waltz's Marx.) The ideas are there, but they have no handles for us to hold and turn, due in large part to what Colin Wight has noted: "the state may not be an agent at all but a structure" (1999, 136), More specifically:

1) one cannot explain current identity by examining only system-level phenomena;

2) one cannot explain identity formation (where current identities came from) by examining only system-level phenomena; and

3) one cannot explain identity change (what current identities are becoming next) by examining only system-level phenomena.

Checkel rightly notes, "without more sustained attention to agency, [constructivist] scholars will find themselves unable to explain where their powerful social structures come from in the first place, and, equally important, why and how they change over time. Without theory, especially at the domestic level, constructivists will not be able to explain in a systematic way how social construction actually occurs or why it varies cross-nationally" (1998, 339). Though one could make a case for each of the above three points of inadequacy, let us just take the last, for its importance is greater than a first glance would suggest. The end of the Cold War allowed for the constructivist turn in IR because it was apparent that you could get meaningful change in the system absent any material change. (Of course, die-hard neorealists answer that there was no meaningful change in the system, but since this stance puts them outside the pale of common sense, this serves only to open the window wider for alternative approaches [Waltz, 2000].) Something ideational had to be going on.

The salient theoretical question then becomes, How is it that ideas can change the behavior of agents? Wendt spends an entire chapter of his book (1999), ironically entitled "Process and Structural Change," evading this very question. He discusses how four master variables might facilitate such change, but admits tacitly that the effect of these variables cannot take place in the absence of "ideological labor" (1999, 352). Such labor must be undertaken volitionally, and may have to be continued in the face of no reciprocity by others in the system of interaction. Someone has to trust first; someone has to restrain himself first; someone has to conceptualize a common fate first; someone has to read the other's mind first before any mutually constituting behavior can derive from interaction between states. Throughout the chapter, Wendt speaks of "leadership," "bright ideas" (347), framing "entrepreneurs" (353), "ideological labor" (352), imagining of "communities" (355). But *states* are not in a position to do any such things—which is why Wendt is left with these generally agent-obscuring circumlocutions to explain how change really does occur. But these contortionist's moves only cause us to see what he would rather we not, which is: only human agents working through a state apparatus can do something first in a state system.

Wight hits the nail on the head:

Wendt advocates a structurationist solution to the agent-structure problem at the level of the state and state system, and a structuralist solution at the level of the individual and the state. . . . But the state, as a constructed social form, can only act in and through individual action. State activity is always the activity of particular individuals acting within particular social forms. . . . None of this is to deny of a common intention, or collective action, which individuals try to realize in their practices. Nor is this to deny the reality of social structures that enable common action. Nor does denial of the "state-as-agent" thesis entail that there can be no common and coordinated action which is a bearer of causal powers greater than that possessed by individuals acting individually. But such causal power that does emerge as a result of the cooperative practices of collectives can only be accessed by individuals acting in cooperation with others. . . . The theory of the state articulated by the agent-structure writers, on the other hand, neglects these points and there is no space for human agency (1999, 128).

This is a special handicap for Wendt, who aspires to a reflexive practice of IR: "the possibility of thinking self-consciously about what direction to go in" (1999, 375). He hopes there can be "engineering" or "steering" of the states system, a "design orientation to international life . . . which would give students of facts and students of values in world politics something to talk about" (1999, 376–77). But how can his theory in its current formulation bring us closer to such a realization? After all, there is no ghostly Structural Engineer; there is no ghostly Structural Steering Force—in the end, *there is only us.* There is only human agency. Theories that pull a veil over that human agency hurt our ability to go in a preferred value direction. Such theories impoverish our agency, for they blind us to its reality and its power. FPA-style theories provide a helpful corrective to this theoretical conundrum.

For example, consider research by Barbara Farnham that testifies to this real power of agency. Farnham's work concerns the Reagan side of the ideational change that finished the Cold War. (The quotes that follow are all from Farnham, 2002). IR scholars such as Jeffrey Checkel have illuminated the intra-Russian politics of the time, and he is able to point out to us which actual human beings in which role positions chose to become policy entrepreneurs, and how their activities affected Mikhail Gorbachev (Checkel, 1993). Farnham takes the U.S. side of the story, showing that none of Reagan's core beliefs prepared him to trust Gorbachev. Indeed, many of his closest advisors who shared those beliefs never would. Only Reagan himself was willing to trust first. From the Moscow summit of 1988, we hear Reagan say, "Systems can be brutish, bureaucrats may fail. But men can sometimes transcend all that, transcend even the forces of history that seem destined to keep them apart." We hear him comment, "perhaps the deepest impression I had during this experience and other meetings with Soviet citizens was that they were generally indistinguishable from people I had seen all my life on countless streets in America."

For Gorbachev, the emotions ran equally deep. Farnham says, "years later, Edmund Morris asked Gorbachev what he saw when he looked up into Ronald Reagan's eyes [the first time]. 'Sunshine and clear sky. . . . At once I felt him to be a very authentic human being.'" The translator tries to explain further that the Russian term Gorbachev used means "someone of great strength of character who rings true, all the way through to his body and soul. . . . He has—'Kalibr,' said Gorbachev, who has been listening intently." Gorbachev further explained to the Politburo,

> In Washington, perhaps for the first time, we understood so clearly how important the human factor is in international politics. . . . For us, Reagan appeared as a representative of and a spokesman for the most conservative part of the most conservative segment of American capitalism and the military-industrial complex.
>
> But . . . policymakers . . . also represent purely human qualities, the interests and aspirations of common people, and that they can be guided by purely normal human feeling and aspirations. . . . *This is an important aspect of the new international thinking, and it has now produced results* [Italics added].

How is it that accounting for human agency is not an important aspect of the new International *Relations* thinking? Our IR data is impregnated through and through with human agency—how is it we do not feel obliged to include it in our theories, even after we have seen its spectacular power displayed right before our very eyes so recently? What else could IR be for? And that, in a nutshell, is why FPA exists, and why it must exist as an integral part of IR theory.

A ROAD MAP OF FPA: FPA'S BEGINNINGS AND THREE PARADIGMATIC WORKS

What are the origins of FPA? In one sense, FPA-style work has been around as long as there have been historians and others who have sought to understand why national leaders have made the choices they did regarding interstate relations. But FPA-style work within the field of International Relations per se is best dated back to the late 1950s and early 1960s.

Three paradigmatic works arguably built the foundation of Foreign Policy Analysis:

- *Decision-Making as an Approach to the Study of International Politics* by Richard C. Snyder, H. W. Bruck, and Burton Sapin (1954: also see Snyder, Bruck, and Sapin, 1963; reprinted in 2002).
- "Pre-Theories and Theories of Foreign Policy" by James N. Rosenau (a book chapter written in 1964 and published in Farrell, 1966).

- *Man-Milieu Relationship Hypotheses in the Context of International Politics* by Harold and Margaret Sprout (1956: expanded and revised in article form in 1957 and their 1965 book *The Ecological Perspective on Human Affairs with Special Reference to International Politics*).

The work of Richard Snyder and his colleagues inspired researchers to look *below* the nation-state level of analysis to the players involved:

We adhere to the nation-state as the fundamental level of analysis, yet we have discarded the state as a metaphysical abstraction. By emphasizing decision-making as a central focus we have provided a way of organizing the determinants of action around those officials who act for the political society. Decision-makers are viewed as operating in dual-aspect setting so that apparently unrelated internal and external factors become related in the actions of the decision-makers. Hitherto, precise ways of relating domestic factors have not been adequately developed (Snyder, Bruck, and Sapin, 1954, 53).

In taking this approach, Snyder and his colleagues bequeathed to FPA its characteristic emphasis on foreign policy *decisionmaking* (FPDM) as versus foreign policy *outcomes*. Decisionmaking was best viewed as "organizational behavior," by which the basic determinants would be spheres of competence of the actors involved, communication and information flow, and motivations of the various players. Desirable explanations would thus be both multicausal and interdisciplinary.

James Rosenau's pre-theorizing encouraged scholars to systematically and scientifically tease out cross-nationally applicable generalizations about nation-state behavior.

To identify factors is not to trace their influence. To understand processes that affect external behavior is not to explain how and why they are operative under certain circumstances and not under others. To recognize that foreign policy is shaped by internal as well as external factors is not to comprehend how the two intermix or to indicate the conditions under which one predominates over the other. . . . Foreign policy analysis lacks comprehensive systems of testable generalizations. . . . Foreign policy analysis is devoid of general theory (1966, 98–99).

General, testable theory was needed, and the intent of Rosenau's article was to point in the direction it lay. However, the general theory Rosenau advocates is not the grand theory of Cold War IR: the metaphor Rosenau used in this work is instructive in this regard—FPA researchers should emulate Gregor Mendel, the father of modern genetics, who was able to discern genotype from phenotype in plants through careful observation and comparison. Are there genotypes of nation-states, knowledge of which would confer explanatory and predictive power on our models of foreign policy interaction? What Rosenau was encouraging was the development of middle-range theory: theory that mediated between grand principles and the complexity of reality. At the time Rosenau wrote this article, he felt the best way to uncover such midrange generalizations was through aggregate statistical exploration and confirmation. Rosenau also underscored the need to integrate information at several levels of analysis—from individual leaders to the international system—in understanding foreign policy. As with Snyder, the best explanations would be multilevel and multicausal, integrating information from a variety of social science knowledge systems.

Harold and Margaret Sprout contributed to the formation of the field by suggesting that understanding foreign policy outputs, which they associated with the analysis of power capabilities within an interstate system, without reference to foreign policy undertakings, which they associated with strategies, decisions, and intentions, was misguided. "Explanations of achievement and estimations of capabilities for achievement invariably and necessarily presuppose antecedent undertakings or assumptions regarding undertakings. Unless there is an undertaking, there can be no achievement—and nothing to explain or estimate" (1965, 225). To explain undertakings, one needs to look at the *psycho-milieu* of the individuals and groups making the foreign policy decision. The psycho-milieu is the international and operational environment or context as it is perceived and interpreted by these decisionmakers. Incongruities between the perceived and the real operational environments can occur, leading to less than satisfactory choices in foreign policy. The sources of these discongruities were diverse, requiring once again multicausal explanations drawing from a variety of fields. Even in these early years, the Sprouts saw a clear difference between foreign policy analysis and what we have called actor-general theory:

> Instead of drawing conclusions regarding an individual's *probable* motivations and purposes, his environmental knowledge, and his intellectual processes linking purposes and knowledge, on the basis of *assumptions* as to the way people are likely on the average to behave in a given social context, the cognitive behavioralist—be he narrative historian or systematic social scientist—undertakes to find out as precisely as possible how specific persons actually did perceive and respond in particular contingencies (1965, 118).

The message of these three works was powerful in its appeal to certain scholars: the particularities of the human beings making national foreign policy were vitally important to understanding foreign policy choice. Such particularities should not remain as undigested idiosyncrasies (as in traditional single country studies), but rather be incorporated as instances of larger categories of variation in the process of cross-national middle-range theory building. Multiple levels of analysis, ranging from the most micro to the most macro, should ideally be integrated in the service of such theory. The stores of knowledge of all the social sciences must be drawn upon in this endeavor. The process of foreign policymaking was at least as important, if not more important, than foreign policy as an output. The substance of this message was and continues to be the "hard core" of FPA.

Other parts of the message were more temporally bounded. As we shall see, certain methodological stances that perhaps seemed self-evident in the early 1960s would not stand the test of time. These would engender troubling paradoxes that would plague the field and lead to a temporary decline in some areas in the mid- to late 1980s until they were satisfactorily resolved. Despite these paradoxes, the first bloom of FPA, lasting from the late 1960s to the aforementioned decline, was a time of great intellectual effort and excitement.

CLASSIC FPA SCHOLARSHIP (1954–1993)

The energy and enthusiasm of the first generation of work in FPA (1954–1973) were tremendous. Great strides in conceptualization, along with parallel efforts in data collection and methodological experimentation, were the contributions of this time period. The second generation of work from about 1974 to 1993 expressly built upon those foundations. Though it is always difficult to set the boundaries of a field of thought, the overview that follows includes a representative sampling of classic works in the first and second generation that both examined how the "specifics" of nations lead to differences in foreign policy choice/behavior, and put forward propositions in this regard that at least have the potential to be generalizable and applicable cross-nationally.

Group Decisionmaking

Snyder, Bruck, and Sapin had emphasized the process and structure of groups making foreign policy decisions (Snyder extended his work with case studies in collaboration with Glenn Paige; see Snyder and Paige, 1958; Paige, 1959; Paige, 1968). Numerous scholars echoed this theme in their work, which ranged from the study of foreign policymaking in very small groups to the study of foreign policymaking in very large organizations and bureaucracies.

Small group dynamics. Some of the most theoretically long-lived work produced during this period centered on the consequences of making foreign policy decisions in small groups. Social psychologists had explored the unique dynamics of such decision setting before, but never in relation to foreign policy decisionmaking, where the stakes might be much higher. The most important work is that of Irving Janis, whose seminal *Victims of Groupthink* (simply *Groupthink* in later editions) almost single-handedly began this research tradition. In that volume, and using studies drawn specifically from the realm of foreign policy, Janis shows convincingly that the motivation to maintain group consensus and personal acceptance by the group can cause deterioration of decision-making quality. The empirical research of Leana (1975), Semmel (1982), Semmel and Minix (1979), Tetlock (1979), and others extended this research using aggregate analysis of experimental data, as well as case studies. Groupthink becomes one outcome of several possible in the work of Charles F. Hermann (1978). Hermann categorizes groups along several dimensions (size, role of leader, rules for decision, autonomy of group participants) and is able to make general predictions about the likely outcome of deliberations in each type of group.

The work of the second wave moved "beyond groupthink," to both refine and extend our understanding of small group processes. Representative work includes 't Hart, Stern, and Sundelius, 1997; Herek, Janis, and Huth, 1987, 1989; McCauley, 1989; Ripley, 1989; Stewart, Hermann, and Hermann, 1989; and Gaenslen, 1992.

The second wave also brought with it a new research issue: How does a group come to understand, represent, and frame a given foreign policy situation? Works include those by George Breslauer, Charles F. Hermann, Donald Sylvan, Philip Tetlock, and James Voss (Vertzberger, 1990; Breslauer and Tetlock, 1991; Voss, Wolfe, Lawrence, and Engle, 1991; Billings and Hermann, 1994). Turning to efforts by individual scholars, we will highlight the work of Khong (1992) and Boynton (1991).

Boynton wishes to understand how human agents in groups come to agreement on the nature of a foreign policy situation. In his 1991 piece cited above, he uses the official record of congressional committee hearings to investigate how committee members make sense of current events and policies. By viewing the questions and responses in the hearing as an unfolding narrative, Boynton is able to chart how "meaning" crystallizes for each committee member, and how they attempt to share that meaning with other members and with those who are testifying. Boynton posits the concept of "interpretive triple" as a way to understand how connections between facts are made through plausible interpretation—in effect, ascertaining which interpretations are plausible within the social context created by the hearings.

Khong's 1992 book, *Analogies at War*, has a similar aim but a different focus: the use of analogies to guide problem framing by foreign policymakers. In this particular work, Khong demonstrates how the use of conflicting analogies to frame the problem of Vietnam led to conceptual difficulties in group reasoning about policy options. The "Korea" analogy gained ascendance in framing the Vietnam problem, without sufficient attention paid to the incongruities between the two sets of circumstances.

Organizational process and bureaucratic politics. This first period also saw the emergence of a strong research agenda that examined the influence of organizational process and bureaucratic politics on foreign policy decisionmaking. The foundations of this approach can be traced back to Weber's *The Theory of Social and Economic Organizations* (from the 1920s). First-period research showed how "rational" foreign policymaking can be upended by the attempt to work with and through large, organized governmental groups. Organizations and bureaucracies put their own survival at the top of their list of priorities, and this survival is measured by relative influence vis à vis other organizations ("turf"), by the organization's budget, and by the morale of its personnel. The organization will jealously guard and seek to increase its turf and strength, as well as to preserve undiluted what it feels to be its "essence" or "mission." Large organizations also develop standard operating procedures (SOPs), which, while allowing them to react reflexively despite their inherent unwieldiness, permit little flexibility or creativity. These SOPS may be the undoing of more innovative solutions of decisionmakers operating at levels higher than the organization, but there is little alternative to the implementation of policy by bureaucracy. The interface between objectives and implementation is directly met at this point, and there may be substantial slippage between the two, due to the incompatibility of the players' perspectives.

Although the articulation of this research agenda can be found in works such as Huntington (1960), Hilsman (1967), Neustadt (1970), and Schilling, Hammond, and Snyder (1962), probably the most cited works are Allison (1971) and Halperin (1974; additional works coauthored by Halperin include Allison and Halperin [1972] and Halperin and Kanter [1973]). In his famous *Essence of Decision*, Graham Allison offers three cuts at explaining one episode in foreign policy—the Cuban missile crisis of 1962. Investigating both the U.S. and the Soviet sides of this case, Allison shows that the unitary rational actor model of foreign policymaking does not suffice to explain the curiosities of the crisis. Offering two additional models as successive "cuts" at explanation, the organizational process model and the bureaucratic politics model (one of intraorganizational factors, one of interorganizational factors), allows Allison to explain more fully what transpired. His use of three levels of analysis also points to the desire to integrate rather than segregate explanations at different levels.

Halperin's book *Bureaucratic Politics and Foreign Policy* (1974) is an extremely detailed amalgam of generalizations about bureaucratic behavior, accompanied by unforgettable examples from American defense policymaking of the Eisenhower, Kennedy, and Johnson years. It should be noted that bureaucratic politics research gained impetus from the Vietnam

War ongoing during this period, because the war was seen by the public as defense policy run amok due, in part, to bureaucratic imperatives (see, for example, Krasner, 1971).

Comparative Foreign Policy

Those who took up James Rosenau's challenge to build a cross-national and multilevel theory of foreign policy and subject that theory to rigorous aggregate empirical testing created the subfield known as comparative foreign policy (CFP). It is in CFP that we see most directly the legacy of scientism/behavioralism in FPA's genealogy. Foreign policy could not be studied in aggregate: foreign policy *behavior* could. Searching for an analog to the "vote" as the fundamental explanandum in behavioralist American political studies, CFPers proposed the foreign policy "event": the tangible artifact of the influence attempt that is foreign policy, alternatively viewed as "who does what to whom, how" in international affairs. Events could be compared along behavioral dimensions, such as whether positive or negative affect was being displayed, or what instruments of statecraft (e.g., diplomatic, military, economics, etc.) were used in the influence attempt, or what level of commitment of resources was evident. Behavior as disparate as a war, a treaty, and a state visit could now be compared *and aggregated* in a theoretically meaningful fashion.

This conceptualization of the dependent variable was essential to the theory-building enterprise in CFP. To uncover lawlike generalizations, one would have to conduct empirical testing across nations and across time: case studies were not an efficient methodology from this standpoint. However, with the conceptual breakthrough of the "event," it was now possible to collect data on a variety of possible explanatory factors and determine (by analyzing the variance in the events' behavioral dimensions) the patterns by which these independent variables were correlated with foreign policy behavior (see McGowan and Shapiro, 1973). Indeed, to talk to some scholars involved in CFP research, it seemed that their goal was nothing less than a GUT (grand unified theory) of all foreign policy behavior for all nations for all time. Some set of master equations would link all the relevant variables, independent and dependent, together, and when applied to massive databases providing values for these variables, would yield r-squares approaching 1.0. Though the goal was perhaps naive in its ambition, the sheer enormousness of the task called forth immense efforts in theory building, data collection, and methodological innovation that have few parallels in International Relations.

Events data. The collection of "events data" was funded to a significant degree by the United States government. Andriole and Hopple (1981) estimate that the government (primarily Defense Advanced Research Projects

Agency [DARPA] and the National Science Foundation [NSF]) provided over $5 million for the development of events data sets during the time period 1967–1981. Generally speaking, the collection effort went like this: students were employed to comb through newspapers, chronologies, and other sources for foreign policy events, which they would then code according to rules listed in their coding manuals, have their coding periodically checked for intercoder reliability, and finally punch their codings up on computer cards. So, for example, if we wanted to code an event such as "The United States invaded Afghanistan," we would code a date (DDMMYYYY), the actor (United States), the subject (Afghanistan), and some code or series of codes that would indicate "invasion." A series of codes might work like this: the code for invasion might be "317," the "3" indicating this was a hostile act, the "1" indicating it was a military act, the "7" indicating in more specific fashion invasion. Many other variables could also be coded; for example, we might code that the United Nations facilitated the act by sponsoring a Security Council Resolution; we might link in previous events such as Mullah Omar's refusal to turn in Osama bin Laden, and so forth. Events data sets, then, contain thousands or even millions of lines of code, each of which is a foreign policy "event."

The acronyms of some of these events data projects live on: some because the data are still being collected (see, for example, Gerner et al., 1994; some collection was funded by the DDIR [Data Development for International Research] Project of the NSF), others because the data are still useful as a testing ground for hypotheses: WEIS (the World Event/Interaction Survey), COPDAB (the Conflict and Peace Data Bank), CREON (Comparative Research on the Events of Nations), and so forth. KEDS (Kansas Event Data System) is more of a second wave effort, in that the Kansas team has developed machine coding of events, leading to much more reliable and capacious data collection and coding than was possible in the first wave of events data (Schrodt, 1995).

Integrated explanations. In contrast to the other two types of FPA scholarship being discussed, CFP research aimed explicitly at *integrated multilevel* explanations. The four most ambitious of these projects were those of Michael Brecher (1972) and his associates of the Interstate Behavior Analysis (IBA) Project (Wilkenfeld et al., 1980), of the Dimensions of Nations (DON) Project (Rummel, 1972, 1977), of the Comparative Research on the Events of Nations (CREON) Project (East, Salmore, and Hermann, 1978; Callahan, Brady, and Hermann, 1982), and of Harold Guetzkow's Internation Simulation (INS) Project (Guetzkow, 1963). Independent variables at several levels of analysis were linked by theoretical propositions (sometimes instantiated in statistical or mathematical equations) to properties or types of foreign policy behavior. At least three of the four attempted to confirm or disconfirm the propositions by aggregate empirical testing. Unfortunately, the fact that the empirical results were not all that had been hoped for ushered in a period of disenchantment with all things CFP, as we will see in a later section.

The Psychological and Societal Milieux of Foreign Policy Decisionmaking

The mind of a foreign policymaker is not a tabula rasa: it contains complex and intricately related information and patterns, such as beliefs, attitudes, values, experiences, emotions, traits, style, memory, and national and self-conceptions. Each decisionmaker's mind is a microcosm of the variety possible in a given society. Culture, history, geography, economics, political institutions, ideology, demographics, and innumerable other factors shape the societal context in which the decisionmaker operates. The Sprouts (1956, 1957, and 1965) referred to these as the milieu of decisionmaking, and scholarly efforts to explore that milieu were both innovative and impressive during this first period. Michael Brecher's work cited above (1972) belongs in this genotype as well. Brecher's *The Foreign Policy System of Israel* explores that nation's psycho-cultural environment and its effects on Israel's foreign policy. Unlike Brecher's integrative approach to the psychosocial milieu, most works in this genotype either examined the psychological aspects of FPDM, or the broader societal aspects of it.

Individual characteristics. Would there be a distinct field of Foreign Policy Analysis without this most micro of all explanatory levels? Arguably not. It is in the cognition and information processing of an actual human agent that all the explanatory levels of FPA are in reality integrated. What sets FPA apart from more mainstream IR is this insistence that, as Hermann and Kegley put it, "(a) compelling explanation (of foreign policy) cannot treat the decider exogenously" (1994, 4).

Political psychology can assist us in understanding the decider. Under certain conditions—high stress, high uncertainty, dominant position of the head of state in FPDM—the personal characteristics of the individual would become crucial in understanding foreign policy choice. The work of Harold Lasswell on political leadership was a significant influence on many early pioneers of political psychology with reference to foreign policy (see Lasswell, 1930, 1948). Joseph de Rivera's *The Psychological Dimension of Foreign Policy* (1968) is an excellent survey and integration of early attempts to apply psychological and social psychological theory to foreign policy cases. Another early effort at a systematic study of leader personality effects is the concept of "operational code," an idea originating with Leites (1951) and refined and extended by one of the most important figures in this area of research: Alexander George (1969). Defining an operational code involves identifying the core political beliefs of the leader about the inevitability of conflict in the world, the leader's estimation of his or her own power to change events, and so forth, as well as an exploration of the preferred means and style of pursuing goals (see also Johnson [1977], O. Holsti [1977], Walker [1977]). It should be noted that George's influence on the field is by no means confined to his work on operational codes; he has offered useful suggestions on methodological issues (see George on process tracing [1979]), on the demerits of abstract theorizing versus actor-specific theory (see George and Smoke, 1974 and George, 1993), and on the need to bridge the gap between theory and practice in foreign policy (see George, 1993, 1994).

The work of Margaret G. Hermann is likewise an attempt to typologize leaders with specific reference to foreign policy dispositions. A psychologist by training, she was also involved in a CFP project (CREON). However, the core of her research is leaders' personal characteristics (1970, 1978). Using a modified operational code framework in conjunction with content analysis, she is able to compare and contrast leaders' beliefs, motivations, decisional styles, and interpersonal styles. Furthermore, Hermann integrates this information into a more holistic picture of the leader, who may belong to one of six distinct "foreign policy orientations." Orientation allows her to make more specific projections about a leader's behavior in a variety of circumstances. In the second wave of research, scholars began to explicitly compare and contrast the findings of different personality assessment schemes (Winter, Hermann, Weintraub, and Walker, 1991; Singer and Hudson, 1992; Snare, 1992).

The role of perceptions and images in foreign policy was a very important research agenda in this first generation of FPA. The work of both Robert Jervis and Richard Cottam deserve special mention here. Jervis's *Perception and Misperception in International Politics* (1976) and Cottam's *Foreign Policy Motivation: A General Theory and a Case Study* (1977) both explicate the potentially grave consequences of misperception in foreign policy situations by exploring its roots. Deterrence strategies can fail catastrophically if misperception of the other's intentions or motivations occurs (see also Holsti, North, and Brody's stimulus-response models, 1968). Like Janis, Halperin, and others, the work of Jervis and Cottam is consciously prescriptive: both include advice and suggestions for policymakers. Work in the late 1980s continuing this tradition included scholarship by Janice Gross Stein, Richard Ned Lebow, Ole Holsti, Alexander George, Deborah Welch Larson, Betty Glad, and Stephen Walt (Jervis, Lebow, and Stein, 1985; Martha Cottam, 1986; George and Smoke, 1989; O. Holsti, 1989; Lebow and Stein, 1990; Larson, 1985, 1993; Glad, 1989; Walt, 1992). An excellent example of work in this period is that of Richard Herrmann (1985, 1986, 1993), who developed a typology of stereotypical images with reference to Soviet perceptions (the other as "child," as "degenerate," etc.) and began to extend his analysis to the images held by other nations, including American and Islamic images.

The work on cognitive constraints was informed by the work of scholars in other fields, including that of Herbert Simon (1985) on bounded rationality, Heuer (1999, but written 1978–1986) on cognitive bias; and Kahneman, Slovic, and Tversky (1982) on heuristic error. Many other important cognitive and psychological studies that came forth during the 1970s and early 1980s dealt with a diversity of factors: motivations of leaders (Barber, 1972; Winter, 1973; Etheredge, 1978); cognitive maps, scripts, and schemas (Shapiro and Bonham, 1973; Axelrod, 1976; Carbonell, 1978); cognitive style (Suedfeld and Tetlock, 1977); life experience of leaders (Stewart, 1977); and others. Good edited collections of the time include Hermann with Milburn (1977) and Falkowski (1979).

National and societal characteristics. Kal Holsti's elucidation of "national role conception" spans both the psychological and the social milieu (1970). With this concept, Holsti seeks to capture how a nation views itself and its role in the international arena. Operationally, Holsti turns to elite perceptions of national role, arguing that these perceptions are arguably more salient to foreign policy choice. Perception of national role is also influenced by societal character, a product of the nation's socialization process. Differences here can lead to differences in national behavior as well (see, for example, Bobrow, Chan, and Kringen, 1979; Broderson, 1961; Hess, 1963; Merelman, 1969; Renshon, 1977). The methodology of national role conception was continued in the 1980s by Walker (1987) and others (Wish, 1980; Cottam and Shih, 1992; Shih, 1993).

The study of culture as an independent variable affecting foreign policy was just beginning to be redeveloped near the end of the 1980s, after petering out in the 1960s (Almond and Verba, 1963; Pye and Verba, 1965). Culture might have an effect on cognition (Motokawa, 1989); it might have ramifications for structuration of institutions such as bureaucracies (Sampson, 1987). Conflict resolution techniques might be different for different cultures, as well (Cushman and King, 1985; Pye, 1986; Gaenslen, 1989). Indeed, the very processes of policymaking might be stamped by one's cultural heritage and socialization (Holland, 1984; Etheredge, 1985; Lampton, 1986; Merelman, 1986; Leung, 1987; Voss and Dorsey, 1992; Banerjee, 1991).

The study of the role of societal groups in foreign policymaking can be seen as an outgrowth of the more advanced study of societal groups in American domestic politics. Sometimes an individual scholar used theory developed for the American case to explore the more diverse universe of the international system: for example, it was Robert Dahl's volume *Regimes and Oppositions* (1973) that provided key theoretical concepts necessary to analyze the relationship between domestic political pressure by societal groups and foreign policy choice by the government. Other more country- and region-specific case studies were also developed: see Chittick (1970), Dallin (1969), Deutsch et al. (1967), Hellman (1969), Hughes (1978), and Ogata (1977), among others. In the late 1980s, a new wave of thinking began to explore the limits of state autonomy in relation to other societal groups in the course of policymaking. The work of Putnam (1988) on the "two-level game" of foreign and domestic policy was paradigmatic for establishing the major questions of this research subfield. Other excellent work includes Evans, Rueschmeyer, and Skocpol (1985), Lamborn and Mumme (1989), Levy (1988), Levy and Vakili (1989), Hagan (1987), and Mastanduno, Lake, and Ikenberry (1989). A second wave of research in this area can be seen in the work of Van Belle, 1993; Skidmore and Hudson, 1993; and Kaarbo, 1993 (see also Bueno de Mesquida and Lalman, 1992 for an interesting combination of game theory and FPA to understand domestic political imperatives and their effect on foreign policy).

The second wave work of Joe Hagan deserves special note. Hagan (1993) has compiled an extensive database on the fragmentation and vulnerability of political regimes, with special reference to executive/legislative structures. The set includes ninety-four regimes for thirty-eight nations over a ten-year period. His purpose is to explore the effects of political opposition on foreign policy choice. Using aggregate statistical analysis, Hagan is able to show, for example, that the internal fragmentation of a regime has substantially less effect on foreign policy behavior than military or party opposition to the regime.

Domestic political imperatives could also be ascertained by probing elite and mass opinion (again, piggybacking onto the sophisticated voter-attitude studies of American politics). Though usually confined to studies of democratic nations (especially America, where survey research results were abundant), these analyses were used to investigate the limits of the so-called Almond–Lippman consensus: that is, that public opinion is incoherent and lacking unity on foreign policy issues, and thus that public opinion does not have a large impact on the nation's conduct of foreign policy (see Almond, 1950; Bailey, 1948; Campbell, Converse, Miller, and Stokes, 1964; Converse, 1964; Lippman, 1955; and Lipset, 1966). Opinion data collected during the Vietnam War period appears to have served as a catalyst to reexamine this question. Caspary (1970) and Achen (1975) found more stability in American public opinion concerning foreign policy and international involvement than their predecessors. Mueller (1973) used the Vietnam War to show that although the public may change their opinions on international issues, they do so for rational reasons. Holsti and Rosenau (1979) and Mandelbaum and Schneider (1979) use survey data to identify recognizable ideological positions to which the public subscribes on foreign policy issues. A large amount of research was undertaken to show that public and elite opinion does affect governmental foreign policy decision-making (see Cantril, 1967; Graber, 1968; Yankelovich, 1979; Hughes, 1978; Wittkopf, 1981; Beal and Hinckley, 1984; Verba and Brody, 1970; and Verba et al., 1967).

The study of the effect of national attributes (size, wealth, political accountability, economic system, etc.) on foreign policy was certainly, in a theoretical sense, in the Sprout genotype, but was carried out by scholars and with methods more to be placed in the Rosenau genotype (if you exclude Lenin and others who had never heard of Rosenau!). The propensity to be involved in war was usually the foreign policy dependent variable of choice in this work (see East, 1978; East and Hermann, 1974; Kean and McGowan, 1973; Rummel, 1972, 1977, 1979; Salmore and Salmore, 1978). Are large nations more likely to go to war than small nations? Are rich nations more likely to go to war than poor ones? Are authoritarian regimes more bellicose than democracies? Statistical manipulation of aggregate data, at best a blunt instrument, was unable to uncover any law-like generalizations on this score (though for an interesting and hard-to-classify treatment of the multilevel causes and effects of war, see Beer, 1981). Political economy research on the effects of economic structures and conditions on foreign policy choice are fairly rare: the "culture" of international political economy (IPE) and the "culture" of FPA did not mix well, for reasons explored below. However, the works of Neil Richardson and Charles Kegley (see, for example, Richardson and Kegley, 1980) and of Peter Katzenstein (see, for example, Katzenstein, 1985) are notable as exceptions to this generalization.

However, in the second wave years, one notable exception to the above analysis burst forth upon the scene: democratic peace theory. Democracies, it was noted, tend not to fight one another, though they fight nondemocratic countries as often as other nondemocracies do. This appeared to be an example of how a difference in polity type led to a difference in foreign policy behavior (Russett, 1993a, b). This has been an interesting bridging question for FPA and IR. Why do democracies not fight one another? Here we find more abstract theorists of war (Merritt and Zinnes, 1991; Morgan, 1992; Bremer, 1993; Dixon, 1993; Ray, 1993; Maoz and Russett, 1993) wrestling with a question that leads them into FPA waters and into conversation with FPA scholars (Hagan, 1994; Hermann and Kegley, 1995).

Finally, if it is possible to see the international system as part of the psychosocial milieu in which foreign policy decisionmaking takes place, then the work of much of mainstream IR at this time can be seen as contributing to the FPA research agenda. The effects of system type, as elucidated by Kaplan (1957, 1972), may depend on the number of poles in the system, the distribution of power among poles, and the rules of the system game that permit its maintenance. This structure may then determine to a large extent the range of permissible foreign policy behavior of nations. The work of Waltz was extremely influential in its description of the effects of an anarchical world system on the behavior of its member states (see also Rosecrance [1963]; Hoffman [1961]; Singer, Bremer, and Stuckey [1972]). FPA seemed not to emphasize this type of explanation, primarily because the variation in behavior during the time when a certain system is maintained cannot be explained by reference to system structure because the structure has not changed. Explanation of that variation must be found at lower levels of analysis, where variation in the explanans can be identified. Here, then is one of several sources for the notable lack of integration between actor-general systems theory in IR and FPA.

FPA Self-Reflection in the late 1970s and 1980s

A period of critical self-reflection began in the late 1970s and continued until the mid-1980s in FPA. The effects were felt unevenly across FPA; CFP was affected the most: it is here we see the most pruning, both theoretical and methodological, which will be discussed in a moment. In decision-making studies, there was a period of rather slow growth due to methodological considerations. The information requirements to conduct a high quality group or bureaucratic analysis of a foreign policy choice are tremendous. If one were not part of the group or bureaucracy in question, detailed accounts of what transpired, preferably from a variety of primary source viewpoints, would be necessary. Because of security considerations in foreign policy, such information is usually not available for many years (e.g., until declassified). The question facing decision-making scholars became: Is it possible to be theoretically and policy relevant if one is relegated to doing case studies of events twenty or more years old? If so, how? If not, how is it possible to maneuver around the high data requirements to say something meaningful about more recent events? (See Anderson, 1987.) Scholars wrestling with this issue came up with two basic responses: (a) patterns in group/bureaucratic processes can be isolated through historical case studies, on the basis of which both general predictions of and general recommendations for present day foreign policy decisionmaking can be made; and (b) innovative at-a-distance indicators of closed group/bureaucracy process can be developed, which allow for more specific explanation/ prediction of resultant foreign policy choice.

FPA work at the psychological level actually expanded during this time period, but work at the societal level arguably contracted on some research fronts. The reason for this bifurcation in the genotype was a methodological one: psychology provided ready-made and effective tools for the study of political psychology; political science did not offer the foreign policy analyst the same advantage. To understand how the broader sociocultural-

political context within a nation-state contributes to its governmental policymaking (whether domestic or foreign) is, perforce, the domain of comparative politics. It is hopefully not controversial to aver that the theories
and methods of comparative politics in this period of time were not quite
as highly developed as those of psychology. The attempt to graft "scientific"
statistical analyses of variance onto the underdeveloped theory of comparative politics of the 1970s and 1980s was a failure. More successful were
efforts to spin existing comparative politics work on a particular nation to
the cause of explaining factors that contribute to that nation's foreign policy—for example, borrowing techniques from American politics (such as
public opinion surveys) to study domestic political imperatives in the
United States on foreign policy issues. Still missing were the conceptual and
methodological tools necessary to push past the artificial barrier between
comparative politics and international relations that stymied theory development. One of the greatest leaps forward in the present period of FPA is
the innovative work begun on conceptualizing the "two level game" (Putnam, 1988).

As mentioned, CFP dwindled in the 1980s. Indeed, the very term *comparative foreign policy* began to sound quaint and naive. Membership in the
Comparative Foreign Policy Section of the International Studies Association plummeted. Public vivisections took place, while Rosenau genotype-
style scholarship became scarce. Both sympathetic and unsympathetic criticism abounded (see, e.g., Ashley, 1976, 1987; Caporaso, Hermann, and
Kegley, 1987; East, 1978; Hermann and Peacock, 1987; Kegley, 1980; Munton, 1976; Smith, 1987). At one point, in exasperation, Kegley (1980, 12;
himself a CFPer) chides, "CFP risks being labelled a cult of methodological
flagellomaniacs."

This searing criticism and self-criticism revealed a number of inconsistencies in the CFP approach, which needed to be sorted out before any progress could be contemplated. The stumbling blocks included the following:

1. You can't have your parsimony and eat it, too. The tension between
the desire of some CFPers for a hard science–like grand unified theory and
the assumption that micro-level detail is necessary if one really wants to
explain and predict foreign policy behavior became unbearable. Rosenau's
"Pre-theories" article, when reviewed from this vantage point, sets the
genotype up for an inevitable dilemma about parsimony. To what should
we aspire: richly detailed, comprehensively researched microanalyses of a
few cases, or conceptually abstract, parsimonious statistico-mathematical
renderings of thousands of events? One can see the problem in desiring
richly detailed, comprehensively researched microanalyses of thousands of
events: a lifetime would be over before a theorist had collected enough data
to do the first big "run"! But many CFPers rejected the case study approach
as unscientific and too much like the soft, anecdotal research of the "tradi-

tionalists" (Kegley, 1980). CFPers wanted to be behavioralists and to be scientific, and a hallmark of this was aggregate empirical testing of cross-nationally applicable generalizations across large N sizes. At the same time, they were fiercely committed to unpacking the black box of decisionmaking, so the detail of their explanans grew, and with it, their rejection of knee-jerk idealization of parsimony. Push had to come to shove at some point: CFP methods demanded parsimony in theory; CFP theory demanded nuance and detail in method.

2. To quantify or not to quantify? A corollary of large N size testing is the need for more precise measurement of data: indeed, quantification of variables is essential to linear regression and correlation techniques, as well as to mathematical manipulations, such as differential equations. However, the independent variables of CFP included such nonquantifiables as perception, memory, emotion, culture, and history, all placed in a dynamic and evolving stream of human action and reaction that might not be adequately captured by arithmetic-based relationships. To leave such nonquantifiable explanatory variables out seems to defeat the very purpose of microanalysis; to leave them in by forcing the data into quasi interval-level pigeonholes seems to do violence to the substance CFP sought to capture. CFPers began to ask whether their methods were aiding them in achieving their theoretical goals or preventing them from ever achieving those goals.

3. A final inconsistency centered in policy relevance. As mentioned earlier, CFP had received a large amount of money from the government to create events data sets. CFP researchers successfully argued that such an investment would yield information of use to foreign policymakers. Specifically, events data would be used to set up early warning systems that would alert policymakers to crises in the making around the world (as if they do not also read the same sources from which events data come!). Computerized decision aids and analysis packages with telltale acronyms began to appear—EWAMS (Early Warning and Monitoring System), CASCON (Computer-Aided Systems for Handling Information on Local Conflicts), CACIS (Computer-Aided Conflict Information System), XAIDS (Crisis Management Executive Decision Aids) (see Andriole and Hopple, 1981). Unfortunately, these could never live up to their promise: the collected events could be had from other sources and so were nothing without the theory to explain and predict their occurrence. The methodological paradoxes explicated above resulted in theory that was stuck, by and large, at the level of globally applicable but specifically vacuous bivariate generalizations such as that "large nations participate more in international interactions than small nations" (see McGowan and Shapiro, 1973). Again, CFP found itself pulled in two opposed directions: Was the research goal to say something predictive about a specific nation at a specific time in a specific set of circumstances (which would be highly policy relevant, but which

might closely resemble the output of a traditional country expert)? Or was the goal a grand unified theory (which would not be very policy relevant, but would qualify you as a scientist and a generalist)? Attempts to accomplish both with the same research led to products that were unsatisfactory in a scholarly as well as a policy sense.

Hindsight is always 20/20: it does seem clear in retrospect that change was necessary. Left behind were the aim of a grand unified theory and the methodological straitjacket imposed by the requirement of aggregate empirical testing. In 1980, Kegley spoke of the need to come down from the rarified air of grand theory to middle-range theory, and to capture more of the particular:

> To succeed partially is not to fail completely. . . . Goals (should be) downgraded to better fit capacities. . . . This prescribes reduction in the level of generality sought, so that more contextually-qualified, circumstantially bounded, and temporally/spatially-specified propositions are tested. More of the peculiar, unique, and particular can be captured at a reduced level of abstraction and generality (12, 19).

To be fair, this was arguably Rosenau's original aim, and the CFP community had to reach a consensus to return to its founding vision. The conference on New Directions in the Study of Foreign Policy, held at Ohio State University in May of 1985, probably represents a finalization of these changes for the CFP group (see the resulting volume, Hermann, Hermann, and Hagan, 1987; see also Gerner, 1992).

FOREIGN POLICY ANALYSIS FROM 1993 TO THE PRESENT

As FPA was being liberated from its inconsistencies in the late 1980s, the world was being liberated from the chess match of the Cold War. This was a felicitous coincidence for FPA and was an added source of vigor for its research agenda. The significance of this temporal coincidence can be understood by remembering what types of IR theory were in ascendance at the time: neorealist systems structure theory and rational choice modeling. Indeed, the dominance was so overwhelming that to take an IR theory course during this time, one would think these two were the sumum bonum of all thinking in International Relations (at least in the United States). This state of affairs was natural for American thinkers: America was one of two poles of power in the Cold War international system. A bipolar quasi-zero-sum rivalry lends itself relatively well to abstract, actor-general analysis focused primarily on the macro-constraints imposed by the system.

Furthermore, actor-general theory was more practical for scholars during the Cold War, because so little was known of the black box of the closed Soviet, Chinese, and Eastern bloc foreign policy decision-making bodies.

However, when the bipolar system collapsed with the fall of the Soviet bloc regimes, an important theoretical discovery was made: *it is impossible to explain or predict system change on the basis of system-level variables alone.* Along the same lines, in a period of great uncertainty and flux, lack of empirically grounded inputs to rational choice equations is deadly in terms of the usefulness of such analysis. Our intuitive understanding of the collapse involves variables more to be found in FPA: the personalities of Gorbachev, Havel, Walesa; the activities of transnational groups such as the Lutheran Church and the Green Movement; the struggles between various domestic political players, such as the military, the Communist Party, the bureaucrats; the role of economics and societal needs in sparking the desire for change. With the fall of the Iron Curtain, the need for an "actor-specific" complement to mainstream IR theory became stark in its clarity.

FPA in the post–Cold War era retains the distinctive theoretical commitments that demarcated at its inception. Included among these are:

- a commitment to look below the nation-state level of analysis to actor-specific information.
- a commitment to build middle-range theory as the interface between actor-general theory and the complexity of the real world.
- a commitment to pursue multicausal explanations spanning multiple levels of analysis.
- a commitment to utilize theory and findings from across the spectrum of social science.
- a commitment to viewing the process of foreign policy decisionmaking as important as the output thereof.

Nevertheless, FPA has evolved in sophistication of questions asked, and in means of answering those questions. Indeed, FPA's ability to ask new questions is perhaps more promising in relation to its future theoretical potential than any other indicator. Einstein and Infeld (1938) commented that "(t)he formulation of a problem is often more essential than its solution which may be merely a matter of . . . skill. To raise new questions, new possibilities, to regard old problems from a new angle, requires creative imagination and works real advance in science."

In order to see this advance, let us examine some of the new questions that have evolved from the old. We will start at the more micro-levels of analysis and move toward the more macro-levels.

When studying the effects of leaders on foreign policy decisionmaking, can we extend our understanding of how a leader's personality affects foreign policy through determining its effect on choice of advisors, preference for issues, preference for certain group processes, and so forth? Can we integrate different analytical schemes for analyzing leader personality and its effects? What are the ramifications of new breakthroughs in neuroscience for FPA? How do various leader personality types shape the structure and process of groups serving them? What role do emotions play in FPDM?

Turning now to the group level, how are problems recognized as such by the group? How are situations "framed" and "represented"? How are options developed? How does a group come to share an interpretation of the situation? How does a group change an established interpretation? How does a group learn? How is the group's potential for creativity enhanced or dampened? How does group memory affect group action? How do groups become players in the "two level game"? How are group structure and process a function of societal culture?

Moving to the level of society and political competition, can we uncover the societal sources of change in shared perceptions? How do attitudes of leaders and publics change as context changes? Can national role conception be reconfigured to serve as the theoretical interface between a society and the individual members of that society that come to lead it and make its foreign policy decisions? Can we specify the effect on foreign policy of domestic political competition? Can we complete the theoretical circle, and specify the effects on domestic politics of the implementation of a certain foreign policy choice? How can we discern culture's influence on foreign policy? Does the type of political system impact foreign policy? What is the effect of systemic change on foreign policy?

Methodologically speaking, there are quite a few important questions to be addressed. These include, can events data be reconceptualized to be of use to contemporary FPA? Can FPA utilize methods created to simulate human decisionmaking as a means of integrating complex, nonquantifiable data? Can we think of nonarithmetic ways to relate variables? Can rational choice models be altered to accommodate actor-specific idiosyncrasies with regard to utility, choice mechanisms, and choice constraints? Can we create models that will allow us to use as inputs the actor-specific knowledge generated by country/region experts? When is the detail of actor-specifics necessary, and when is actor-general theory sufficient to explain and project FPDM? How could one instantiate a model of the "two level game"? Can discursive analysis or interpretivism be used to introduce the dynamics of evolving understanding in FPDM?

These are exciting new questions to be asking and answering. Doubtless some of you will be involved in this work. It is a wonderful time to become engaged in FPA, a time of new horizons.

To help you on your way, the rest of this textbook will be devoted to the classic and contemporary theory in FPA that has helped shape the field thus far, organized around six levels of analysis and issues of integration. Of course, it is simply not possible to cover *all* pertinent theory in the subsequent chapters. There is simply too much to cover. We will have to make do with a selection of earlier and later theorizing, and I apologize for the fact that I, a very fallible mortal, had to make painful decisions about which theories to discuss, and which not to discuss. Nevertheless, for each level of analysis, we will cover selected important work from earlier periods (1954–1993), but we will also discuss selected important advances made around the turn of the twenty-first century (1994–2004), which were not enumerated in this introductory chapter on the history of FPA (see Hudson, 2005 for a brief overview of work in the modern period). In this way, you will have a solid, if not perfectly comprehensive, foundation upon which to build in your own research.

NOTE

Sections of this paper were previously published and reprinted by permission, including "Foreign Policy Analysis Yesterday, Today, and Tomorrow" (with Christopher Vore; *Mershon International Studies Review*, 39, Supplement 2, 1995:209–38), and "Foreign Policy Decision-Making: A Touchstone for International Relations Theory in the Twenty-First Century," in Richard C. Snyder, H. W. Bruck, and Burton Sapin (eds.), *Foreign Policy Decision Making (Revisited)* (New York: Palgrave-Macmillan, 2002, 1–20).

II

LEVELS OF ANALYSIS

2

The Individual Decisionmaker: The Political Psychology of World Leaders

Do leaders matter? In International Relations (IR), this question has been answered differently in different time periods. In the 1930s, it was not uncommon to see the use of "the Great Man" approach, where almost naught but leadership mattered in explanations of foreign policy. During the Cold War, Great Man approaches fell into disfavor, and the most important elements in understanding at least superpower behavior seemed to be defined at the level of state or system attributes. After the Cold War, crises such as those involving Iraq and North Korea inclined specialists to look once again at leader characteristics to help understand the foreign policy of these nations.

While the academy has been more tentative about the value of leader analysis, the government is much less tentative. An office of leadership analysis was created in the CIA in the 1970s, and continues to offer analysis and briefings about world leaders to presidents and high-level diplomats to this day. As one commentator put it, "policymakers desperately want to understand just what kinds of adversaries they are facing" (Omestad, 1994). Strategies of deterrence and negotiation depend significantly upon an understanding of the other's worldview. Communication between nations can also be affected in important ways by leadership idiosyncrasies. The desperate desire of policymakers to understand their counterparts in other nations is not without foundation.

However, a better question to ask might be, When do leaders matter? Surely not every foreign policy decision carries the imprint of the leader's distinctive personal characteristics and perceptions. A related question might be, Which leaders matter? Government personnel other than the top leader may leave more of an impression on a particular foreign policy. It is to these questions that we now turn.

WHEN AND WHICH?

Under what conditions might it be more fruitful to examine leader characteristics? A variety of hypotheses come to mind.

First, regime type may play a role in answering this question. Different regime types offer different levels of constraint on leader control of policy. It might be more imperative to assess leader characteristics in one-man dictatorships, such as Kim Jong Il's North Korea, than it would be to examine them in some long-established parliamentary democracies. Nevertheless, it must be kept in mind there is no regime type that precludes a leader's personal influence on policy altogether.

Second, it matters whether a leader is interested in foreign policy. Leaders uninterested in foreign policy may delegate a large measure of authority to subordinates, in which case it would be vital to identify and examine their characteristics as well. For example, after World War II, Francisco Franco openly commented on his disinterest in foreign affairs, delegating most decisionmaking power to his foreign minister. Nevertheless, over the years his foreign minister began to make choices that did not sit well with Franco, and eventually was dismissed. Even a disinterested leader can become interested if the context is right. Leaders who have an emotional response to the issues under discussion because of prior experience or memory are also likely to leave more of a personal imprint on foreign policy.

Part of that context may provide us a third scope condition: crisis situations will invariably be handled at the highest levels of government power, and almost by definition top leaders will be involved regardless of their general level of interest in foreign affairs. However, an important caveat must be mentioned here. If the crisis is so extreme that the country's survival is at stake, a leader may try to keep his or her psychological predispositions in check in order to avoid making any unnecessary mistakes. But for every example of such restraint (John F. Kennedy and the Cuban missile crisis), we can find numerous examples of how crisis situations brought a leader's predispositions to the fore in a very strong way (Richard Nixon and Watergate).

A related context that may allow a leader's personal characteristics to play more of a role in decisionmaking is in ambiguous or uncertain situations, our fourth contextual variable. When advisors are unable to "read" a situation because information is sparse or contradictory, a leader may be called upon to exercise his or her judgment so that a basis for foreign policy decisionmaking is laid. One subcategory of these types of situations are those involving long-range planning, where sweeping strategic doctrines or approaches to particular problems are decided for an uncertain and unpredictable future.

Margaret Hermann has proffered a fifth contextual variable, namely, the degree to which a leader has had diplomatic training (1984). Hermann argues that leaders with prior training have learned to subordinate their personal characteristics to the diplomatic requirements of the situation at hand. Untrained leaders, especially those with what she has termed "insensitive" orientations to the international context, are likely to rely more on their personal worldviews in any foreign policy response.

Expertise in a particular issue area or region of the world may also signal that a particular leader, even if he is not the top leader, may leave a personal imprint on the policy eventually chosen. It is not uncommon in the post-Vietnam era for U.S. presidents to defer to military leaders when conflict is being discussed as an option. Indeed, in a number of cases it is the military leadership that makes the strongest case against intervention options being weighed by the president. Patterns of deference to acknowledged experts must be tracked in order to identify which leaders bear further examination in any particular case, and this constitutes a sixth condition to consider.

A seventh variable concerns the style of leadership: does the leader like to delegate information processing and decision tasks? Or does the leader prefer to sort through the intelligence himself or herself, providing a much more hands-on style of leadership? There are pros and cons to each style, but clearly the hands-on style of leadership lends itself to a much more prominent effect on decisionmaking of the leader's personality.

Finally, a fuller exploration of the eighth contextual variable must wait until the next chapter, when we discuss group interactions. Groups, whether small or large, tend to evolve into contexts in which particular individuals play a given role on a fairly consistent basis. For example, one person may play the devil's advocate role, while another views himself as a loyal "mindguard." Still others may view themselves as advocates of particular policies, or as the group's diplomats, frequently brokering agreements. Examination of the top leadership must not overlook the advantage provided by examining it not only in isolation, but also in group settings.

EXPLORING THE COMPONENTS OF THE MIND

Before we can understand FPA scholarship on leaders, we must first adopt a language based in psychology that allows us to name and relate components of an individual's mental framework. It must be acknowledged at the outset that there are many schools within the field of psychology, and many of the terms we will use here have subtle or not-so-subtle differences in definition and interpretation between these schools. Nevertheless, to effect the kind of analysis desired in FPA, we must start somewhere.

The following diagram outlines the key concepts that we will be exploring in this chapter.

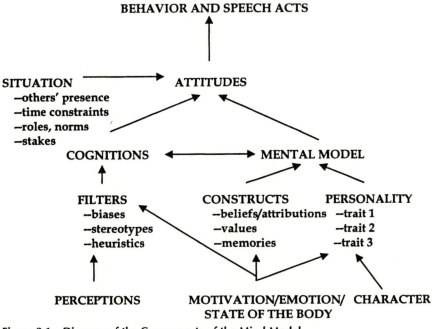

Figure 2.1   Diagram of the Components of the Mind Model

Perception and Cognition

It is through our senses that our minds make contact with the world around it. Some psychologists have posited a mental capacity for the brief storage of sensory information as it is processed, usually a quarter of a second in duration. However, our senses take in vastly more information than the mind is ever capable of processing. If we label those sensory inputs **perception,** than we perceive more than we notice. The mind apparently builds a "filter" that helps it decide which sensory inputs are worthy of more detailed processing, which processing we would call **cognition**. These filters might include **stereotypes, biases,** and **heuristics**. These are all shortcuts to help the mind decide which sensory inputs should be focused on in a given situation. Each person has an individually tailored set of filters that arise from the person's larger experiences. Young children have fewer filters than adults, and often "see" more in a situation than their parents. I often ask my students if they can say what color shoes I am wearing without looking. The majority of students cannot. In their assumptions about what to pay attention to in a college classroom, the color of the professor's shoes is considered to be unimportant. Therefore, although their retinas surely did register the color of my shoes as I walked around the classroom, their minds deemed the information irrelevant.

These perceptual filters can trip us up, however. In some cases, our filters don't help us in a particular situation. For example, the serial killer turns out to be the nice, quiet man with the immaculate lawn next door. Our stereotypes about serial killers do not include such innocuous characteristics. In other cases, our filters are so strong that they prevent us from receiving accurate sensory perceptions. As Jervis notes, new information may be assimilated into existing images. For example, in one famous experiment, subjects were tasked with playing cards in multiple rounds. At one point, the researchers substituted cards wherein the hearts and diamonds were black, and the spades and clubs were red. At first, it was hard for the subjects to identify that something was amiss. When alerted to the mismatch between suit and color, it was then very difficult for them to play with the abnormal cards (Brunner and Postman, 1949). We perceive what we expect to perceive.

In a very real way, then, our human capacity to be rational is bounded. Herbert Simon, the Nobel laureate, notes that our **bounded rationality** stems from our inability to know everything, think everything, and understand everything (including ourselves). We construct a simplified mental model of reality and behave fairly rationally within its confines, but those confines may be quite severe. Mental models are inescapable, but they do have their downsides. They are hard to change, and they are based only upon what we know. Mind-sets and categories based on these mental models are quick to form and resistant to change. Thus, we are attempting to reason through the use of mental hardware that is profoundly constrained. For example, let's look at some common heuristics, or ways of processing information.

Heuristic Fallacies

There are several excellent works on heuristic fallacies, with favorites being Richards Heuer's *The Psychology of Intelligence Analysis* (1999), and *Judgment under Uncertainty: Heuristics and Biases* by Daniel Kahneman, Paul Slovic, and Amos Tversky (1982). Each of these works tackles the human brain as it is, rather than as we would like to believe it is. Our brains evolved over long millennia to use particular mental "machinery." We have an almost limitless storage capacity in our long-term memory, but most of our day-to-day mental activity involves short-term memory and associative recall. **Short-term memory** has a limited capacity, usually defined at approximately five to seven items. Once you exceed the limits of your short-term memory, some of the items will be dropped from active consideration in your mind. These will be dropped according to some mental definition of priority. Though for a few days you may have vivid recall of a striking experience, you may be unable to remember what you had for breakfast yesterday. After a week, even a vivid experience may fade, and you may only be able to remember generalities about the event. That is why it is not uncommon for two people who have lived through the same event to disagree over the facts of what happened.

If deemed important enough, items in short-term memory can be stored in **long-term memory**. The advantage of long-term memory is that it is of almost limitless capacity (although unless the experience was traumatic, you are unlikely to be able to recover raw sensory data about a memory—what you will recover instead is an interpretation of the memory). The disadvantage is that usually the only way to retrieve such information is through associative recall. Have you ever tried to remember where you put your keys, or what you named a computer file you created six months ago? What follows is typically an indirect and laborious process of remembering other things you were doing or thinking while you were holding your keys or working on the file. Oftentimes, we have to "sleep on it," with the mind processing the retrieval request through the night and recalling it upon waking.

One common approach to overcoming this problem is to bunch several items in long-term memory together, into a "**schema**." For example, you may have a schema about renewing your driver's license, in which memories and knowledge about the process are bundled together and recalled together as a template. As Schrodt puts it, "recall usually substitutes for reasoning" (Hudson, Schrodt, and Whitmer, 2004). This is so because the human brain is hardwired to find patterns in complexity. While logic and deductive reasoning take a lot of mental energy for a human being, recall and pattern recognition are almost effortless.

While effortless, however, we do develop "rules" to govern our mental activity, allowing us to become "cognitive misers" concerning our limited cognitive resources. Often these rules are shortcuts that allow for recall or interpretation with a minimum of inputs, thus minimizing reaction time. These heuristics usually help us; occasionally they can trip us up. Let's look at a few examples.

Some of the most common heuristic fallacies involve the estimation of probabilities. Humans turn out to be pretty bad at this task, which is no doubt why the gambling business is so lucrative. The "availability fallacy" notes that people judge something to be more probable if they can easily recall instances of it from memory. Thus, if certain types of events have happened more recently, or more frequently, or more vividly, humans will judge these events to be more probable, regardless of the underlying causal factors at work. The "anchoring fallacy" points out that when trying to make an estimation, humans usually begin at a starting point that may be relatively arbitrary. After setting that initial estimate, people use additional information to adjust the probability up or down from that starting point. However, the starting point, or anchor, is a drag on the estimator's ability to make adjustments to their estimate. In one experiment cited by Heuer, students were asked to estimate what percentage of the membership of the United Nations were African countries. Students who started with low anchors, say 10 percent, never guessed higher than 25 percent despite additional information. On the other hand, students who started with high anchors, say 65 percent, could not lower their estimate by very much even with the additional information, settling on approximately 45 percent as their final estimate. Thus, although each was given the same additional information, their anchors limited their final estimates (Heuer, 1999).

Humans are also notoriously bad at the calculation of joint probabilities. Take the scenario where I wish to perform well on a test, and a series of things must occur for this to happen. I have to get up when my alarm clock rings (90 percent probability), my car has to start (90 percent probability), I have to find a parking space in time (80 percent probability), and I have to perform to my capacity on the test (80 percent probability). Most will say that the probability of me doing well on the test is about 80 percent. That is, they take the lowest single probability and extend it to the entire scenario. But this would be incorrect. The probability of this scenario is the joint probability defined as the product of the individual probabilities. The true probability of my doing well on the test is .90 x .90 x .80 x .80, or about 52 percent.

But probabilities are not the only thing that humans are not very good at evaluating. Humans are also fairly bad at evaluating evidence, which no doubt accounts for the persistence of even rudimentary scams and frauds in our societies. Humans are eager, even impelled, to seek causal explanations for what is happening in their environment. When you present a person with a plausible causal stream to explain a certain event, for example, "bad" cholesterol causes heart disease because it promotes inflammation and clogging of arteries, if the person "gets" the explanation—that is, if the person exerts effort to understand the explanation as given—it will be almost impossible to disabuse that person of that causal inference. Even if you told the person a *lie*, they will still cling to that causal understanding even when told it was a lie. Because it made sense to them once, it will not stop making sense to them after such a revelation (for a dramatic example, see Festinger, Riecken, and Schachter, 1956). Many conspiracy theories retain adherents for long periods of time because of this heuristic pitfall. Furthermore, if a person has a prior belief that two things are unrelated, they may not perceive evidence of a relationship; likewise, if a person has a prior belief that two things are related, they may not perceive evidence that there is no relationship (Fiske and Taylor, 1984, 264). Apparently, humans tune in to information that supports their beliefs and tend to ignore information that is discrepant with their beliefs (Zimbardo and Leippe, 1991, 144), and humans interpret mixed evidence as supporting their prior beliefs (163). This speaks volumes about human ability to evaluate the evidence for an explanation.

This conclusion even applies to self-interpretation. Psychologists note that humans are terrible at figuring out why they themselves do what they do (Nisbett and Wilson, 1977, 231–59). Humans appear to have little or no access to their own cognitive processes, and attributions about the self are notoriously inaccurate. We cannot even effectively analyze evidence about ourselves.

The bottom line is that humans are not very picky about evidence, because their first priority is to "get" the explanation, that is, to understand their world. Stopping the explainer every other word to demand empirical evidence for their assertions is not standard human practice. For example, researchers now ask whether the conventional distinction between "bad" and "good" cholesterol even makes sense. Other researchers are not sure that the inflammation in heart disease is caused primarily by the cholesterol ratios; they now wonder whether it isn't low-level infections that are the chief culprit. Generally speaking, only a modicum of evidence is sufficient to "sell" a causal story. The best evidence, research shows, is evidence that is vivid and anecdotal, and resonates with personal experiences the listener has had. Abstract, aggregate data pales in comparison. When selling weight-loss products, a couple of good testimonials accompanied by striking before-and-after photos will outsell large N-trials every time.

A second problem with evidence has to do with its representativeness. When we see those two weight-loss testimonials, our mind assumes that such results (if true) represent what the average person could expect from using the product. This is an erroneous assumption. The two testimonials may be the only two positive testimonials the company received.

Similarly, humans are predisposed to work *within* a given framework of understanding, which also limits their ability to evaluate the evidence for a particular explanation. In the aforementioned example concerning heart disease, if we stick to the framework of "bad" cholesterol and "good" cholesterol and of cholesterol-induced inflammation, the story outcome is predetermined. "Bad" cholesterol is going to be bad for you, and is going to cause inflammation, and by golly we'd better do something about it. But if you start asking questions that upset the framework, the story gets fuzzier—

what if there's no valid reason to call one type of cholesterol "bad"? What if inflammation has many causes, and could these other causes be operating in heart disease? Asking such questions is going to cripple your ability to reach closure on a causal explanation, however. Because humans are hard-wired to explain the world around them in order to feel a sense of control, reaching such closure provides mental and emotional satisfaction. Therefore, it is not strange that humans are poor at evidence evaluation; they are more interested in the emotional relief of explanations than in the evidence.

Finally, our use of heuristics, as inevitable and natural as it may be, actually leads to the fallacy of "overconfidence." When we first try to, say, make a prediction with limited information, we may feel unsure about its accuracy. As we obtain more and more information, our confidence in our predictions rises. Interestingly, psychological experiments have shown that this level of confidence is *unrelated* to the actual accuracy of our predictions. Confidence was related solely to how much information the predictor obtained. Perhaps this interesting emotional response is necessary in providing humans with enough confidence to act upon what they believe they know. But the lack of correlation to accuracy means there will also be a steep learning curve from the mistakes invariably made as a result. Or not: Kruger and Dunning (1999) point out that students in the bottom quartile on grammar tests still felt they had scored above average *even when they were allowed to see the test papers of the students in the top quartile.* Apparently, if you are not competent in a particular task, you are not competent to know you are not competent—and hence, no matter the feedback provided, everyone thinks of themselves as above average!

Emotion and Reason

In the same way that cognitive constraints affect reasoning, so do emotions. Though an important topic of research in psychology, the implications for foreign policy decisionmaking are only beginning to be explored. This is because most decisionmaking theories in IR have either ignored emotion or seen it as an impediment to rational choice. However, psychologists are now beginning to assert that decisionmaking depends upon emotional assessment. McDermott notes that "individuals who cannot reference emotional memory because of brain lesions are unable to make rational decisions at all" (2004, 153). McDermott also points out that "emotions can facilitate motivation and arousal. . . . Emotion arouses an individual to take action with regard to an imagined or experienced event. Emotion can also direct and sustain behavior in response to various situations" (167). Emotion is one of the most effective ways by which humans can change goal emphasis: I might be focused on getting to work on time, but if there is a car accident occurring in front of me, emotional arousal will sweep that goal from my mind that I may concentrate on the more immediately important goal of avoiding the accident. The effects of emotion on decisionmaking are diverse, and not all effects are yet understood. Intangible inputs to rational choice equations, such as level of trust, are clearly emotionally based. Studies have also shown that emotion-based attitudes are held with greater confidence than those that are not connected to emotion.

Future advances in the study of emotion will be facilitated by new methodologies. For example, developing fields of neuroscientific inquiry help us to understand that emotion is as important to decisionmaking as cognition is. "Seeing" the limbic system "light up" on an MRI as a person makes a difficult decision gives us a whole new way of thinking about decisionmaking. McDermott is optimistic that "neuroscientific advances might bridge rationally and psychologically-oriented models" (186).

Behavioral economists such as Robert Shiller argue that emotional factors, such as the fear of being left out, or optimistic gut feelings, or media hype producing a sense of confidence and control, all substitute for reasoned analysis on the part of investors. "I can present my research and findings to a bunch of academics and they seem to agree," Shiller said. "But afterward at dinner, they tell me they are 100 percent in stock. They say: 'What you argue is interesting, but I bet stocks will go up. I have this feeling'" (Uchitelle, 2000, 1).

Psychologist Barry Schwartz and colleagues have described the paradox of choice, wherein proliferation of choices leads to lower satisfaction and greater regrets than fewer choices. This may even lead to a situation where, frustrated by the plethora of choices available, decisionmakers find it impossible to make a choice and so do nothing. For example, Schwartz notes that one of his colleagues discovered that as the number of mutual funds in a 401(k) plan offered to employees goes up, the likelihood they will choose any mutual fund plan actually goes down (2004b, 27).

Other psychologists, such as Daniel Gilbert, suggest that humans really do not understand their own emotions. When asked to estimate how a particular event would affect their lives for better or worse (such as winning $1 million on a game show), respondents overestimated how such an event would affect them and for how long. Each person appears to have a happiness "set point" and, over time, will return to that set point no matter their circumstances. Both bad and good events turn out to have less intense and briefer emotional effects than people generally believe. Studies have shown that over time lottery winners were not happier and persons who became paraplegics not unhappier than control groups (Kahneman, 2000, 673–92). Both Midwesterners and Californians describe themselves as similarly happy, but both groups expect that Californians will report themselves happier. Gilbert calls this misunderstanding of happiness "miswanting": the inability to really understand what their own feelings would be in a particular situation. For example, Gilbert says, "If you ask, 'What would you rather have, a broken leg or a trick knee?' they'd probably say, 'Trick knee.' And yet, if your goal is to accumulate maximum happiness over your lifetime, you just made the wrong choice. A trick knee is a bad thing to have" (Gertner, 2003, 47).

This misunderstanding of our emotions is especially acute when comparing "hot" emotional states (rage, fear, arousal) to more composed emotional states. In experiments conducted about unprotected sexual behavior, people in composed emotional states would generally state they would never engage in such risky behavior. But when subject to arousal most would, in fact, so engage. In a sense, our decisionmaking has the potential to produce profoundly different outcomes depending upon our emotional state. And it also turns out that we are not good at predicting that such differences would ever occur.

Humans also seem to be hardwired to detect unfairness, and the presence of unfairness makes humans very upset. Reaction to unfairness elicits a strong, persistent negative emotional response. When members of a team are presented with the choice to have one of their members win $50 and the rest win $5 each, or to have none of their team members win anything, most persons chose the latter. They would rather not gain at all then acquiesce to an obviously unfair situation in which they would still gain something.

The Body and Reason

Emotions are not the only thing capable of altering our normal cognitive function. Our cognition operates in the context of a physical body, and what happens to that body can affect our decisionmaking.

Mental illness can strike leaders. Indeed, political psychologist Jerrold Post believes that certain mental illnesses are overrepresented in the population of world leaders (2003), such as narcissism and paranoia. Narcissists, for example, may be more willing than a normal person to pay any price to become a leader. Post also hypothesizes that the stresses and power of national leadership may cause a predisposition to mental illness to bloom into a pathological state, especially in systems where the leader's power is unchecked. This was true, for example, in the case of Saddam Hussein, whom Post diagnoses as a malignant narcissist. As Saddam Hussein's power became ever greater within his society, his mental illness began to overtake his normal powers of judgment. He could not admit ignorance, and so could not learn. He could not brook dissent, and so received no dissonant information from his advisors. His power fantasies, lack of impulse control, willingness to use force, and absence of conscience warped his decision-making to the point where what was good for Saddam Hussein was defined as the national interest of Iraq. An unhealthy obsession with power and control appears as part of the mental illnesses most often suffered by world leaders, with one estimate that up to 13 percent of world leaders express this trait (Weiner, 2002).

The body's experience of stress may also alter decisionmaking. Stress's effect on the body appears to follow a U-shaped curve: our mental acuity seems best when under a moderate amount of stress. We function at less than our peak capacity when under higher (and, ironically, lower) levels of stress. Chronic, high-level stress not only impairs judgment, but induces fatigue and confusion. The body's hormonal, metabolic, and immune functions are also compromised by chronically high levels of stress. Under chronic high stress, the mental effort required to think something through may seem unattainable. Studies show that a rat exposed to repeated uncontrollable stressors cannot learn to avoid an electric shock: the stress has caused it to become helpless and incapable of becoming motivated enough to expend the mental energy to learn (Sapolsky, 1997, 218). The predisposition may be to decide a matter quickly on gut instinct, or to not make a decision at all. And it is interesting to consider common sources of stress: an overabundance of information is a reliable stressor, one that probably plagues most foreign policy decisionmakers every day. One study asserts that the life spans of American presidents are significantly shorter than controls, and that most have died from stress-related causes (Gilbert, 1993).

Though it is always a matter of speculation whether our leaders have used illicit drugs, there is no shortage of evidence that leaders commonly use licit drugs, such as alcohol, caffeine, and prescription medications. A fairly famous case in point is that of Richard M. Nixon, who, while abusing alcohol, was also self-medicating with relatively high doses of Dilantin in addition to taking prescribed medication for depression and mood swings. Dilantin causes memory loss, irritability, and confusion. President George H. W. Bush's use of Haldol as a sleep aid around the time of Desert Storm was also a focus of speculation concerning its effects on his decisionmaking. President John F. Kennedy's use of steroids and high-dose pain medication for his back problems is not as well known as his suffering from Addison's disease, but may also have affected his cognition.

Physical pain and suffering from disease and its treatment must also be mentioned as a bodily experience that may alter decisionmaking. Living with high levels of chronic pain often induces irritability and frequent changes of opinion. Certain types of pathology, such as cerebral strokes, may in fact change cognitive function permanently, as it did with President Woodrow Wilson in the last part of his presidency. Recent research points to a syndrome of lowered impulse control in patients that have undergone bypass surgery, ostensibly due to the mechanical rerouting of the blood-stream. The devastating side effects of chemotherapy and radiation treatment can cause temporary depression. But we must not forget that even ordinary physical ailments, such as jet lag, the flu, and gastric distress, may be distracting and serve to diminish acuity.

Many world leaders are elderly. Aging may bring wisdom, but research tells us that aging may also bring rigidity and overconfidence, difficulty in dealing with complexity, and a preference for extreme choices. Once again, the hardware we have been given in the form of our embodied mind provides some significant constraints on our reasoning.

The Situational Context

The particulars of the situation in which the person finds themselves are also very pertinent to the final choice of action. One germane characteristic is the presence or absence of others. For example, when a person has been seriously injured, psychologists have shown that the actions of bystanders depend on how many of them there are. Counterintuitively, the greater the number of bystanders, the less likely it is that someone will come forward to help the injured person. Everyone among the bystanders is thinking, "Surely someone in this crowd is more qualified than I to help this person," and so they fail to act. EMT training emphasizes that the person who does step forward to help (finally) should make specific assignments to bystanders: "You there, call the police"; "You there, get a blanket out of your car"; and so on. Pressures to conform are also part of the influence of others' presence. A high school kid may find that everyone in his circle of friends drinks alcohol; the resulting social pressure may be so great that the kid will begin to drink alcohol even if he has no personal desire to do so, or even if he actively does not want to drink.

In a series of famous experiments in the 1950s, Solomon Asch assembled groups of male college students where all but one person in the groups were actually working for Asch. The groups were asked to determine relative length of parallel lines, and the real subject would always answer last. When the others in the group gave clearly erroneous answers, over 70 percent of real subjects would conform at least once to the erroneous answer (Zimbardo and Leippe, 1991, 56–57). The need for social acceptance is very deeply rooted in most human beings, and may cause abnormal or even irrational behavior in many individuals given a relevant social situational context. In Asch's experiments, only 25 percent of the real subjects never conformed.

There is also the issue of time constraints. The reaction to a situation is going to be somewhat different if it is an emergency-type situation in which action must be taken quickly. There may not be time for an extensive information search; there may not be time for extended deliberation. In such a situation, the role of emotions, or "gut feelings," may be prominent. In a threatening situation with time constraints, even more basic responses, such as the "fight or flight" (male) or "tend and befriend" (female) reactions, may occur without much conscious reasoning.

The stakes of the situation are also formative. When one is risking nuclear war, a more careful deliberation process may occur than when a situation is routine and of little consequence. Furthermore, gains and losses that arise from a situational context may be processed differently in the human brain. Prospect theory tells us that humans do not like situations where one alternative is a certain loss. If I gave you a choice between losing $5 for sure, or betting $5 in a gamble with 1000 to 1 odds of keeping your $5, you would always choose the gamble over the sure loss, though there is little practical difference in outcome. Humans also prefer sure wins to riskier higher gains. If I offered you a choice of $5 or a 1 in 100 chance of winning $500, you would probably take the $5. Prospect theory also tells us that previous wins and losses affect our subsequent behavior. If I have just experienced a sure loss, I will be more willing to engage in riskier behavior in the next round of play to make up my previous loss (Thaler, 2000). An interesting corollary of prospect theory with relevance for international negotiations is that we process the concessions of others as having less value than any concessions we ourselves make (McDermott, 2004). Psychologists believe the discounting of other's concessions may be as high as 50 percent, meaning that the other person would have to concede twice as much to make the concessions feel as valuable to you as the concession you are making.

Social roles and rules can also affect decisionmaking, especially as they tie in with existing schema. I helped to organize a conference once, and in the middle of one of the presentations, a member of the audience stood up and began to verbally harass the speaker. Now, this was not a large and public group, but a small private group of approximately fifty persons, where such aggressive heckling would typically not take place, according to social rules. Most of the participants simply sat there, wondering what to do. But one member of the audience was a security contractor for the government. He got up, deftly pinned the man's arm behind his back without hurting him, escorted him from the room, and made sure that he left the building. His social role gave him a precise and effective schema for handling this situation that had so perplexed the other members of the audience.

Attitudes and the Mental Model—and What Lies Beneath

Though all of us possess the type of cognitive constraints enumerated above, we are not all the same. Each of us is a unique mix of genetic information, life experience, and deeply held values and beliefs. Political psychologists who study world leaders are interested in these deeper elements of personality, as well. We have spoken of how perception is filtered through to cognition, but a person's reaction to a cognition in a particular situational context—their **attitudes** (easily accessed mental judgments or evaluations) that will shape their immediate response—are largely shaped by their **mental model** of the world. That model will contain elements such as beliefs, values, and memories, which are drawn upon to form these attitudes. We have already examined characteristics of memory, short-term, long-term, and memory "schema." However, we need to say a few words about beliefs and values.

Beliefs are often called **attributions** in the psychological literature. These are beliefs about causality in the world. For example, person A might believe that when his neighbor B mowed down a flower in A's yard that was very near their joint property line, B was acting from malicious intent. "He mowed down the flower because he holds malice toward me and acted on that malicious intent." A different person in A's shoes might believe that B's mind was on other things and the mowing-down of the flower was accidental, not intended, and not even noticed. Still another person might believe that B was impaired by alcohol when mowing his lawn and attribute the flower-mowing to alcohol abuse. Why things happen, or what causes what, are crucial elements in our understanding of the world.

Psychologists often speak of a "fundamental attribution error," fundamental in this case meaning common to virtually all humans. Almost all of us attribute our behavior to situational necessity, but the behavior of others to free choice or disposition. Thus, in the example above, if *we* had mowed our neighbors' flower down, we would tend to think it was because we had no choice—but if *he* mowed our flower down, we would tend to think that he wanted to mow it down. One could see how this fundamental attribution error could play out in international relations: North Korea feels it has no choice but to build nuclear weapons given U.S. policy; the United States, on the other hand, believes that North Korea is building nuclear weapons not because it has to, but because it wants to. The North Koreans believe that the U.S. policy of denuclearization of North Korea is a choice based on antipathy; Americans believe their stance is forced by the situation of having to protect themselves and allies from a madman intent upon obtaining nuclear weapons and long-range delivery capabilities.

Values, our final component of the mental model, may be created fairly early in life. Values refer to the relative ranking individuals use to justify preferring one thing over another. These values cannot exist without attribution, attribution cannot exist without memory of experience, but probably it is values that allow us to make judgments—to hold attitudes in a particular situation that will lead to our speech and behavioral actions. Values, in a sense, "energize" our mental model. Values are also very much influenced by our motivations and emotions. "Values" are often used when discussing morality: we "value" honesty and prefer it to dishonesty, and so we are not going to lie in situation X. But values may also be about things that may have little reference to moral issues: a president may value the advice of his or her ANSA (special assistant to the president for National Security Affairs) over the advice of the secretary of defense. In situation X, then, the advice of the ANSA may be more influential on the president's decision than the advice of the secretary of defense.

To summarize a bit at this point, perceptions are filtered, and only certain perceptions become cognitions. Cognitions are both new inputs and a function of the existing mental model that makes them possible in the first place. The mental model itself is quite complex, containing previously constructed elements such as attributional beliefs (beliefs about what causes what), values and norms created or assimilated from the larger cultural context, and memories, along with a categorization and relational scheme probably unique to the individual that allows the model to both persist and change over time. Important to this conceptualization is the understanding that change in any part of this system of perception/cognition/mental theory/attitude can lead to change in other elements. Belief change can cause attitude change; attitude change can cause behavioral change; change in cognition can cause attitude change; attitudes and cognitions can even change beliefs (Zimbardo and Leippe, 1991, 34).

While we can conceptualize the mental model's structural components to be beliefs/attributions, values, and memories, the mental model is also shaped by the **personality** of the leader, with personality being the constellation of **traits** possessed by the leader. Though personality is undoubtedly shaped by one's experiences and background, it is also true that some elements of personality seem genetically determined. For example, scholars now assert that a predisposition toward social conservatism may be inherited. Specific traits of personality might be the person's overall level of distrust of others, the individual's level of conceptual complexity in understanding the world around them, the individual's level of loyalty to relevant social groups (such as the nation), the individual's degree of focus on task completion. Other traits might include energy level, sociability, emotional stability, or degree to which the individual can control his or her impulses.

Furthermore, we cannot overlook the broad influence of emotions, motivations, and the state of the body on personality, but also on mental constructs formed and even cognitions. We have previously discussed emotions and the state of the body, but we must also mention here that there are several psychological models of human **motivation**. One conceptual framework that has recently been applied to world leaders is that of David

Winter, based upon previous work of McClelland (McClelland, 1985). Winter postulates three fundamental human motivations, which can exist to greater or lesser degree in any individual. These motivations include need for power, need for affiliation, and need for achievement. For example, according to Winter's scoring system (1990), the strongest motivation for John F. Kennedy was need for achievement. But these motivations are not one-dimensional. Nixon's need for affiliation was almost as great as his need for achievement, and Nixon rates rather average on need for power in Winter's scoring.

The deeper element of **character** may contain underlying structural parameters of the individual's personality. Character is relatively underconceptualized in psychology, but most psychologists use the term to refer to some deep organizing principles of the human psyche. One example could be the individual's predisposition toward abstractive versus practicalist reasoning. Another example might be integrity, here meaning the degree to which constructs, emotions, beliefs, and attitudes are consistent in the individual. A related concept might be the degree to which the individual is able to tolerate dissonance between beliefs and action. Such dissonance is often termed **cognitive dissonance**, and this concept can inform our concept of mental models.

To understand the concept of cognitive dissonance, it is useful to discuss an example. Suppose a person is absolutely convinced that smoking harms you. And yet that person smokes. If the person's deep character is not shaken by this inconsistency because his or her character has a high tolerance for it, the person may simply both continue to smoke and continue to think it will harm them. However, if the person's character has a low tolerance for inconsistency, the person may be forced to either change his or her actions and stop smoking, or may be forced to change, add to, or delete certain attributional beliefs about smoking. Interestingly, empirical study seems to demonstrate that the likeliest course of action in a case of cognitive dissonance is a change in belief, as it is less costly than a change in behavior.

APPROACHING LEADERS

Most empirical work in psychology derives from experiments and simulations, some of which are embedded in survey instruments and some of which take place in laboratory settings. Most work examining particular individuals' psychology is performed using standard psychological profile testing and/or in-depth psychoanalytic examination. All of it is fascinating. However, its applicability to the assessment of the personalities and views of world leaders is obviously limited. Most leaders refuse to take personality tests. Most leaders refuse to participate in psychoanalysis. Some of us are old enough to remember when Thomas Eagleton had to drop out as a vice presidential candidate because years previously he had visited a therapist to help him cope with a family loss (and, worse yet, had undergone electroshock treatments). He also happened to shed a few tears once during an interview that touched upon that loss. There are real costs to a leader of letting someone assess their personalities and views. As a result, there are several FPA scholars that do use experiments and simulations to probe general psychological phenomena in FPDM; for example, the decision board approach of Alex Mintz et al. (1997), or the FPDM simulations of the ICONS Project (ICONS, 2004).

Nevertheless, the assessment of leader personality, with a concomitant understanding of a leader's mental model, is clearly a high priority for political psychologists and foreign policy analysts. The problem is that one does not have the luxury of extended person-to-person contact with world leaders. At-a-distance measures are required for this task. The two primary at-a-distance methodologies in use by those who wish to study the personality and views of world leaders are psychobiography and content analysis.

Psychobiography

There have been many examples of "psychologizing" leaders by examining their lives. Sigmund Freud (1967) himself psychoanalyzed Woodrow Wilson based upon biographical material, and Wilson was reanalyzed in a famous psychobiography by Alexander and Juliette George (1956). Numerous others have attempted to psychoanalyze leaders such as Hitler and Stalin. One of the benefits of psychobiography is the ability to bring to light emotional factors that play a role in motivation and decisionmaking. In this section, we will concentrate on the work of two scholars who have famously employed psychobiography in the study of world leaders: James David Barber and Jerrold Post.

James David Barber, who died in 2004, is most famous for the successive editions of his book, *The Presidential Character*. Barber was of the opinion that we should not elect leaders with dysfunctional personalities. He developed a fourfold categorization scheme for leaders using two axes: active-passive and positive-negative. The active-passive dimension taps into the leader's energy level and sense that personal effort can make a difference in human affairs. The positive-negative dimension addresses the leader's motivation for seeking office and overall outlook on life, probing whether the leader was basically optimistic or pessimistic, trusting or suspicious, motivated by feelings of neediness or shame or obligation or motivated by feelings of confidence and joy in the work to be done. Barber believed that these two traits, or elements of personality, were shaped long before a president is elected to office. In Barber's view, a careful examination of the leader's background, upbringing, early successes and failures, and career could provide insight into what type of leader an individual would be.

Not surprisingly, Barber felt that active-positive leaders, such as FDR, Harry Truman, and JFK, made the best presidents. They are not driven by twisted and dark motives, and are willing to work hard to effect improvements. They are also willing to reverse course when things do not turn out well, for they are not constrained by a rigid ideology, but rather motivated by the sense that they should search for policies that actually produce the results they desire.

On the other hand, Barber fervently wished that Americans would not elect leaders who were active-negative in orientation. Leaders thus categorized include Woodrow Wilson, Herbert Hoover, Lyndon B. Johnson, and Richard M. Nixon. These leaders are compelled to power by deep-seated feelings of inadequacy and fear of humiliation and ostracism. They become rigid in thinking and in action, and cannot relate to others with genuine warmth and empathy. They may be feared, but they are not loved—and they know it. They may be willing to circumvent convention or even rules and laws in order to maintain or increase their power.

Of the remaining two types of leaders, passive-positive and passive-negative, Barber actually prefers the passive-negatives. These are leaders who take the mantle of leadership out of a sense of obligation or duty, not out of a desire for power and control. At the same time, passive-negatives may have a hard time effecting significant change, given their lower level of activity. Barber identifies Calvin Coolidge and Dwight D. Eisenhower as passive-negative presidents. Interestingly, new research seems to indicate that Coolidge only became passive-negative, as versus active-positive, after the death of his son in 1924, which caused Coolidge to become clinically depressed (Gilbert, 2003).

Passive-positive leaders, while not as great a danger as active-negative leaders, present a persistent risk of scandal and corruption. So focused as they are on issues of affiliation and acceptance, while also dependent upon others for reassurance, support, and even direction, passive-positive leaders may find that others are willing to take advantage of their emotional neediness and willingness to turn a blind eye to their own excesses and those of their friends. William Howard Taft, Warren G. Harding, and Ronald Reagan were passive-positive presidents, according to Barber.

Jerrold Post was one of the founders of the CIA's Office of Leadership Analysis in the 1970s. Having spent the better part of his career analyzing foreign leaders, Post has developed a fairly systematic approach to the task. He calls his methodology *anamnesis,* and believes that a good political psychological analysis will contain several parts. The first part is a psychobiography that compares the time line of the leader's life to the time line of events taking place in the nation and the world. The family saga must be understood, as well as birth order and relationship among siblings. Has the family emigrated from another land? Is the family wealthy, or have they lost wealth over the generations? Have family patriarchs been war heroes? Have there been traumatic deaths in the family? Early heroes and dreams are important to examine. For example, Post notes that Indira Gandhi's favorite childhood game was to be the commanding general over her forces of toy soldiers. The leader's education, mentors, and adolescent life experiences should be examined for influences that will shape the leader's personality. For example, when FDR's mother or father would forbid him to do something, he would find a way to please them while still doing what he wanted to do. Early successes and failures are often a template for high-stakes decisions later in the leader's career.

The second part of the anamnesis concerns the leader's personality. A recounting of the leader's balance between work and personal life is useful, as well as an investigation of his health and habits, such as drinking and drug use. The leader's intellectual capacity, knowledge, and judgment will be probed. Emotional stability and motivations, conscience and values, and the quality of interpersonal relationships with family, friends, and coworkers will also be noted. The leader's reaction to criticism, attack, or failure will be important to discover.

The third part of the anamnesis inquires about the actual substantive beliefs held by the leader about issues such as the security of the nation, or about the nature of power. But other beliefs, such as political philosophy or ideology, will be examined. The fourth part of the analysis surveys the leader's style, examining factors such as oratorical skill, ability to communicate to the public, aspects of strategy and tactics preferred in particular situations, and negotiating style. As we have noted previously, Post, as a trained psychiatrist, is also alert to the presence of mental illness in world leaders.

Post is then able to use this four-part analysis to project a leader's reaction to various possible situations in international relations. Which issues will be most important to the leader? What is the best way to deter such a leader? To persuade such a leader to change his mind? What type of negotiating stance will this leader prefer? How will this leader cope with high-stress, high-stakes crises? The type of analysis Post was able to offer to the CIA no doubt finds parallel in the intelligence establishments of other nations (Post, 2003).

Content Analysis

Content analysis is another at-a-distance measure for analyzing the traits, motivations, and personal characteristics of world leaders. It can be a complement, or an alternative, to psychobiographical techniques. The artifacts of one's personality must include the things one has said and written. There must be some relationship between these and personality. This is the primary assumption upon which content analysis as a methodology is based.

However, there are important reasons to believe that this assumption is not always valid. Politicians lie, and sometimes for good reasons, such as reasons of national security. Much of what politicians say in public has been ghostwritten. A politician may say different things—and differently—to different audiences. And even in spontaneous interviews, the answers given may be shaped, sometimes unnaturally, by the manner in which the question is posed.

Scholars who use content analysis try to get around these perturbing factors in several ways. First, spontaneous live interviews are the most preferred source of text. Second, diaries, letters to confidantes, and automatic tape recordings (such as existed in the Kennedy, Johnson, and Nixon administrations) are very useful. Last, it is important to obtain a large amount of text, spanning different time periods, audiences, and subjects, in order to get a fairly accurate result from content analysis.

There are two primary forms of content analysis: thematic content analysis and quantitative (or "word-count") content analysis. In the first technique, the scholar develops a categorization of themes he or she wishes to investigate. Sometimes the dependent variable is the appearance or frequency of a theme within the text; at other times, the scholar creates a variable from the theme and records the value of the variable. For example, Ole Holsti, in his content analysis of John Foster Dulles, secretary of state under Eisenhower, was interested in four themes. These were Dulles's views on Soviet policy, Soviet capabilities, and Soviet success, and Dulles's overall evaluation of the Soviet Union. Each of these themes allowed for variation. For example, text commenting on Soviet policy could characterize that policy as friendly or hostile or something in between. Soviet capabilities could be seen along a continuum from strong to weak. Soviet policy might be, overall, successful or unsuccessful in Dulles's eyes. Dulles's evaluation of the Soviet Union could range from good to bad.

Interestingly, what Holsti found was that regardless of how Dulles viewed Soviet policy, capabilities, or success, Dulles's overall evaluation of the Soviet Union remained constant—"bad." Even when directly confronted by an interviewer concerning the Soviet 1956 demobilization of more than a million men, Dulles felt that the move did not lower world tensions because the men might be put to work making, for example, more atomic weapons. Holsti felt his analysis was one methodology whereby the dynamics of a rigid and closed belief system could be identified.

Thematic content analysis is only as meaningful as the analyst's categorization scheme, of course. Word-count content analysis, on the other hand, rests upon a foundation tied to psychological theory. If words are the artifacts of personality, then particular personality traits can be linked to particular word choices. Theoretical literature in psychology can be plumbed to determine such links. Then, while parsing text, the presence and the absence of particular words may be noted, and the presence or absence of traits inferred. For example, researchers have suggested that use of the words *I, me, my, mine*, and *myself* might indicate the trait of self-confidence.

In order to use this proposition, we must go through several steps. First, in addition to noting the presence of these words, we must also be able to notice their absence. Hermann postulates that these words indicate self-confidence when used in such as way as to demonstrate that the speaker is an instigator of an activity ("This is my plan"), or as an authority figure ("Let me explain"), or as the recipient of something positive ("You flatter me"). In the case that these words are used without any of these three connotations, it would indicate the absence of the trait ("He hit me").

Second, there must be a means of computing a score for the trait. A simple way is to simply sum the total instances where these words were used, and then determine what proportion of uses corresponds to the three expressions of self-confidence. Third, the score by itself means nothing without comparison. We cannot tell if a raw score is high or low or average without a group to which to compare it. A sample population to which the leader can be compared—usually a sample of other regional or world leaders—must be available. Scores are standardized and then compared to see how many standard deviations from the mean they are. For example Hermann uses the comparison table on the following page.

Next, the analyst must think again about the usage of the words in question for contextual validity. For example, while teaching a class on political psychology many years ago, one of my students, performing just such a word-count content analysis, announced that François Mitterand was extremely lacking in self-confidence! Knowing just a little about Mitterand, I pronounced that impossible. Upon looking at the coded text, it became apparent that Mitterand always used the "royal we." That is, he referred to himself in the plural to denote that he was representing the nation, as did the French kings of old. Thus, Mitterand would say, "This is our plan; this is what we believe would work best," even though he was referring to himself. When we adjusted for this cultural tradition, the recoding showed Mitterand to be possessed of abundant self-confidence.

Last, the analyst would be well advised to see if trait scores varied significantly by time period, by audience, or by topic. In her analysis of Saddam Hussein, Margaret G. Hermann found that self-confidence swung widely according to time period—that is, if Hussein was pre-invasion or postinvasion (Hermann in Post, 2003). A more nuanced view of such differences

Table 2.1   Adapted from Hermann, 2003.

Personality Traits	87 Heads of State	122 Political Leaders
Belief in ability to control events	Mean = .44 Low < .30 High > .58	Mean = .45 Low < .33 High > .57
Need for power and influence	Mean = .50 Low < .37 High > .62	Mean = .50 Low < .38 High > .62
Self-confidence	Mean = .62 Low < .44 High > .81	Mean = .57 Low < .34 High > .80
Conceptual complexity	Mean = .44 Low < .32 High > .56	Mean = .45 Low < .32 High > .58
Task focus orientation	Mean = .59 Low < .46 High > .71	Mean = .62 Low < .48 High > .76
In-group bias (nationalism)	Mean = .42 Low < .32 High > .53	Mean = .43 Low < .34 High > .53
Distrust of others	Mean = .41 Low < .25 High > .56	Mean = .38 Low < .20 High > .56

could avoid the masking effects of using an overall mean score for any particular trait.

Though word-count content analysis has been used by many scholars, one of the best ways of exploring its potential for FPA is to examine the work of Margaret G. Hermann. Trained as a psychologist, Hermann began to work on the CFP CREON Project at its inception. One of her earliest research endeavors was the attempt to determine if personalities mattered in classroom simulations of the outbreak of World War I. She became convinced that they did, and desired to create a means by which the personal characteristics of world leaders could be both assessed and used as the basis for projections of how they would behave and react in particular circumstances. As she developed her framework, which is based on long-standing trait research in psychology (Costa and McCrae, 1992), she was called upon by the leadership analysis office in the CIA to explain her approach. Thus, her work has spanned both the academic and policymaking communities.

As with many researchers who perform content analysis, Hermann prefers spontaneous live interviews across topics, time periods, and audiences. She also states that results should be based on at least fifty interview responses of over one hundred words apiece.

Hermann codes for seven personality traits: (1) belief in one's own ability to control events, (2) need for power and influence, (3) conceptual complexity, (4) self-confidence, (5) task/affect orientation (problem focus or relationship focus), (6) distrust of others, and (7) in-group bias (formerly called nationalism). These seven traits speak to three more general characteristics of personality: whether an individual leader challenges or respects constraints, is open to new information, and is primarily motivated by internal or external forces.

Hermann goes further. These three general characteristics may then be combined into eight possible personality "orientations." For example, an expansionistic leader challenges constraints, is closed to new information, and holds a problem focus. A consultative leader respects constraints, is closed to new information, and exhibits a relationship focus motivation. The following list illustrates her framework:

- Expansionistic: challenges constraints, closed to information, problem focus: focus is on expanding one's power and influence
- Evangelistic: challenges constraints, closed to information, relationship focus: focus is on persuading others to accept one's message and join one's cause
- Incremental: challenges constraints, open to information, problem focus: focus is on maintaining one's maneuverability and flexibility while avoiding the obstacles that continually try to limit both
- Charismatic: challenges constraints, open to information, relationship focus: focus is on achieving one's agenda by engaging others in the process and persuading them to act
- Directive: respects constraints, closed to information, problem focus: focus is on personally guiding policy along paths consistent with one's own views while still working within the norms and rules of one's current position
- Consultative: respects constraints, closed to information, relationship focus: focus is on monitoring that important others will support, or not actively oppose, what one wants to do in a problem situation
- Reactive: respects constraints, open to information, problem focus: focus is on assessing what is possible in the current situation given the nature of the problem and considering what important constituencies will allow
- Accommodative: respects constraints, open to information, relationship focus: focus is on reconciling differences and building consensus, empowering others, and sharing accountability in the process.

One of the most valuable elements of Hermann's framework is that she is able to draw out from the psychology of the orientations hypotheses concerning such varied behavior as the style of the leader, likely foreign policy, nature of preferred advisory group, nature of information search, ability to tolerate disagreement, and method of dealing with opposition. For example, we have mentioned the expansionist leader, who is concerned with increasing his or her control over territory, resources, or people, and who perceives the world as divided into "us" and "them." According to Hermann, an expansionist leader will prefer a very loyal advisory group where the leader's preferences will always prevail. An expansionist's ability to tolerate disagreement will be quite limited, for this will be interpreted as a challenge to authority. An expansionist's usual approach to opposition is to eliminate it. And the nature of an expansionist's information search will be characterized by the desire to find information that supports and confirms what the leader already believes and desires to have happen.

The expansionist's style is prudent and wary, for this type of leader wants to keep one step ahead of leaders and potential opponents. When he or she enjoys a power advantage in a situation, however, the leader will attempt to exercise his or her will, by force if necessary. As a result, the foreign policy of an expansionist is not likely to be very committed unless the situation is one in which the leader's nation holds an undisputed advantage or in which the nation has no alternative but to fight. However, the foreign policy rhetoric of such a leader is likely to be fairly hostile in tone and focused on threats and enemies. The leader may also advocate immediate change in the international system.

Hermann's framework for analyzing leader orientation, then, allows for several layers of derivative analysis that may be of use in forecasting likely behavior over time.

Other Techniques

There are a few other techniques deserving of mention with regard to leader analysis. The first is that of "think aloud" protocols (Purkitt, 1998). Though difficult to use with real world leaders, it can be used with lower-level officials that may be more accessible. In short, the interviewer presents the official with a specific foreign policy problem, and then asks him or her to think out loud while deciding how to react to that problem. Though such responses are manipulable, of course, the intent is to understand what concepts, in what order, and in what relation, arise in the official's mind while thinking the issue through. These transcripts can then be analyzed.

One such method of analysis is cognitive mapping. In cognitive mapping, a visual diagram of a text is constructed. Concepts and variables are coded thematically from the text, and then linkages and relationships are mapped using lines connecting concepts. For example, if a Middle East expert believes that Palestinian suicide bombings are one motivation for the building of security walls by the Israelis, then a line from the first to the second, with a symbol denoting that the relationship is positive, will be drawn. A cognitive map, once drawn, may then be further analyzed in several ways. The consistency of the linkages and valences may be noted. The "tightness" of the conceptual clusterings can be investigated. Change over time in cognitive mapping can be discerned (Shapiro and Bonham, 1973).

Another technique is personality assessment of leaders by scholars. For example, Etheredge (1978) combed scholarly works, insiders' accounts, biographies, and autobiographies and coded presidents and secretaries of state for personality variables. He then masked the identities of the leaders and asked several other scholars to also rank these anonymous individuals along the same personality variables. Intercoder reliability was quite high. M. Hermann performed a variant of this technique in her doctoral dissertation. Wanting to investigate the effect of personality of leaders on the outbreak of World War I, Hermann wished to run simulations of that event with students whose personalities were similar to the leaders involved in World War I, and students whose personalities were different from those same leaders. In order to perform such an analysis, Hermann used standard psychological inventories to assess the students' personalities. But to compare them to the leaders' personalities, she had to come up with a creative way to determine the leaders' scores on those same tests. She immersed herself in the biographical material of each leader, and then took the personality test as if she were the leader in question.

Yet another technique is that of the Q-sort, where subjects are asked to report how strongly they agree or disagree with certain statements that relate to psychological characteristics the researcher wishes to study. These self-reports are then subjected to factor analysis. The resulting factors represent the subject's "narration of self," which can then be analyzed (McKeown, 1984). One can also use this technique at-a-distance by asking leadership experts or even public citizens about their perceptions of a leader's beliefs, much like the aforementioned personality assessments.

Finally, this chapter would be remiss without an introduction to ProfilerPlus, a series of computer interfaces and software developed by Michael Young to effect word-count content analysis as well as cognitive mapping. Young has prepared a demonstration for FPA students to examine, and that demo is available at www.socialscienceautomation.com/hudson/hudson.html.

The demo is narrated and revolves around the idea that automated text coding allows for superior analysis of textual data. The student is first introduced to four types of automated coding: tag and retrieve, frequency analysis, concept coding, and information extraction. Each type is demonstrated by conceptual discussion followed by actual coding results for Presidents

Bill Clinton and George W. Bush for their respective State of the Union addresses to Congress. In one case, an Iranian leader's remarks are coded.

Tag and retrieve is simply the built-in ability to "tag" certain words in texts, retrieving the context in which the words were used.

Frequency analysis "counts" how often particular words are used, sometimes in contrast to divergent sets of words. The demo illustrates frequency analysis in two ways: the Leadership Style Analysis of Margaret G. Hermann, and the Verbal Behavior Analysis (VBA) system of Walter Weintraub. For Hermann's scheme, the conceptual complexity and task orientation scores of Clinton and Bush are presented; for VICS (Verbs in Context System), the use of "feeling" words that might indicate either aloofness or insincerity depending on use are examined for Clinton and Bush.

Concept coding refers to the automated search for patterns in the use of word phrases. Such pattern recognition typically involves more advanced algorithms than frequency analysis. For example, the algorithms would have to distinguish between the use of positive or neutral context phrases surrounding the mention of other entities versus the use of negative context, in order to code level of distrust. Two examples are given: first, the variables of "belief in own ability to control events," "distrust of others," and "need for power" from the Hermann framework, as well as the variables "nature of the political universe," and "preferred strategy for achieving goals" from the Operational Code analysis scheme developed by Stephen Walker, Michael Young, and Mark Shafer (VICS). For President Bush, the Operational Code variables are also displayed in a longitudinal graph, showing the effect of 9/11 on Bush's perceptions.

Information extraction, the final type of automated coding, is illustrated by two approaches: Image Theory (Martha Cottam, 1986, 1992, and 1998) and Cognitive Mapping. Image theory examines larger themes constructed from particular words used to describe other nations. These themes correspond to broad images the speaker has of other entities, with the example given in the demo of "degenerate." This "degenerate" image is demonstrated to be present in the speeches of Iranian leader Ali Khamenei in reference to the United States. Cognitive mapping, on the other hand, restructures the text physically in order to display a visual picture of the relationships between concepts in text. Both sentence-level and speech-level mapping is demonstrated. Valences and/or levels of certainty may also be attached to the relationships outlined in the maps, and change in the map over time is often analyzed by comparing successive speeches.

In conclusion, then, FPA asserts that leaders do matter, and that analysis of perception, cognition, and personality of world leaders is well worth undertaking. In addition, FPA draws upon a wide variety of techniques to make such an analysis possible, despite the unavailability of world leaders for direct observation.

3

Group Decisionmaking: Small Group Dynamics, Organizational Process, and Bureaucratic Politics

No matter how influential or mercenary, a single leader cannot make and implement foreign policy by himself or herself. In fact, in most countries, foreign policy decisions are always made in a group setting. And these policies are virtually always carried out by particular organizations or arrays of organizations (bureaucracies).

We might consider using the following flowchart to help us orient ourselves to the role of groups in foreign policy decisionmaking.

Of course, these distinctions cannot be precisely drawn. Small groups may devolve to bureaucratic politics, depending upon the group's membership. Organizations must implement decisions regarding nonroutine prob-

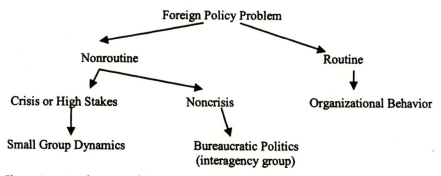

Figure 3.1   Involvement of Groups in Foreign Policy Decisionmaking

lems. Nevertheless, the locus of decision in a particular foreign policy situation is likely to follow tendencies as portrayed in the figure. In the remainder of this chapter, we will investigate Foreign Policy Analysis (FPA) theory regarding each of these types of groups.

SMALL GROUP DYNAMICS

Most high-level foreign policy decisions are made in small groups, meaning approximately fifteen persons or less. This is not to say that only less than fifteen persons are involved in any particular issue, but serious discussion of, say, a crisis situation almost demands that a leader be able to sit around a table with a set of peers and engage in candid and far-ranging debate of policy options. As a result, the study of small group dynamics has received considerable attention in FPA.

We have mentioned in chapter 2 that a leader's personality will play a role in his or her choice of close FP advisors. Some personalities prefer groups that defer to the leader's opinions; others want to hear dissenting views. Some personalities desire a more methodical process of decision-making, while others do not want to take the chance that a methodical process might stifle either creativity or second thoughts.

Charles F. Hermann (1978) asserts that elements of the group's structure, such as the distribution of power within the group as well as the type of role played by the group's members, will have important consequences for group process, which in turn may have ramifications for FP choice. Groups wherein the leader holds primary power will behave differently than groups wherein the president may have considerable power, but must share that power with other members at the table, such as the military chief of staff in a nation heavily dependent on the military's sanction for rule. Likewise, members of the group may view themselves as differing somewhat in their role at the table. Some members may view themselves as loyal staff, whose presence must help facilitate promotion of the leaders' preferences. Others may view themselves primarily as delegates of external entities, whose main purpose in the group is to clarify and argue for the perspective of that entity. So, for example, the director of central intelligence (DCI) may feel less like a staff member and more like the representative of his analysts and agents when part of a National Security Council (NSC) meeting. Still others may view themselves as autonomous actors, who are neither completely beholden to the leader nor to an external entity. These are often some of the most powerful players in the small group, because it is assumed that being beholden to none, their analysis is more clear-sighted, less con-strained, and thus more valuable. Furthermore, the consent of these power-ful players may be necessary to implement any resulting decision. In the

United States, the secretaries of defense and state are often relatively autonomous players in FP decisions. For example, the U.S.-led bombing of Bel-
grade in 1998 over the Kosovo crisis was often called "Madeleine's War"
because of Madeleine Albright's strong, almost single-handed insistence on
retaliatory action against the Serbs, even in the face of a more cautionary
stance taken by the Pentagon and even NATO allies.

Many FP issues are often relegated to interagency committees for initial
discussion, and these are then tasked to report to the higher levels of decisionmakers. Though these interagency committees are often technically
"small groups," we will not consider them in this section because they are
almost always "all-delegate" groups, whose interactions can only be understood by reference to theories concerning bureaucratic politics.

Hermann extended his analysis of groups to talk about a more nuanced
view of member role than the simple staff/delegate/autonomous actor categorization. In later work, Hermann began to develop indicators of whether,
on a particular issue, a member would be an advocate of a specific policy,
a "cue-taker" who would see which way the decision was going and band-
wagon, or a "broker" who would use his or her influence to create a consensus position through coalitions and bargaining (Stewart, Hermann, and
Hermann, 1989). Having identified which members of a small group
would play each of these roles, Hermann then created a set of rules that
helped him decide which members would take what positions, and which
views would prevail as a result. Though the data requirements for such an
exercise are quite high, this exercise is no different in kind than that performed by top-notch investigative journalists as they try to piece together,
say, how the NSC came to a particular FP decision.

The most seminal work on small groups in foreign policy decisionmaking (FPDM), however, is the work of Irving Janis, which focuses on small
group dysfunction in the foreign policy realm. Though not all small groups
are dysfunctional, quite a few are, given the particular characteristics of
FPDM—high stress, high stakes, ambiguity, uncertainty, secrecy, risk (Janis,
1982). Small group dysfunction, which Janis labels "groupthink," feeds
upon just such situations, which elicit a strong emotional response center-
ing around fear. Fear-inducing circumstances prompt us to find the emotional support that will enable us to decrease our fear to manageable levels.
That emotional support is first and foremost sought through the small
group itself, often because the foreign policy issues involved cannot be
revealed outside of the group. Janis feels groupthink is a form of group
derangement, a parallel to the derangement we often note in larger groups
as "mob psychology." Groupthink is a form of dysfunctional group cohesiveness.

In Janis's original theory, groupthink does not arise from conscious
manipulation of group members by the leader for his or her own ends, but

rather from a subtle social dynamic that evolves over time. However, as 't Hart and others have noted (1997), it is quite possible to create groupthink-like processes and outcomes in ways other than those posed by Janis. For example, the context may include a high level of threat from the leader himself or herself. For example, Jerrold Post (1991) relates the anecdote of Saddam Hussein calling together his inner circle for advice at a crucial juncture early in his reign. One minister opined that perhaps Saddam should relinquish leadership for a short while until the crisis at hand passed. Saddam thanked him for his opinion, and later that day the minister's body—chopped into pieces and placed in a plastic bag—was delivered to his wife. Needless to say, such an unusually coercive context will almost certainly promote groupthink as well. Other possibilities that may lead to the development of groupthink-like processes and outcomes would include the presence of a highly charismatic leader who elicits in noncoercive fashion an unusual degree of loyalty; a larger cultural context in which unanimity and consensus are highly valued; or an issue about which the society allows for little deviation in acceptable viewpoint.

Though there are several routes to groupthink, we will examine in greater detail Janis's original conception of the social dynamics of groupthink where the variables noted above are not in play. In the original conceptualization, group dynamics produce subtle constraints, which the leader may inadvertently reinforce, that prevent members of the group from exercising their critical powers and from openly expressing doubts when the majority of the group appears to have reached a consensus. There may certainly be sincere agreement with the emerging consensus, but Janis points out that in a groupthink group, there is a significant degree of insincere agreement as well. We have all participated in group deliberations where we went along with a decision with which we did not feel comfortable and then watched in dismay and sometimes horror when the decision turns out as badly as we thought (to ourselves) that it would. How do rational, educated persons find themselves in such a situation, assuming they are not members of Saddam Hussein's group of advisors?

Janis opens his analysis by means of an illuminating field observation made when he was studying the social dynamics of smokers at a clinic set up to help them stop smoking:

> At the second meeting of one group of smokers, consisting of twelve middle-class American men and women, two of the most dominant members took the position that heavy smoking was an almost incurable addiction. The majority of the others soon agreed that no one could be expected to cut down drastically. One heavy smoker, a middle-aged business executive, took issue with this consensus, arguing that by using willpower he had stopped smoking since joining the group and that everyone else could do the same. His declaration

was followed by a heated discussion, which continued in the halls of the building after the formal meeting adjourned. Most of the others ganged up against the man who was deviating from the group consensus. Then, at the beginning of the next meeting, the deviant announced that he had made an important decision. "When I joined," he said, "I agreed to follow the two main rules required by the clinic—to make a conscientious effort to stop smoking and to attend every meeting. But I have learned from experience in this group that you can only follow one of the rules, you can't follow them both. And so, I have decided that I will continue to attend every meeting but I have gone back to smoking two packs a day and I will not make any effort to stop smoking again until after the last meeting." Whereupon, the other members beamed at him and applauded enthusiastically, welcoming him back to the fold. . . . At every [subsequent] meeting, the members were amiable, reasserted their warm feeling of solidarity, and sought complete concurrence on every important topic, with no reappearance of the unpleasant bickering that would spoil the cozy atmosphere (1982, 8).

This case, because of its extremity, reveals some of the dynamics at work. When a group is formed, two separate forces are set in motion. The formation of the group sets in motion a decision process to tackle the issue or problem at hand. But the formation of the group also sets in motion a social institution that is to be maintained over time. Thus the group has, in a sense, two goals: to effectively address the problem that catalyzed its formation, and to continue to function as a group. These two goals are neither intuitively nor inevitably at odds. But in groupthink groups, such as the smoking clinic, they become at odds over time.

Group cohesiveness is a powerful source of emotional support for small group members. We see this dynamic at work in families, in gangs, in sports teams, in military platoons, in groups of friends, on specialized internet listservs, in business departments, and so forth. The rest of the world may not appreciate you or even like you, but as long as the people who interact with you in a salient small group (and thus arguably know you best) appreciate and like you, what the rest of the world thinks may not cause you psychological distress. Conversely, the capacity to produce psychological distress for its members is heightened in small groups that interact over time. The source of that stress is fear—fear of ostracism by the group.

Consider that fear of failure in addressing the problem that catalyzed formation of the group is compensated for by the emotional support provided by the group itself, but then the prospect of potentially losing that support produces a fear of ostracism that may dwarf the original fear of task failure. Thus maintenance of group cohesiveness may evolve into the group's primary purpose, supplanting the original task-oriented purpose for which the group was formed in the first place. When this occurs, groupthink exists. What one begins to fear most is to be labeled as a deviant from the group.

As noted in the smoking clinic example, if a group member expresses deviance, the other members of the group will try to influence him or her to revise or tone down their dissident views. If they are not successful in bringing the deviant back into the fold, he or she will be excluded from the group—at first subtly, and then more overtly. Insincere agreement to avoid ostracism may then arise.

In addition to the group's purpose being supplanted and insincere agreement occurring, Janis notes several other hallmarks of groupthink. First, the group's standards of judgment are changed and lowered. The group's standards for judging a matter may stray from more objective reasoning to reasoning based on the desire to prevent deviance or lack of cohesiveness and preserve amiability above all else. Second, groupthink groups begin to think very well of themselves and their members. A groupthink group will feel that it and its members are wiser, more powerful, more knowledgeable, and more virtuous than those who do not belong to the group. This inflated self-image may have several consequences. For one, nonmembers may be dehumanized, especially those who are seen as competing with the group. Nonmembers may be seen as inferior or evil, and action that might not usually be considered moral might be deemed appropriate to deal with nonmembers. For another, inflated self-image may lead to the "risky shift": the propensity for groupthink groups to collectively decide on more risky behavior than any one member of the group would have chosen individually (this is sometimes called "group polarization"). An easy analogy is to teenage gangs. Often these gangs are capable of risky, violent, criminal behavior on a level that no one teen in the group would dare attempt.

In sum, Janis asserts that groupthink groups are hard-hearted but soft-headed. This soft-headedness can also manifest itself in sloppy decision practices due to lowered standards of judgment and inflated self-image. In his case studies of foreign policy fiascoes, Janis finds that the groups in questions usually examined only two options to deal with the problem they faced, and that the group would quickly seize on one of the two options that would never again be critically examined for weakness. He also found very little effort on the part of these groups to obtain information from knowledgeable nonmembers, but found instead a selection bias in the evaluation of information to favor the preferred option, and an utter failure to establish contingency plans in case the preferred option was unsuccessful. Sloppy decisionmaking did not induce psychological stress because of compensatory inflated self-image: the groupthink groups thought of themselves as not only omniscient, but also as invulnerable. And immoral decisionmaking likewise did not induce stress, because loyalty to the group had become the highest form of morality.

Janis is quick to note that not all foreign policy fiascoes are produced by groupthink groups. And it is possible for a groupthink group to operate without producing a fiasco. However, ceteris paribus, it is much more likely for a groupthink group to create fiascoes than otherwise, given its dysfunctional attributes. A case in point, argues Janis, is the 1961 Bay of Pigs episode.

That the Bay of Pigs invasion was a fiasco by any standard is not in doubt. On April 17, 1961, about fourteen hundred Cuban exiles, trained by the United States for this purpose, invaded Cuba at the Bay of Pigs. By the second day, the brigade of exiles was completely surrounded by over twenty thousand Cuban troops. By the third day, about twelve hundred (all who had not been killed) were captured and sent to prison camps. About twenty months later, the United States ransomed most of these with $53 million in food and medicine. The European allies, the United Nations, and friendly Latin American regimes were outraged, and the invasion may have been the catalyst for new military agreements between Cuba and the USSR, which would eventually culminate in the Cuban missile crisis. Even John F. Kennedy, president at the time, asked rhetorically, "How could I have been so stupid to let them go ahead?" (Janis, 1982, 16)

Janis points to the underlying dynamics of Kennedy's first foreign policy inner circle, which included Dean Rusk (secretary of state), Robert McNamara (secretary of defense), Robert "Bobby" Kennedy (attorney general and the president's brother), McGeorge Bundy (special assistant for national security affairs [ANSA]), Arthur Schlesinger, Jr. (White House historian), Allen Dulles (DCI), and Richard Bissell (deputy director of central intelligence [DDCI]). Kennedy had only been in office a very short time. He was under stress to perform well in foreign policy, since he was the youngest president ever elected, he was a Democrat, and he was a Catholic. Kennedy was not the only "greenhorn" in the group: McNamara, Bobby Kennedy, Bundy, and Schlesinger were all new to government, not to mention high-level government office. In the recent presidential campaign, his opponent Richard Nixon had painted Kennedy as too young and inexperienced to stand up to the Soviet threat. Was Kennedy tough enough?

Dulles and Bissell, both holdovers from the previous Eisenhower administration, briefed Kennedy on the ongoing plan for the exiles' invasion of Cuba. The plan, therefore, was the plan of his predecessor: Dwight Eisenhower, two-term Republican president, hero of World War II, and a man about whom no one had qualms about "toughness." Fear of failure in standing up to the Soviet threat was to be extinguished for Kennedy via the emotional support he would get from his small group of advisors. But most were newcomers themselves, and had as great or greater fear of failure as he did. Emotional support from Dulles and Bissell, then, would be key. Since they had crafted the invasion plan, this needed emotional support would only be forthcoming if the plan were accepted. This social dynamic set the stage for groupthink.

Janis points to additional factors auguring in favor of groupthink. Kennedy's election had ushered in a sense of elation and invulnerability among his inner circle. Schlesinger later put it this way: "Euphoria reigned: we thought for a moment that the world was plastic and the future unlimited" (Janis, 1982, 35). Janis also identifies Bobby Kennedy as a self-appointed "mindguard" who would attempt to corral deviants who expressed second thoughts privately: in one instance, Bobby accosted Schlesinger about the latter's doubts with, "You may be right or you may be wrong, but the President has made his mind up. Don't push it any further" (Janis, 1982, 40). Furthermore, Schlesinger himself noted at the time "a curious atmosphere of assumed consensus" (38). No one spoke up against the plan in the group's meetings, even though numerous members apparently did harbor doubts. Silence was interpreted as consent.

In this context, then, group decision-making processes deteriorated in quality. Though the press had leaked the invasion plan, the plan proceeded. The State Department and British intelligence contradicted the CIA position that Castro's army and air force were weak, but there was no attempt to discover which position was correct: the CIA's position was accepted uncritically. One assumption of the plan was that the invasion would ignite the Cuban underground, which would then revolt in the cities. Janis points out that not only did no one think to let the underground know that an invasion was imminent, but that since Castro was alerted by U.S. press reports to the plan, he took preemptive measures to round up dissidents. An egregious error was the decision to move the landing site from Trinidad to the Bay of Pigs—without looking at a topographical map that would show that the Bay of Pigs was a swamp far removed from the Escambray Mountains (which is where the invaders were to flee if they ran into trouble).

Though the Bay of Pigs invasion was a fiasco, Janis argues that Kennedy learned invaluable lessons that prepared him for the higher stakes of the Cuban missile crisis. Among other things, ExCom (the small group formed in response) proceeded quite differently in the second crisis. A wide range of options was considered, and Kennedy refused to allow the group to move swiftly to adoption of a preferred option. Experts, particularly from the military, were grilled instead of being shown deference. Dissension was encouraged, and Bobby Kennedy often assumed the role of devil's advocate. Participants were explicitly asked to be skeptical. There was no formal agenda and no protocol. Subgroups of ExCom met with or without President Kennedy. Often lower-ranking officials were asked to meetings to which their bosses were not invited. Contingency plans were extremely detailed. Kennedy fostered an air of discomfort and reminded all of the grave dangers involved. Issues of morality were openly raised. Reversals of judgment were frequent. Kennedy had members role-play Khrushchev and

Castro, pushing for a nonstereotypical view of the enemy alongside themes of non-humiliation and non-underestimation.

Janis argues that if we are pleased with the result in the Cuban missile crisis, part of the credit must go to Kennedy being scrupulous and diligent in avoiding groupthink at all costs. Thus, it is possible to consider measures to head off this pernicious social dynamic. In his research, Janis explores a variety of ways to defuse this all-too-frequent phenomenon. He encourages leaders to avoid homogeneity in the background of group members, to refuse to dissipate stress and discomfort through group amiability. Leaders might do well to appoint a devil's advocate, though that role may have to be rotated over time so that the person's views are not automatically dismissed due to role expectations. Janis urges leaders not to make the group too insular, to invite in outsiders and experts to openly challenge group assumptions. Kennedy's use of subgroup meetings is a good way to make room for dissent, especially if the leader himself is not present. Janis also counsels leaders to hold their opinions to themselves as long as feasible, so as to not inadvertently close off dissent. A checklist of good decision practices might be used to ensure no important steps have been omitted. Role-playing and study of the other nations involved in order to construct realistic alternative scenarios are very useful. And finally, Janis notes that a variety of cultures have norms of the "last chance" meeting, here after a decision is finalized, participants often get drunk (or otherwise lower their social inhibitions) and then meet again to see if they still agree on the decision made.

Though we have spoken very negatively of groupthink, for good reason, it is possible that the attempt to foment group cohesiveness might have its uses. One such documented use was the 1994–1995 talks between Palestinian and Israeli negotiators to work out the details of the Oslo Accord regarding the West Bank. At the Patio Hotel in remote Eilat, the Israelis took the third floor, the Palestinians took the second, and the talks were held on the first—and no one was allowed to leave for months. As an Israeli negotiator put it, "We created a setting in which there was no physical way out without an agreement" (Schmemann, 1995, A1). The article goes on to note:

> "You could watch the peace process develop like one of those American soap operas. You saw who went to whose room, who was negotiating with whom." The delegates ate together, went to the health club together, Israeli generals took saunas with Palestinian guerrillas. "It created a club mentality vis à vis everybody else. We needed a common enemy, and it became the media. We developed a deep understanding of each other's paranoias, we created a certain trust among representatives of total mistrust."

Even here, we see the power of the emotional support that small groups can provide; power enough to overcome historical hatreds (at least temporarily). The influence of small group dynamics on foreign policymaking should never be underestimated, but rather studied, understood, and used to promote functional ends.

There are other scholarly insights on small group dynamics that deserve mention. For example, the psychologist Garold Stasser noted that most small groups tend to rely primarily on information about the problem that is already known to all or nearly all group members before group discussion commences (Carey, 2005, 4:1,3). Important information that only a few members of the group hold will probably not be used, and is likely to be overlooked in the group discussion. Apparently, the easiest psychological route to agreement is not learning new premises for a decision, but discovering common premises that already exist within the group.

Ryan Beasley's work on how small groups come to agree on a problem representation moves the small group dynamics research agenda forward in significant ways (1998). Beasley believes that small groups are not identical: that there is a taxonomy of groups according to characteristics such as the centrality of particular individuals, the complexity of group discussion, the degree of alternation between speakers, the continuity of the discussion, and so forth. Thus, each type of group may be predisposed to a certain style of group decisionmaking. Beasley postulates several varied processes for group aggregation of individual understandings: simplicity ("classic" groupthink), single representation embellishment (leader-drive groupthink), factionalism, common decomposition, common alternatives, and expertise. In a study of meetings of the British Cabinet over the Munich crisis, Beasley found that each of these types of decisionmaking was used over time. Groupthink-style processes occurred in only five of the twelve meetings. Thus there may be more nuance and complexity to small group dynamics than the work of Janis might suggest.

Sylvan and Haddad (1998) suggest also that in cases of group conflict over problem representation, the technique of "story-telling" begins to dominate, in which participants compete with each other to provide the most articulate causal argument concerning a particular problem. The views of those with the most persuasive story will become the basis for decisionmaking by the group.

The fine volume *Beyond Groupthink*, edited by 't Hart, Stern, and Sundelius (1997), suggests that the "group-as-decisionmaker" might be too simplistic. The small group in FPDM may play a variety of roles that should be considered, not just "command center," but also sanctuary, smoke screen, and arena. Furthermore, the effects of leader personality, culture, and institutional context on small group structure and function need further attention. For example, Stern and Sundelius believe the Bay of Pigs fiasco is better explained as "newgroup syndrome" than classic groupthink à la Janis (Stern, 1997). Going further, Hoyt and Garrison wonder why strategic manipulation of a small group by political "gamesmen" has not been researched more fully (1997): tactics such as non-invitation to meetings, non-sharing of information, destroying a member's credibility, casting a member as an insubordinate when they refuse to be silenced or excluded, duplicating another member's assignments to provide alternative information, dropping an item from the agenda, and so forth. Furthermore, Vertzberger suggests that scholars look more deeply into the cultural context of small group dynamics, pointing to the *guru-chela* (teacher-disciple) template for political relationships in India as an example (1997; see also 1990). In conclusion, there is much more ground to be plowed in FPA concerning the analysis of small group dynamics.

ORGANIZATIONAL PROCESS

Though small group dynamics are extremely important in understanding foreign policy behavior, it must not be overlooked that most high-level foreign policy decisions are implemented through large executive organizations, such as departments and agencies. Furthermore, the government's "senses" are these same organizations: the gathering of information and the initial processing of information are performed for the most part by organizations. Governments both perceive and act primarily through organizations.

This situation invites us to explore the degree to which the government is not a unitary rational actor. Given the prominence of organizations in the government's ability to conduct foreign policy, it might be more useful at times to view the government as a matrix of organizations, or, in other words, as a national bureaucracy. There are multiple actors in a national bureaucracy, not one unitary actor. And just as we have found that a collection of individuals within a small group might not act in classically rational fashion, so we can also speculate that the actions of the multiple bureaucratic players might also result in behavior that is less than optimally rational and coordinated. Those who have had the opportunity to work within a large organization, whether that be a government agency, a business corporation, a university or school system, or even an organized religion, inevitably discover that sometimes the collective is less intelligent than the sum of its members.

So why have organizations at all? Organizations exist to provide capabilities that otherwise would not exist. Consider the case of space exploration, such as sending probes to Mars or Saturn's moon Titan. When one details all the subtasks involved in accomplishing those larger tasks, it becomes clear that without large collectives of people pooling resources, knowledge, labor, and leadership, no space exploration would ever have taken place. Tasks such as space exploration, or even the fielding of an army of men, require specialization so that larger tasks may be divided into smaller, more feasible ones. Such endeavors also require a tremendous amount of coordination and communication, with the ability to preserve memory as particular individuals enter and leave the larger organization. Remember that some large organizations relevant to foreign policy, such as the U.S. Department of Defense, may have over one million employees!

A common reaction is to anthropomorphize organizations, and speak in such terms as, "The Defense Department wanted greater authority to collect intelligence, and it got what it wanted." This type of language, again connoting a unitary rational actor but at a lower level of government, conceals a more complex reality. Though large organizations contain many human beings, large organizations are arguably a simpler form of life than a human being. First, they have a constrained functionality related to the purpose of their creation. It is useless to ask NASA to plan the invasion of Afghanistan. It is useless to ask the State Department to send a man to the moon. Of course, some organizations may be interested in expanding their functions, but by and large that cannot happen quickly. Organizations will develop specific skill sets, which will constrain what they are able to do. Second, this will give rise to an organizational culture, which is an understanding by the humans in the organization as to the organization's identity and mission and vision. Morton Halperin calls this an understanding of the organization's "essence," which, once entrenched, is almost impossible to change.

One's essence leads to the staking out of particular "turf," meaning an understanding of which issues the organization can claim a "stake" in, or organizational interest. Concerning some issues the organization may view itself as the primary "stakeholder," and in other issues it may view itself as a lesser stakeholder.

An organization's resources include not only its personnel and their capabilities and talents, but also a standard set of resources such as budget, influence, morale, and autonomy, in addition to turf and essence, all of which we will discuss in due turn.

Essence. An organization's self-understanding of what it is and does is crucial to its ability to function effectively. An organization's sense of identity and mission provides its members with a vision of why what they are doing is important and necessary, and how what they are doing differs from what other organizations are doing. Without this focus and vision, an organization may not develop the special skill set needed to possess influence within the bureaucracy, and it may also lose its ability to instill morale in its members. An organization's essence will lead it over time to develop a distinctive organizational culture, with norms of dress, behavior, thinking, and value prioritization. A legendary case in point is the differing corporate cultures of Microsoft and Apple. Not only can one tell the employees apart, one can also tell the customers apart!

The development of an identity always carries risks however. The most salient risks are empire-building and intra- and interorganizational xenophobia. Though organizations are designed to be tools of a higher-level elected executive, in many ways they are far more powerful than that executive. They are going to last much longer than he or she will; they directly control large sums of money and personnel; they exercise capabilities on the ground; they are not under electoral accountability. It is not surprising, then, that many governmental organizations begin to act as autonomous entities—empires, almost—that are not in the business of obeying directives so much as in the business as negotiating directives with an eye to their organization's advantage. One president (FDR) put it this way:

> "The Treasury is so large and far-flung and ingrained in its practices that I find it is almost impossible to get the action and results I want. . . . But the Treasury is not to be compared with the State Department. You should go through the experience of trying to get any changes in the thinking, policy, and action of the career diplomats and then you'd know what a real problem was. But the Treasury and the State Department put together are nothing as compared with the Na-a-vy. . . . To change anything in the Na-a-vy is like punching a feather bed. You punch it with your right and you punch it with your left until you are finally exhausted, and then you find the damn bed just as it was before you started punching" (Eccles 1951, 336).

Essence can also breed distrust and resentment of those who are different, whether they be in other organizations, or even within one's own organization. The infamous antipathy between the FBI and CIA arguably contributed to some of the intelligence failures that led to 9/11. In the wake of that horrific event, the heads of both agencies publicly accused the other of incompetence and noncooperation. Even the intelligence reform of December 2004, with its creation of a director of national intelligence (DNI) and two new interagency intelligence centers, did not stop the bickering between the two. At the time of this writing, they were feuding over which had the right to recruit foreign nationals in the United States to spy on other nations.

But this xenophobia also extends within the organization. Those who are not "like" those who identify with the essence of the organization may be targeted for harassment and even expulsion. Some scholars have used the term *homosexual reproduction* to refer to an organization's tendency to employ only those who embrace the organization's essence and culture, which may, as a result, become even narrower over time. I once overheard a conversation between two FBI agents, in which was discussed the dismissal of another colleague. One said, "Yeah, he'd show up to work in sandals and chinos. It's true he was very bright—possibly the brightest in the office—but there was no way the Bureau was going to keep him. He just didn't fit in." But it is not just individuals who are targeted in this fashion: sometimes groups of individuals may find themselves marginalized or even expelled because they do not "belong," given the organization's essence. The position of submariners within the Navy has always been somewhat marginalized, because the essence of the Navy is sailing ships on the water, not under the water. Likewise, the Army was eager to be rid of the Army Air Corps in the wake of World War II, because the pilots were seen as undermining the essence of the Army: boots on the ground.

Turf. Essence will help shape "turf," referring to the substantive and skill domains in which the organization believes it has a primary claim to influence and expertise within the national bureaucracy. As we have just noted, sometimes an organization's essence leads it to shun or treat lightly particular turf that it sees as unimportant or subversive to that essence. But much more often than not, organizations are greedy for additional turf, and jealously guard what turf they already possess. The reason is simple: more turf means a larger sphere of influence, more personnel, a larger budget, perhaps even greater autonomy. Losing turf means a concomitant loss in each of these areas. Thus, though the Navy and the Air Force do not view sealift and airlift in support of the Army as expressing their respective essences, the two services resist efforts by the Army to create its own lift capabilities, such as the TSV (theater support vessel). Turf battles over close air support of troops between the Air Force and the Army and over amphibious operations between the Army and the Marines are long-standing and legendary. Issues of turf can also determine access to information within the bureaucracy. Since access to information is a form of power and control, fights over such access can become especially intense. An organization cannot afford to have its policy stances ignored because it is perceived as not knowing what is really going on.

Budget and Personnel. The size of an organization, operationalized as the amount of funds allocated for its budget and the number of personnel assigned to the organization, is a primary indicator of the strength an organization can bring to bear in bureaucratic battles. The budget of the entire CIA is less than one-tenth that of the Pentagon. Civilian employees of the Department of Defense (DoD) alone number over seven hundred thousand, with military personnel adding almost one million more. Estimates of the number of CIA employees range from twenty-five thousand to thirty thousand. Though popular perception, promulgated through Tom Clancy novels and the like, might lead one to conclude that the CIA is on an organizational par with the DoD, nothing could be further from the truth.

Compared to the CIA, the DoD is an eight hundred-pound gorilla, and the social dynamics of interagency working groups reflect this. With regard to budget, it is also worth remembering that relative budget increase is as important to track as total budget figures. The proportion of the armed services budget that goes to each of the three major services is arguably more an issue of contention between the services than is total level of funding. Often a wary peace develops where entities keep bureaucratic conflict under control by a de facto agreement to keep budget proportionality static. This conflict-avoidance measure can readily undercut the ability of the secretary of defense to make significant alterations in the nation's fighting force.

Influence. One of the objectives of any governmental organization is influence; influence with policymakers and comparative influence on matters affecting one's turf within the bureaucracy. For example, even though the CIA is a considerably smaller organization than the DoD, until the DNI office was established, it was CIA personnel who provided the president with his daily morning security briefing (the PDB). This unparalleled access provided the CIA with influence far in excess of what its size would forecast. Now that it appears the office of the DNI will take over this function, the CIA will probably lose influence as an organization. Sometimes influence is obtained not through access to policymakers, but through acquiring an interagency reputation. The very small INR office of the State Department (the Bureau of Intelligence and Research) maintains influence completely out of proportion to its size because it has developed a reputation for skewering the intelligence estimates of its larger sister organizations, particularly the DoD and CIA. Because they are so small, they have nothing to lose and everything to gain by questioning the estimates of these larger organizations. If the INR is proved right, as they sometimes are, this further establishes their reputation as being hard-nosed objectivists who operate unconstrained by organizational pressures to conform their analyses to the accepted or acceptable wisdom. Nevertheless, it is still true as a generality that the larger and more well-funded an organization, and the larger the scope of its expertise and turf, the more likely that organization will have veto power over other organizations in interagency working groups.

Morale. Morale, though less tangible an asset than funding or personnel, is still vitally important to organizations. Demoralization can lead to an exodus of personnel, or a decrease in productivity among those who remain. A demoralized organization is in a weaker position within the bureaucracy, and may have to fight harder to retain what influence, turf, and budget it once had. Sometimes organizational attention to morale can take unusual, sometimes counterproductive forms. Halperin recounts how it was issues of morale that led the Army to implement shorter tours of duty of officers than enlisted personnel during the Vietnam War (Halperin,

1974). Officers who aspired to a long career in the Army needed combat experience to qualify for field grade rank. The Army felt that providing combat experience for the maximum number of officers possible would thus boost morale. Unfortunately, it led in some cases to resentment by seasoned enlisted personnel of "green" officers looking for glory and willing to engage in risky operations to get it. There were reports that especially gung ho junior officers were as much at risk from their own platoons as they were from the Viet Cong.

Autonomy. It is very difficult for two or more organizations to jointly plan an operation. Each has a different culture, different skills, different procedures, different equipment, and different priorities. Furthermore, each is vying with the others for influence and turf in matters where these overlap between organizations. Thus, one objective of organizations is to operate as autonomously as possible. An excellent example of this was the political jockeying over the creation of the DNI position. The 9/11 Commission, which spurred the creation of this new position, wanted the DNI to have budgetary authority over all intelligence units scattered throughout the federal bureaucracy, as well as the power to set priorities for intelligence gathering by these units. The major opponent to this conceptualization of the DNI's power was the DoD, naturally enough: these proposed DNI powers would severely cut into their autonomy. The DoD fought and won the concession that military requirements could override DNI requirements when the lives of American military personnel were at stake. Given the DoD's preference for autonomy, we would expect that exceptional condition to become a chronic condition.

Combined with this understanding of what drives organizations, it is now important to understand how large organizations operate. At their most fundamental, organizations exist to reduce complexity. There are several aspects to this complexity: complexity of information processing and decisionmaking, complexity of task execution, and the complexity of coordinating the efforts of the organization's numerous human employees.

The attack an organization makes on complexity is a simple one: break up a complex whole into pieces that are easily understandable, easily executable, and easily standardized. In a way, the last thing an organization really wants to do is have to think about something from scratch. More efficient is to view something new as an instance of something already known, or something new to do as an extension of something the organization already does. This approach is not irrational in the least: remember that typical government organizations may have hundreds, thousands, or even hundreds of thousands of human employees. And these employees are not static over time; on any given day, some employees are leaving, some are staying, and some are entering employment with the organization for the first time. No one human being within the organization can know all there is to know about it. No one human being possesses complete institutional memory concerning what the organization has done in the past. No one human being has the skills and know-how that the complete organization has. If the organization is to function, such global knowledge must be made as irrelevant as possible.

Though the organizational approach is not irrational, it is decidedly different than what we consider to be normal behavior for a human being, where global knowledge is prized. Let us consider some of the major differences.

Organizations are simply not very responsive to change. Inertia is a strong force within organizations, which may result in a lack of creativity, a lack of flexibility, and a lack of adaptability to new circumstances. The National Security Agency (NSA) admitted it had hundreds of hours of captured pre-9/11 conversations among individuals suspected of having planned or taken part in those attacks that still had not been translated months afterwards because it did not have enough Arabic translators. The FBI spent several years and over $170 million to update its computerized file management systems to allow easier dissemination of information across units, only to scrap the entire project and decide to start all over. Nearly two years after the 2003 invasion of Iraq, Special Operations forces were finally given permission to pay field informants cash. Armor for humvees and body armor for soldiers were not provided in sufficient quantities for the Iraqi invasion because the working assumption was that most troops would not encounter enemy forces. The notion of a hardcore insurgency that would attack American troops anywhere within Iraq, even within "secured areas," was apparently not a scenario seriously considered during contingency planning.

Responsive learning can be painfully slow, imperiling important priorities. Usually incremental learning is the norm for large organizations, where baby steps toward change are undertaken over a significant time period. The most reliable guide to organizational action at time t is organizational action at time t-1. For example, the journalist Fred Kaplan notes it took twenty-one months after 9/11 for the DoD to come up with a nineteen-page planning document to improve language skills pertinent to the war on terror. This document called for another eleven months to come up with guidance to create new programs, thirteen months to come up with an index to measure readiness in language, sixteen months to establish a database of current language capabilities, nineteen months to enunciate language requirements, twenty-eight months to disseminate a language aptitude test, thirty-seven months to establish crash courses for deploying personnel, and forty-nine months to create a personnel information system containing data on language skill. By forty-nine months after the original planning document, no actual language training programs outside of the crash course for deploying personnel would actually have been established. Kaplan points out that seventy months after 9/11 we still were not yet offering additional language training to meet national priorities—almost six years! He notes it took far less time than that for the Americans to enter World War II and help defeat the Axis powers, and far less time for America to undertake profound reforms after the Soviet launch of Sputnik in 1957. When the time period is this extended, incremental learning almost becomes no learning at all (Kaplan, 2005, www.slate.msn.com/id/2116330).

Organizations interpret orders according to their existing understandings and capabilities, which results in an implementation gap between what policymakers believe they have ordered and what organizations actually do to execute such orders. March and Simon have called this the "logic of appropriateness," where actions are chosen on the basis of pattern recognition from knowledge already stored in the system (March and Simon, 1993). For example, when John F. Kennedy ordered the Navy to quarantine Cuba, the Navy heard "blockade," because that was the closest match in their knowledge base. But there were several key differences between what Kennedy wanted the Navy to do and what the Navy thought a blockade entailed. For example, the Navy wanted to force Soviet subs in the area to surface, and determined to sink ships that refused to stop or be boarded. Kennedy did not want either to occur. Fortunately, Kennedy was able to recognize these differences and intervene to clarify in very precise terms what would and would not happen during the quarantine.

Organizations develop standard operating procedures (SOPs) in place of thinking through every new situation from the ground up. However, in addition to simple mismatch of definitions, as noted above, there is also the possibility that the existence of an SOP has short-circuited acknowledgment of obvious extenuating circumstances, resulting in wildly inappropriate behavior on the part of the organization. In his book *Essence of Decision*, Allison recounts such a case concerning the camouflage of Soviet intermediate-range ballistic missiles (IRBMs) and medium-range ballistic missiles (MRBMs) during the Cuban missile crisis. The missiles were extremely well camouflaged during transportation and unloading at Cuban ports. However, once dispersed to their construction sites, the missiles were not camouflaged at all. They were constructed in the very same configuration as missile sites in the USSR, allowing for easy identification from U-2 imagery. Some U.S. officials even speculated that the USSR *wanted* the United States to know about the presence of these missiles as they were being emplaced. That was not the case, however. According to Allison, the excellent in-transit camouflage was due to the efforts of Soviet intelligence. But once ashore, the missiles were placed under the Group of Soviet Forces in Cuba, whose commander placed them in control of his staff from the Strategic

Rocket Forces (SRF). Now, the SRF had never placed missiles outside of the Soviet Union. Here they were, thousands of miles away from the USSR on a small tropical island. What to do? What they knew how to do: SOP for missile placement in the Soviet Union, which SOP did not include camouflage but did include a standard configuration for the silos. After the Americans announced they had discovered the presence of the missiles, camouflage was hastily improvised. The DCI at the time, John McCone, could not help but wonder how much worse the situation would have been if the missiles had not been discovered before the IRBMs could be made operational. Fortunately, we will never know.

SOPs also create an explicit chain of command. The degree to which hierarchy permeates decisionmaking within an organization has been related by scholars to both the organization's culture and the culture of the larger society in which it is embedded. In some cultures, "jumping" the chain of command can be grounds for termination. Even serious questioning of a superior's decisionmaking assumptions or information, let alone the actual decision, may cause career disruption. Though all members of the organization in a sense comprise the brain of the organization, possessing some knowledge that may not be duplicated in the knowledge base of others, some brains may be more valued than others. Unfortunately, it tends to be those most removed from the "ground" whose judgment prevails. This creates the undesirable circumstance in which higher-level decisionmakers within the organization may not even know what they lack in terms of important information about a particular situation. And subordinates may feel discouraged from bringing this lack to their superior's attention, for fear of personal repercussions. This catch-22 is, of course, the basis for federal and state protection of "whistle-blowers."

Organizations are motivated primarily by factors discussed above, such as essence, budget, influence, and autonomy. These will not be sacrificed for the sake of executing orders or requests for information issued by policymakers. For example, there is no doubt that organizational reporting on the situation in Vietnam during the Vietnam War was inhibited by the memory of the "China Hands" in the State Department who had been sacked during the McCarthy era for having written the truth about the relative strength and popularity of the Communist and Nationalist forces. Organizations were very leery about reporting the weaknesses of the South Vietnamese regime or the strengths of the North Vietnamese forces. That such "altered" reporting did nothing for the quality of U.S. decisionmaking during this era was not uppermost in the calculations of these organizations.

In conclusion, then, organizations are necessary to government. Yet, organizations often produce unintended negative consequences on a regular basis and often at the most inopportune moments. How can foreign policymakers use organizations without being undermined by them? First, it is crucial that leaders and their staff delve into the arcane structure and SOPs of organizations through which they are trying to implement policy. In this way, leaders can work with SOP rather than against it, by finding appropriate units and more closely matched SOPs within the organization and steering executive orders in that direction. Second, leaders can try to force a change on an organization through budgetary "feast or famine." Offering more money to do something new can be attractive to an organization. Taking money away—especially if it upsets budgetary "truces" between organizational units—can also be a catalyst for change. Leaders can also be alert to scandal and egregious failure within an organization, which can be the justification for extreme change. For example, the Federal Emergency Management Agency (FEMA) will probably not survive as an organization, given its abysmal handling of the Hurricane Katrina disaster. Third, a leader can use turf wars to his advantage, by putting two or more organizations in competition and tying factors like turf, budget, and personnel to the outcome of that competition. Finally, a leader can give up and create a new organization to do what the old organization cannot or will not. This was a major consideration in the creation of the Directorate for National Intelligence. In the end, leaders cannot do without organizations, and must be prepared to deal with them on their own terms in order to effectively use them—and not be used by them.

An excellent way to see how these principles play out when violated is the extensive report on the *Columbia* shuttle disaster of 2003 (NASA, 2003). The crew of the *Columbia* space shuttle was lost on February 1, 2003, when their reentry vehicle disintegrated because of a breach in the wing caused by a foam strike eighty-one seconds into launch. The foam strike was noticed in the launch footage two days after the launch. NASA ultimately treated the foam strike as an event that would not compromise flight safety. How did they come to this conclusion? The following excerpts from the Columbia Accident Investigation Board (CAIB) Report provide a tragic summary of that organizational decision, and make plain the problems inherent in organizational decisionmaking. As you read these report excerpts, pay close attention to how the panel, which included scholars of organizational behavior, points to several of the factors that we have discussed in order to explain the tragedy.

Upon learning of the debris strike on Flight Day Two, the responsible system area manager from United Space Alliance and her NASA counterpart formed a team to analyze the debris strike in accordance with mission rules requiring the careful examination of any "out-of-family" event. Using film from the Intercenter Photo Working Group, Boeing systems integration analysts prepared a preliminary analysis that afternoon. (Initial estimates of debris size and speed, origin of debris, and point of impact would later prove remarkably accurate.) As Flight Day Three and Four unfolded over the Martin Luther King Jr. holiday weekend, engineers began their analysis. One Boeing analyst used Crater, a mathematical prediction tool, to assess possible damage to the Thermal Protection System. Analysis predicted tile damage deeper than the actual tile depth, and penetration of the RCC coating at impact angles above 15 degrees. This suggested the potential for a burn-through during re-entry. Debris Assessment Team members judged that the actual damage would not be as severe as predicted because of the inherent conservatism in the Crater model and because, in the case of tile, Crater does not take into account the tile's stronger and more impact-resistant "densified" layer, and in the case of RCC, the lower density of foam would preclude penetration at impact angles under 21 degrees.

On Flight Day Five, impact assessment results for tile and RCC were presented at an informal meeting of the Debris Assessment Team, which was operating without direct Shuttle Program or Mission Management leadership. Mission Control's engineering support, the Mission Evaluation Room, provided no direction for team activities other than to request the team's results by January 24. As the problem was being worked, Shuttle managers did not formally direct the actions of or consult with Debris Assessment Team leaders about the team's assumptions, uncertainties, progress, or interim results, an unusual circumstance given that NASA managers are normally engaged in analyzing what they view as problems. At this meeting, participants agreed that an image of the area of the wing in question was essential to refine their analysis and reduce the uncertainties in their damage assessment.

Each member supported the idea to seek imagery from an outside source. Due in part to a lack of guidance from the Mission Management Team or Mission Evaluation Room managers, the Debris Assessment Team chose an unconventional route for its request. Rather than working the request up the normal chain of command—through the Mission Evaluation Room to the Mission Management Team for action to Mission Control—team members nominated Rodney Rocha, the team's Co-Chair, to pursue the request through the Engineering Directorate at Johnson Space Center. As a result, even after the accident the Debris Assessment Team's request was viewed by Shuttle Program managers as a non-critical engineering desire rather than a critical operational need [above paragraphs from p. 167]. . . .

At 8:30 a.m., the NASA Department of Defense liaison officer called US STRATCOM and cancelled the request for imagery. The reason given for the cancellation was that NASA had identified its own in-house resources and no longer needed the military's help. The NASA request to the Department of Defense to prepare to image *Columbia* on-orbit was both made and rescinded within 90 minutes.

The Board has determined that the following sequence of events likely occurred within that 90-minute period. Linda Ham [head of the Mission Management Team—author] asked Lambert Austin [NASA's systems integration manager—author] if he knew who was requesting the imagery. After admitting his participation in helping to make the imagery request outside the official chain of command and without first gaining Ham's permission, Austin referred to his conversation with United Space Alliance Shuttle Integration manager Bob White on Flight Day Six, in which White had asked Austin, in response to White's Debris Assessment Team employee concerns, what it would take to get Orbiter imagery.

Even though Austin had already informed Ham of the request for imagery, Ham later called Mission Management Team members Ralph Roe, Manager of the Space Shuttle Vehicle Engineering Office, Loren Shriver, United Space Alliance Deputy Program Manager for Shuttle, and David Moyer, the on-duty Mission Evaluation Room manager, to determine the origin of the request and to confirm that there was a "requirement" for a request. Ham also asked Flight Director Phil Engelauf if he had a "requirement" for imagery of *Columbia's* left wing. These individuals all stated that they had not requested imagery, were not aware of any "official" requests for imagery, and could not identify a "requirement" for imagery. Linda Ham later told several individuals that nobody had a requirement for imagery.

What started as a request by the Intercenter Photo Working Group to seek outside help in obtaining images on Flight Day Two in anticipation of analysts' needs had become by Flight Day Six an actual engineering request by members of the Debris Assessment Team, made informally through Bob White to Lambert Austin, and formally in Rodney Rocha's e-mail to Paul Shack [director of the shuttle integration office and Rocha's superior—author]. These requests had then caused Lambert Austin and Wayne Hale [Space Shuttle Deputy Program Manager—author] to contact Department of Defense representatives. When Ham officially terminated the actions that the Department of Defense had begun, she effectively terminated both the Intercenter Photo Working Group request and the Debris Assessment Team request. While Ham has publicly stated she did not know of the Debris Assessment Team members' desire for imagery, she never asked them directly if the request was theirs, even though they were the team analyzing the foam strike.

Also on Flight Day Seven, Ham raised concerns that the extra time spent maneuvering *Columbia* to make the left wing visible for imaging would unduly impact the mission schedule; for example, science experiments would have to stop while the imagery was taken. According to personal notes obtained by the Board: *"Linda Ham said it was no longer being pursued since even if we saw something, we couldn't do anything about it. The Program didn't want to spend the resources."* Shuttle managers, including Ham, also said they were looking for very small areas on the Orbiter and that past imagery resolution was not very good. The Board notes that no individuals in the STS-107 operational chain of command had the security clearance necessary to know about National imaging capabilities. Additionally, no evidence has been uncovered that anyone from NASA, United Space Alliance, or Boeing sought to determine the expected quality of images and the difficulty and costs of obtaining Department of Defense assistance. Therefore, members of the Mission Management Team were making critical decisions about imagery capabilities based on little or no knowledge [above paragraphs from pp. 153–54]. . . .

Debris Assessment Team members speculated as to why their request was rejected and whether their analysis was worth pursuing without new imagery. Discussion then moved on to whether the Debris Assessment Team had a "mandatory need" for Department of Defense imaging. Most team members, when asked by the Board what "mandatory need" meant, replied with a shrug of their shoulders. They believed the need for imagery was obvious: without better pictures, engineers would be unable to make reliable predictions of the depth and area of damage caused by a foam strike that was outside of the experience base.

However, team members concluded that although their need was important, they could not cite a "mandatory" requirement for the request. *Analysts on the Debris Assessment Team were in the unenviable position of wanting images to more accurately assess damage while simultaneously needing to prove to Program managers, as a result of their assessment, that there was a need for images in the first place.*

After the meeting adjourned, Rocha read the 11:45 a.m. e-mail from Paul Shack, which said that the Orbiter Project was not requesting any outside imaging help. Rocha called Shack to ask if Shack's boss, Johnson Space Center engineering director Frank Benz, knew about the request. Rocha then sent several e-mails consisting of questions about the ongoing analyses and details on the Shuttle Program's cancellation of the imaging request. An e-mail that he did not send but instead printed out and shared with a colleague follows.

"In my humble technical opinion, this is the wrong (and bordering on irresponsible) answer from the SSP and Orbiter not to request additional imaging help from any outside source. I must emphasize (again) that severe enough damage (3 or 4 multiple tiles knocked out down to the densification layer) combined with the heating and resulting damage to the underlying structure at the most critical location (viz., MLG door/wheels/tires/hydraulics or the X1191 spar cap) could present potentially grave hazards. The engineering team will admit it might not achieve definitive high confidence answers without additional images, but, without action to request help to clarify the damage visually, we will guarantee it will not. Can we talk to Frank Benz before Friday's MMT? Remember the NASA safety posters everywhere around stating, 'If it's not safe, say so'? Yes, it's that serious." [SSP = Space Shuttle Program, MLG = Main Landing Gear, MMT = Mission Management Team]

When asked why he did not send this e-mail, Rocha replied that he did not want to jump the chain of command. Having already raised the need to have the Orbiter imaged with Shack, he would defer to management's judgment on obtaining imagery [above paragraphs from p. 157]. . . .

Mission Control personnel thought they should tell Commander Rick Husband and Pilot William McCool about the debris strike, not because they thought that it was worthy of the crew's attention but because the crew might be asked about it in an upcoming media interview. Director Steve Stitch sent the following e-mail to Husband and McCool and copied other Flight Directors [p. 158]. . . .

The impact appears to be totally on the lower surface and no particles are seen to traverse over the upper surface of the wing. Experts have reviewed the high speed

*photography and there is no concern for RCC or tile damage. We have seen this same
phenomenon on several other flights and there is absolutely no concern for entry
[p. 159]. . . .*

At the Mission Management Team's 8:00 a.m. meeting [on January 24,
when a final decision about the return flight was to be made—author], Mission
Evaluation Room manager Don McCormack verbally summarized the Debris
Assessment Team's 7:00 a.m. brief. It was the third topic discussed. Unlike the
earlier briefing, McCormack's presentation did not include the Debris Assessment Team's presentation charts. The Board notes that no supporting analysis
or examination of minority engineering views was asked for or offered, that
neither Mission Evaluation Room nor Mission Management Team members
requested a technical paper of the Debris Assessment Team analysis, and that
no technical questions were asked [p. 161]. . . .

According to a Memorandum for the Record written by William Readdy,
Associate Administrator for Space Flight, Readdy and Michael Card, from
NASA's Safety and Mission Assurance Office, discussed an offer of Department
of Defense imagery support for *Columbia*. This January 29 conversation ended
with Readdy telling Card that NASA would accept the offer but because the
Mission Management Team had concluded that this was not a safety-of-flight
issue, the imagery should be gathered only on a low priority "not-to-interfere"
basis. Ultimately, no imagery was taken [p. 166]. . . .

[S]afety personnel were present but passive and did not serve as a channel
for the voicing of concerns or dissenting views. Safety representatives attended
meetings of the Debris Assessment Team, Mission Evaluation Room, and Mission Management Team, but were merely party to the analysis process and
conclusions instead of an independent source of questions and challenges.
Safety contractors in the Mission Evaluation Room were only marginally aware
of the debris strike analysis. One contractor did question the Debris Assessment Team safety representative about the analysis and was told that it was
adequate. No additional inquiries were made. The highest-ranking safety representative at NASA headquarters deferred to Program managers when asked
for an opinion on imaging of *Columbia*. The safety manager he spoke to also
failed to follow up [p. 170].

Notice in the account several of the factors we have discussed previously:
the inflexibility of SOPs, the chilling effect of hierarchy, the compartmen-
talization of knowledge, the indifference by more senior personnel to the
re-synthesis of that compartmentalized knowledge, the issue of organizational "face" vis à vis the Pentagon, the façade of attention to safety belied
by the actual organizational culture of "can do." The full report on the
Columbia shuttle disaster is over six hundred pages long, and is a testament
to the inherent problem of creeping dysfunctionality in large organizations.
It is well worth the effort for the foreign policy analyst to peruse this report.

Thus, despite elaborate organizational charts to ensure that all aspects of
a problem would be considered, despite overt rhetoric about the impor-

tance of safety and speaking up, despite the personnel of NASA being highly accomplished in their respective fields, the same old issues of turf, lack of communication, SOP, and organizational culture directly contributed to the deaths of the *Columbia* crew. Without the benefits provided by large organizations, there would have been no shuttle program. Without the disadvantages of large organizations, the lives of these astronauts might not have been lost.

BUREAUCRATIC POLITICS

Bureaucratic politics is a complex intersection of small group dynamics, organizational process, and domestic political forces. Most bureaucratic politics takes place in interagency groups, which are one of the foremost means for important, but noncrisis situations to be addressed within government. Though positions taken by the participants in such interagency groups may be roughly predictable, predicting which position(s) will prevail is sometimes possible, sometimes impossible, but always an extremely complex calculation. Though important matters are generally tasked to an interagency group to develop a series of options or recommendations for higher-level small groups, such as the NSC, to address, it is still likely that the interagency group is not only subject to influence attempts by the participating organizations, but also vulnerable to domestic political pressure and even electoral imperatives. Further complicating matters is the impact of diverse personalities assigned to the interagency group, as well as underlying networks of friendship and conflict that enmesh these personalities. In short, bureaucratic politics produce the most intriguing soap operas to be found in government. Allison and Zelikow put it this way:

> Choices by one player (e.g., to authorize action by his department, to make a speech, or to refrain from acquiring certain information), resultants of minor games (e.g., the wording of a cable or the decision on departmental action worked out among lower-level players), resultants of central games (e.g., decisions, actions, and speeches bargained out among central players), and foul-ups (e.g., choices that are not made because they are not recognized or are raised too late, misunderstandings, etc.)—these pieces, when stuck to the same canvas, constitute government behavior relevant to an issue. To explain why a particular formal governmental decision was made, or why one pattern of governmental behavior emerged, it is necessary to identify the games and players, to display the coalitions, bargains, and compromises, and to convey some feel for the confusion" (1999, 257).

Some key concepts help us frame the dramas, large and small, produced by bureaucratic politics:

Stakeholders. Stakeholders, sometimes called "players," are those whose roles, expertise, or sheer political power coupled with strong interest allow them to affect a bureaucratic outcome. Stakeholdership itself may be the subject of politicking. For example, well-credentialed government nuclear scientists propounding that current nuclear warheads are not reliable and must be replaced have been disinvited from key interagency meetings where the future of the U.S. nuclear arsenal is discussed. Thus the very composition of interagency groups, and other issues such as chairmanship of such a group, are subject to political forces. In general, sheer political power trumps role stakeholdership, and role trumps expertise stakeholdership. For example, Congressman Dan Burton, the grandfather of a child with autism, was able to force the Food and Drug Administration (FDA) to reinvestigate links between thimerosal in childhood vaccines and autism, but the FDA was simultaneously able to effectively marginalize the views of physician-researchers who felt they could show such a link empirically. But there are plenty of exceptions to this generalization, and we will deal with these in the section on "equalizers."

Another generalization about stakeholders is the adage "where you stand depends upon where you sit," implying that at least in the case of role stakeholders, organizational affiliation will largely determine the stance taken in bureaucratic negotiations. In interagency discussion between the FBI and CIA, we are not surprised when the one argues for greater powers vis à vis the other. Furthermore, we are not surprised when outsiders demand greater cooperation between organizations and try to institutionalize that through standing interagency "centers," such as the National Counterterrorism Center. But then we are also not surprised when assignment to such centers is regarded as the kiss of death for one's career within one's home organization.

Action Channels. Those of us who work in large bureaucracies know that the only way to be an effective player is to know the action channels—whom to see and where to go and what to do to make something happen. For example, just to make something trivial happen at my university—getting a new key to a new office—requires that I find the proper form, obtain the signature of my chair and my dean, and walk the form over to a particular obscure building on the margins of campus to pay a fee and get the key. Changing from PC to Mac in my university office? I must give a statement to my chair saying why the change is needed, my chair must write a statement justifying my justification, the result must be forwarded to the college computing committee by a particular date, and the committee must in turn relay its decision to the comptroller who buys the equipment. We are all familiar with the plethora of procedures and committees facing us when attempting to do most anything within the bureaucracies of our universities. So it is within government and the foreign policy establishment.

Though it is always instructive to look at organizational charts, "boxology" does not tell you how to actually get something done. For example, how do you get the official U.S. government opinion to be that Saddam Hussein has weapons of mass destruction (WMD)? This is actually quite complicated. The president just can't say, "Saddam Hussein has WMD." No, the president asks the DCI if Saddam Hussein has WMD. The DCI asks the Intelligence Community Executive Committee, which asks the National Foreign Intelligence Board, which asks each of its member intelligence organizations to independently answer the question. After each intelligence organization hashes out its own answer, interagency committees are set up to debate the answer among agencies. The resulting opinions and minority opinions and dissenting opinions will then be sent to the Board, which will discuss them and send them up to the Executive Committee. The Intelligence Community Executive Committee will further discuss the issue and then make a report to the National Intelligence Council. The NIC will make their own investigation of all the facts and analysis put forward by the intelligence community. At some point, the particular member of that office charged with oversight of the broad issue area of proliferation will issue a National Intelligence Estimate. That official NIE is then presented to the president, who can now say, "Saddam Hussein has WMD." If you don't know the action channels, you cannot act.

Resultants. Those who study bureaucracy are often reluctant to call the outcomes of bureaucratic politics "decisions." After every stakeholder has pulled and hauled to the best of their power in a particular direction, what is left over is better seen as something less than a *decision*, which term connotes some processual rationality. *Resultant* connotes that the outcome would probably not coincide with one chosen by any unitary rational actor. It is usually the lowest common denominator outcome; the outcome upon which a majority of the participants in the process can agree. In general, of course, unless there is a threatening emergency, most resultants can be characterized as incremental change based upon a papering over of key differences. The vaguer the proposal, the greater the convergence of agreement around it.

Framing, Rules, Deadlines, and Agendas. Effective political players within large bureaucracies not only know all the action channels—they are also masters at group manipulation. The most important tools of manipulation, especially if one can occupy a position of authority within the group such as a chairmanship, are the use of framing, rules, deadlines, and agendas to obtain one's desired ends.

Framing is a process by which a group comes to understand a situation and define its decision-making task. Framing is not only a psychological process for an individual; when it involves persuasion of group members to adopt one's frame, framing also becomes a very political act. Is a fetus "uterine material" or a "pre-born person"? Were the contras in Nicaragua during the Reagan administration "freedom fighters" or "terrorist guerrillas"? Is Iran exercising its rights under the Nuclear Nonproliferation Treaty (NPT) with its uranium enrichment program or undermining the NPT? Ryan Beasley (1998) notes that framing may actually be more important to study in bureaucratic politics than the final decision-making process, for choice is constrained by the frame adopted by the group. Beasley finds that a particular frame is more likely to be adopted if it is simple, if it is backed by a strong leader or a member of the group that can claim special expertise in the area, and if it lends itself to a fairly clear-cut course of action. Another aspect is whether the frame of action can be characterized as an incremental outgrowth of what has been done in the past. Frames, once adopted, tend to "set" fairly quickly, and it may take the addition of new personnel to the bureaucratic mix to rethink a long-standing frame.

A famous example of "a frame not taken" occurred near the beginning of ExCom's deliberations during the Cuban missile crisis. When ExCom was presented with the photographic evidence that missile silos were being placed in Cuba, Robert McNamara, the secretary of defense, opined that any such missiles would have little military significance. As such, they would not be worth taking forceful action that would risk a nuclear war. McNamara had the expertise to make such a claim, and yet his frame was swiftly rejected by Kennedy. Kennedy felt that the Soviets' move had great political consequences, ranging from the fate of Berlin to his own electoral prospects. Kennedy's strong opinion that the missiles were a grave threat would frame the rest of ExCom's meetings.

The rules under which the group operates are also an extremely significant factor in understanding group behavior. Consider the differences between a bureaucratic group that operates by majority rule and one that operates on the principle of unanimity. In the former, coalitions will be important; in the latter, every single individual can be a deal breaker. A group under rules of unanimity will probably make fewer and less specific decisions than a group with rules of majority voting. But voting itself can become quite complicated. For example, in the U.S. Congress, parliamentary rules are coupled with rules on filibuster, cloture, committee passage before floor vote, attachment of bills to other bills for vote, necessity of two-thirds majority for particular votes and for overturning vetoes, reconciliation of House and Senate versions of the same bill, and so forth. A legislator who has mastered the rules by which Congress works is at a significant advantage over one who has not. Other types of rules that may play into group deliberations include weighted voting, such as in the International Monetary Fund (IMF); permanent versus nonpermanent status, such as in the UN Security Council; and the power to initiate hearings or investigations.

Deadlines also play a role in group process. The very presence of a deadline can profoundly alter deliberations. Less powerful members of the group can use the deadline as leverage to extract concessions from more powerful members. On the other hand, more powerful members can use the deadline to paint others as obstructionists who are likely to cause the group to miss its deadline. Deadlines can force premature closure of discussion on an issue, but on the other hand, deadlines can also create incentive to compile as much information as quickly as possible in an attempt to carry the discussion and sway undecideds before the deadline occurs.

The manipulation of group agendas is a skill that is highly prized in the political arena. In most groups, the chairman decides the agenda, but in some groups the group may actually vote on the agenda. The reason the agenda may become political is that it determines the course of group discussion. Items may be purposefully not placed on the agenda so that they will not be discussed, for example. But other types of manipulation are possible. The chair may set a time limit on the discussion of each item, which may allow him or her to cut off discussion of a contentious issue before all have had the opportunity to speak. This is a common tactic in public hearings where input from citizens or other interested parties is allowed. Another tactic is to allow lengthy discussion of items placed first on the agenda, and thus limit or even prevent any discussion of issues coming later in the agenda.

Coalitions. Unless there is near unanimity on a particular issue, most group interactions become examples of coalition politics at work. Within the constraints of rules and deadlines, the group is usually tasked with making some type of determination or decision. This requires getting agreement among enough group members so that a particular determination or decision carries the day.

There are generally three ways to assemble a coalition. The first is through compromise, where a minimum winning coalition is built around a position with which coalition members feel comfortable, if not completely satisfied. The second is through quid pro quo arrangements where support on Z's pet issue A by member Y is linked to support on Y's pet issue B by member Z, ensuring a win-win scenario for all. The third is through implicit or explicit coercion, where a particular faction uses intimidation, threats, media attention, manipulation of rules, or other means to wilt any opposition to or possible compromise of their preferred position. Needless to say, the first two types of coalition-building efforts are comparatively more stable than the last because those who voted for the particular position have no vested interest in seeing it fail.

A large part of the complexity of coalition building is that each coalition member has multiple interests, and therefore the membership of a particular voting coalition has the potential to change as new or different interests are perceived to be at stake. Likewise, particular individuals in the coalition may play multiple roles within the government. For example, does the secretary of state represent the president or the State Department? The answer may depend on the issue at hand, and may also be subject to change as circumstances change.

Subversion and Equalizers. Though the individual cog in the bureaucratic machine may have very little power, there are time-honored tactics that can help level the playing field somewhat. Let us suppose you are a middle-level bureaucrat who strongly disagrees with the direction adopted by those at a higher level. What could you do?

Actually, quite a lot. First, you could simply not implement the directives you have been given, without raising a fuss. Oftentimes, officials in high positions may not have the time to check that each and every one of their directives has been carried out. If queried, one could blame overriding circumstances for an unforeseen delay. You could also do something different from what you have been ordered to do, and if questioned suggest that a misunderstanding occurred. You could implement cosmetic, not substantive change, or obey the letter but not the spirit of the orders. Or you could implement your orders in an overzealous fashion so as to showcase the faults you see in the directive.

There are other approaches that can be taken. You could insist upon a personal hearing before implementing your orders, and suggest reasons for reconsidering. You could make it known that you are keeping a detailed paper trail and journal of what is happening. You could resign, or at least threaten to resign. You could attempt to make your directives public, either by going to the media, to Congress, to another government, or by writing your own book about the situation.

This is not to say that subversion is always the right thing to contemplate. There are certainly times when subordinates taking matters into their own hands is exactly the wrong thing to do: think, for example, of the human rights violations at Abu Ghraib. But there are some times when the actions individuals may take on their own initiative may improve the performance of their government. Halperin offers this example from the memoirs of Henry S. Villard, a foreign service officer (FSO) who was ambassador to Libya back when that nation had a king:

> The Libyan Prime Minister had resigned and flown off to Rome, his nerves frayed by the thankless task of guiding a newborn state. The King was ill, in seclusion; there was a rumor in the bazaars that he might abdicate. The whole government structure seemed about to collapse. I had just reached a vital point in negotiations for an air-base agreement. So when the Libyan cabinet asked me to fly to Italy and persuade the Prime Minister to return, I cabled the Department urgently for permission to make the try.

Time was of the essence, yet the hours ticked by without response. In Washington, the wheels ground methodically. Committee met with committee, weighing the pros and cons of my recommendation. The Pentagon had to be consulted. Policy factors had to be considered; so did tactics, in light of the progress to date on the air-base negotiations. Suggestions at a lower level had to be referred to a higher level for further discussion. I sent a second cable. No reply.

Finally, I decided to act on my own. I boarded the plane of my Air Attache, flew to Rome, and called on the Prime Minister at his hotel. With all the eloquence I could muster, I urged him to come back and steer the ship of state through the storm, pointing out that the fate of his country—and our delicate negotiations—rested in his hands alone. He heard me in silence, still smarting from the political wounds which had caused him to resign. He would think it over; he would give me his answer that evening.

At eight o'clock I was again at the Prime Minister's door. His face was wreathed in smiles. He would do as I asked, and to mark the occasion he invited me to dine with him downstairs. With a load like lead off my mind, I was enjoying the repast when I spied an officer of our Rome Embassy discreetly waving a piece of paper from behind the potted palms. I made my excuses, rose, and went over to receive the message—a priority cable to Tripoli, repeated to Rome for information. At long last, Washington had moved. There were my orders. Under no circumstances was I to follow the Prime Minister to Rome for that, the Department feared, might be interpreted as interference in the domestic affairs of a sovereign country. (Halperin, 1974, 277–78)

The Games. In seeking to understand bureaucratic politics, it must also be recognized that many games are being played simultaneously, and the set of players in any one game only partially overlaps the set of players in another. At the most micro-level, there may be clashes of personality or will between two or more individuals. There may be conflicts between different offices within one organization. There may be a struggle between two or more organizations within a bureaucracy over turf or budget. There may be a contest for influence among the president's closest advisors. The larger electoral context between political parties is always a backdrop, and in election years may move to the foreground. And then there are the games in the international arena played out between allies, rivals, nongovernmental organizations (NGOs), international financial organizations (IGOs), and so on. In other words, just identifying stakeholders in a particular issue is not enough. One must know how many boards a stakeholder is playing on, and who the other stakeholders on each board are.

Example: Detention of Foreign Terrorists at Guantanamo

In order to see some elements of bureaucratic politics in action, we will examine a particular case study of recent importance. The *New York Times* published a series of articles in 2004 that detailed how a new system of military justice was created in the wake of the 9/11 attacks (Golden, 2004 a and b). This system was used to detain suspected terrorists at Guantanamo Bay, Cuba, in a military prison setting. One of the chief lightning rods of the system was the assertion that the men detained did not possess rights as prisoners of war under the Geneva Convention. Over time, this new military system came under attack from many quarters, including the military's own lawyers.

The assertion of the *Times* is that bureaucratic manipulation to achieve long-standing ideological aims on the part of key players was the engine driving the creation of this new system. In this recounting, we will refrain from assessing ideological motives and concentrate on the analysis of elements of groupthink, organizational process, and bureaucratic politics. Pay close attention to who "sat" where, who knew whom, who knew what, who was included, who was excluded, and how perceived domestic political imperatives affected the process.

The cast of players included Timothy Flanigan, deputy White House counsel; John Yoo, in the Justice Department's Office of Legal Counsel; William Barr, the former attorney general when Flanigan served as head of that same office; David Addington, counsel to the vice president; Alberto Gonzales, White House counsel; Pierre-Richard Prosper, the State Department's ambassador-at-large for war crimes issues; Patrick Philbin, a deputy in Justice's Office of Legal Counsel; William J. Haynes II, general counsel to the secretary of defense; and John Bellinger, legal adviser to the National Security Council, along with a bevy of higher-ranking officials and lower-ranking attorneys.

The events of September 11, 2001, set the stage for the U.S.-led war on global terrorism. A key question was how the United States could adopt an aggressive stance toward terrorism and yet negotiate the U.S. legal system, which provides many rights to accused persons, and the international legal system, which also provides significant rights to prisoners of war under the Geneva Convention. The best legal minds in government would be tasked with reconciling what on first glance appeared to be irreconcilable.

The White House counsel's office became the locus of initiative concerning the development of a new legal paradigm for the war on terror. Flanigan was apparently assigned the lead on this assignment. Flanigan contacted Yoo, a friend, who wrote a twenty-page reply opining that in the context of terrorist attacks, Fourth Amendment rights might not apply.

Flanigan then put in a call to his old boss, William Barr, to ask advice. Barr apparently reminded him that the Justice Department had researched the idea of special military tribunals to oversee trials of suspected terrorists almost ten years previously when Pan Am 103 had been blown up over Scotland. Flanigan felt that military tribunals, later reworded as military "commissions," would strike precisely the right posture in the new global war on terror. As commander in chief, it would ultimately be the president who would control what these commissions did.

At some point, Flanigan apparently shared his ideas with Addington and Gonzales, who both concurred. Gonzales decided to establish an inter-agency working group to hammer out options concerning the prosecution of terrorists—already knowing which option he would try to ensure pre-vailed. Pierre-Richard Prosper from State was assigned to chair the group, and according to the *Times* account, it was made clear to him by Gonzales that military commissions would be one of the options.

The Prosper interagency group saw three alternatives for prosecuting ter-rorists: federal courts, military tribunals, and Nuremberg-style tribunals with both military and civilian members. The Justice Department's repre-sentatives to the group insisted that federal courts were adequate. The vari-ous counsels from the White House were united in their disagreement. After the options had been researched and debated for approximately a month, the White House pulled the plug on Prosper's group, and Flanigan was again in charge of developing the new legal framework.

This time, the framework would be worked out among the various White House counsels before it was revealed to any other agencies. This is a very risky bureaucratic maneuver. Leaving out whole hosts of lawyers situated across a dozen relevant agencies and departments would virtually invite attack. As we will see, the most damning attack would come from those lawyers who were asked to actually implement the framework's particulars.

On November 6, 2001, Patrick Philbin in the Justice Department's Office of Legal Counsel sent, by request, a thirty-five-page confidential memoran-dum to Gonzales. In it, citing a 1942 case where Franklin D. Roosevelt ordered on his own authority a military tribunal to try eight Nazi sabo-teurs, Philbin argued that the president had the inherent authority to set up the desired military commissions. He further argued that rights of due process would not necessarily apply in the context of war (including the war on terror).

Based on this memorandum, the various counsels at the White House drafted an executive order, which was apparently approved by John Ash-croft, the head of the Justice Department, and also Donald Rumsfeld, secre-tary of defense (through his counsel William J. Haynes II). Interestingly, it had been the criminal division of the Justice Department that had argued against military commissions in the Prosper interagency group. How did Ashcroft overcome their opposition? He did not. Ashcroft did not tell Michael Chertoff, the head of Justice's criminal division, about the new order. Chertoff, who later became secretary of homeland security, only saw the orders when they were published. Ditto for the State Department and even the National Security Council.

In the meantime, a group of Army lawyers had tried to meet with Haynes to prevent a fait accompli. Probably sensing that not meeting with them at all would be contrary to public relations interests, Haynes called their leader into his office on Friday, November 9, and allowed him to review the proposed order for exactly thirty minutes. He was not allowed to take notes, according to the *Times* report.

The next day, Saturday, the Army's judge advocate general called together a group of senior military lawyers for an emergency meeting. Their purpose was to draft a response that would result in modifications to the order before it was published. But that very same day, the vice president, the attorney general, Haynes, Gonzales, Flanigan, Addington, and others were finalizing the order. The *Times* reports that Dick Cheney felt the order should not be shown in advance to Colin Powell, secretary of State, or Condoleezza Rice, the ANSA. The vice president and the president discussed the order over a lunch, and the president signed the order on Tuesday, November 13. No press conference was held.

In bureaucracies, however, as we have discussed in this chapter, "faits" are only "accomplis" when play has ceased—or at least become dormant—on the multiple boards of play. The maneuvering of Flanigan and others to make only one board, the White House board, count was doomed to failure.

The Senate Judiciary Committee immediately called for hearings. (Ironically, according to the *Times* account, the administration tasked Prosper and Chertoff to represent the administration's view, even though both men had argued against the policy and eventually were excluded from deliberations.) The Department of Defense parried this new attack in preemptive fashion by leaking the draft concerning implementation of the new system, indicating that critics' concerns had been taken into account. Rumsfeld also assembled a group of external legal experts to offer advice, and some of these held credibility for having worked on the Nuremberg and Tokyo tribunals.

For a moment, it appeared that play had stalled, and the administration's gambit had worked. However, it would turn out that the Pentagon had overlooked a very important game board. It was not the Senate or the American Civil Liberties Union (ACLU) that the Pentagon should have worried about. It was their own lawyers, military lawyers, over whom they should have lost sleep. Unfortunately, the approach that Haynes took toward the military lawyers was exclusionary. In one exchange reported by the *Times*, the Navy judge advocate general, Admiral Guter, confronted Haynes directly, "'We need more information.' Mr. Haynes looked at him coldly. 'No, you don't.'" Guter would retire soon after, and then sign a "friend of the court" brief on behalf of Guantanamo detainees appealing their detention.

In the meantime, a new issue had been put into play. Could detainees appeal their detention in federal court? Numerous critics had argued detainees must have this right, and then of course the federal courts would judge whether the new legal framework of military commissions was constitutional. The White House team of lawyers saw this chain of reasoning for what it was: a bureaucratic Trojan horse designed to derail the entire military commission idea. Philbin and Yoo from Justice were again tasked with providing relevant legal arguments, this time that detainees could not make such an appeal. Their memorandum dated December 28, 2001, suggested an overseas detention site in order to argue that the detentions were not taking place on American territory. Guantanamo was chosen in accordance with this logic. The first detainees would arrive on January 11.

Furthermore, the White House legal team, again turning to Justice's Office of Legal Counsel for support, had argued that the Geneva Conventions did not apply to terrorists. Yoo had argued, and Gonzales and Addington concurred, that even the Taliban could be considered terrorists. In fact, even if interrogators could not identify any link to terrorism per se, detainees would be held as "enemy combatants," with the identity of the enemy force left undefined.

At this point, however, excluded players began to emerge and make their presence felt. Condoleezza Rice wondered why the National Security Council and its legal team had not been involved. Colin Powell complained that given the number of allied nations involved in the situation, State had to be in the loop, too. The FBI and the criminal division of Justice had their own complaints.

In order to reconstruct unity among his bureaucratic players on these important issues, President Bush asked two of the NSC's staff, including legal counsel John Bellinger, to bring the players together and have them work out the kinks in an interagency committee. Apparently, however, the various players began asking some rather difficult questions, such as how Defense knew these people were enemy combatants. Defense's first position against such probing was to stonewall. One former Defense official told the *Times* that "he and others went into interagency meetings on Guantanamo with a standard script, dictated by their superiors: 'Back off—we've got this under control.'" Since Defense was following the November order drafted by the White House legal team and approved not only by the president, but also the powerful vice president, this tactic worked—for a while.

According to the *Times*, in August 2002, the ANSA, through the NSC, made her move. Rice's NSC staff sent its own Arab-speaking representative, reportedly a "senior intelligence analyst," to Guantanamo to assess conditions and speak to detainees. His or her report was given to Rice, and the report was purportedly very damning of what appeared to be a completely ad hoc operation. Rice took it to Powell. She also took it to Tom Ridge, adviser to the president on Homeland Security. And, in the coup de grâce, she took it to the criminal division of Justice. She began to build a counter-force to Rumsfeld and Cheney on the issues of detainment and military commissions.

On October 18, members of the cabinet involved with national security affairs met in a high-level showdown. Rice and Powell argued that what was going on in Guantanamo was not what the president had had in mind. They called for most of the detainees to be released. Rumsfeld apparently backed down. He was not interested in being a jailer; he was a warrior. Rumsfeld agreed to brief other agencies about the situation at Guantanamo, and agreed that the other cabinet members had the right to approve or disapprove plans for prosecution or release of the remaining detainees.

This last promise was to become the Trojan horse that the White House team had effectively warded off earlier. Now Justice, State, the NSC, the FBI, and other agencies all had to agree to a particular detainee's prosecution before Defense could proceed. As the *Times* puts it, "The internal struggle over the prisoners' fate began to play out in dysfunctional weekly meetings at which officials from across the government assembled by secure video link to consider individual detainees put forward by the Pentagon for outright release or transfer to the custody of their home governments." Readers of this chapter will not be surprised to learn that these dysfunctional weekly meetings produced almost no transfers, releases, or prosecutions.

Months later, in the spring of 2003, the military commissions had still not tried even one case. But after the Supreme Court agreed to hear a case challenging the legality of the detentions, the Pentagon decided to move forward with a few prosecutions. But they had underestimated their own lawyers.

Military lawyers assigned to defend the detainees took an aggressive stance. They filed a "friend of the court" brief with reference to the afore-mentioned Supreme Court case. They publicly challenged Pentagon rules that they were not to speak with the media. One military defense lawyer filed suit in a federal district court to block the military commissions.

On June 28, 2003, the Supreme Court ruled that detainees had the right to petition federal courts for their freedom. Since then, a significant number of detainees have been transferred to the custody of their home governments, where many have simply been released from custody. The military commission framework has never become fully operational. In July 2006, the Supreme Court ruled that military tribunals had to be explicitly authorized by legislation adopted by Congress before they could be formed, and the White House conceded that the detainees would retain their rights under the Geneva Convention. And when William Haynes was nominated to the federal bench, a whole host of military lawyers signed a letter to Congress urging his rejection.

This case study is a fascinating tale of groupthink, organizational behavior, and bureaucratic politics all rolled together into what ended up a policy failure. Consider the personal ties that permitted members of the White House counsel team to work effectively with certain members of the Justice Department, perhaps initiating groupthink. But consider further how intra-organizational cleavages within Justice and Defense undermined the resultant policy. Examine also how tactics to exclude potential naysayers from process, from information, and from access were effectively used in the short-term, but then backfired over time. Keep in mind the roles played by the various branches of government, with moves by the executive branch affected by the opening of Senate hearings and rulings by the Supreme Court. Note also the role of organizational essence, with the Pentagon eventually deciding that it was not in the penitentiary business. Do not overlook the role of public embarrassment as military lawyers and judges voiced their open opposition to the plan. Consider finally the larger context of the game played amongst Rice, Powell, Rumsfeld, and Cheney for influence and access. Finally, reflect upon the fact that the end-stage of interagency meetings, where all naysayers were included, predictably resulted in a de facto gutting of the policy through sheer inability to reach consensus. This episode offers the foreign policy analyst an insightful glimpse into the complex levels of group forces at work in foreign policy decisionmaking.

4

Culture and National Identity

During the Cold War, it was possible for scholars to overlook the effects of culture and national identity on foreign policy: one could argue the constraints of the bipolar rivalry dwarfed, in large part, the domestic idiosyncrasies of nations. However, in the post–Cold War era, that luxury no longer exists. National identity and culture shape the domestic motivations and imperatives that now seem as or more important than international balance-of-power considerations in foreign policymaking. When we inquire concerning the belief systems of political leaders, as we did in chapter 1, we simply cannot ignore the political socialization the leader received in his national culture. That socialization, filled with history and legend, heroes and enemies, successes and failures, God and luck, form much of the basic architecture of political belief systems.

Since we know this at an intuitive level, frameworks that explain foreign policy differences on the basis of differing cultures can be quite persuasive. A clear case in point is the work of political scientist Samuel Huntington, who has argued that the post–Cold War world will see a clash of civilizations (1993, 1996). More specifically, Huntington predicts that a Confucian–Islamic axis will oppose the West and its allies. Huntington points out that the borders of Islamic civilization are "bloody," with open conflicts from Bosnia to Bangladesh, from Nigeria to Xinjiang. China is rising as a possible new challenger to the might of the Western superpower. An alliance of convenience may serve the interests of both Islamic and Chinese culture, and glimpses of it may be seen in China's courting of Iran, Sudan, and other Islamic nations.

In addition to this meta-game of global dominance, there are more regionally focused cultural games as well. How could one interpret contemporary Asian politics without knowledge of the deep resentment held by many in Asia against Japan and Japanese culture, for example? Or the cultural antipathy between India and China, which broke out in the hostilities of 1962? Huntington would suggest that most conflicts in the world have cultural roots.

However, upon looking a bit deeper, one finds that culture turns out to be as elusive as it is intuitive. Actually using culture as part of a rigorous explanation turns out to be a much harder task than first imagined. Let us see how Foreign Policy Analysis (FPA) has struggled to incorporate national identity and culture into its explanations of foreign policy and foreign policy decisionmaking.

The research agenda of the field of Foreign Policy Analysis should be well suited to address questions of culture and identity in foreign policy, striving as it does for actor-specific theory, which combines the strengths of general theory with those of country expertise. Nevertheless, one of the least developed angles of analysis in the subfield, in my opinion, is the study of how societal culture and issues of identity affect foreign policy choice.

This is not terribly surprising, for several reasons. First, the study of how cultural differences affect behavior has been, for the most part, the domain of social sciences other than International Relations (IR). Most scholarly work on culture is to be found in the journals of anthropology, sociology, social psychology, organizational behavior, and other related disciplines. In part, the paucity of such literature in International Relations stems from the now-discredited work on national character from earlier this century. Though a few substantial works have been written since that time in International Relations and comparative politics, the trouble is, according to the author of several such works, Lucian Pye, that culture quickly becomes "the explanation of last resort" (Pye, 1991, 504). Everything that cannot be explained by existing theories in Foreign Policy Analysis is ascribed to "cultural differences." Explanations of last resort, however (e.g., "The Chinese act that way because that is the Chinese way"), are virtually never explanations at all (Pye, 1988, 6; see also Gaenslen, 1997).

In this chapter we will overview the evolution of thinking about culture and national identity as they relate to foreign policy. First, however, we must clarify our central concepts.

CONCEPTUALIZING CULTURE AND NATIONAL IDENTITY

When we speak of culture and national identity as they relate to foreign policy, we are seeking the answers that the people of a nation-state would give to the following three questions: "Who are we?", "What do 'we' do?", and "Who are they?"

Though it is possible each citizen would give more or less different answers, still each has some conception of, say, what it means to be an American or a Turk or a Russian. And that conception is also tied to an understanding of what it is Americans or Turks or Russians would do in certain foreign policy situations. Furthermore, we have conceptualizations of other nations and their peoples. Often, these are very different from how the people of that other nation conceive of themselves. Think of how Americans view Mexico and Mexicans, or Israel and Israelis—and vice versa.

Who are "we"? There are times, particularly in the wake of great systemic or subsystemic change, when a nation-state may encounter profound uncertainty on this point. When there is great uncertainty about who "we" are, various power nodes within the nation-state will begin to answer that question according to their political aims. To be successful in steering that discussion, these forces will have to tap into deep cultural beliefs actively shared or lying dormant among a large majority of the populace. In such times, the primacy of the question "who are 'we'?" may trump all other questions of success or failure or risk in foreign policy.

What is it "we" do (or should do)? Part of defining who "we" are is to define what "we" typically do or what "we" should do, given who "we" are. The noblest elements of what Breuning (1997) calls the nation's "heroic history" will be called upon during these times. Nations may choose actions more in line with their heroic history than with more dispassionate norms of strategy and rational choice. There may also be times when a nation is more confused about what "we" do than about who "we" are. Perhaps that is the lot of the United States in foreign policy now, given the polarizing debate over the invasion of Iraq. In such cases, it may not only be our heroic history that is called upon to help guide our actions, but our notable failures as well. We have already seen the invocation of lessons learned from the Vietnam War in the national debate over Iraq.

Who are "they"? Culture not only alleviates concern over our own identity, it helps alleviate concern over whom we are dealing with. In all stories, myths, and histories, there are "others" who have played important roles, good, bad, or indifferent. In understanding who a new "they" are, it is often helpful to conceive of the other as playing one of these more well-known roles. Notice how Saddam Hussein was "another Hitler," but then Slobodan Milosevic can be "another Saddam Hussein" as well as "another Hitler." Not only can "they" be external to the nation, but there may also be subnational forces that can be scripted to play certain culturally understood roles—the Quisling role, the Neville Chamberlain role, the Jimmy Carter role, the Lyndon Johnson role, and so forth.

These aspects of national identity are not carved in stone, nor do they spring from tablets of stone. Rather, national identity is political and is being shaped and reshaped every moment by society. Discourse and interaction within our society are the engines of national identity. The jokes we tell ourselves on late-night television, the op-ed columns in our newspapers, the blogs, the radio talk shows, the books and movies, our dinner table conversations—all of these inform and over time help change the answers to the three questions noted above. We often term the transitory results of all of this social discourse "culture." Thus we speak of "culture wars," and "culture change."

In a way, we cannot speak of issues of national identity without reference to culture as it arises from the continual process of social discourse.

Culture is simultaneously one of the most elusive and most easily understood concepts in social science. It is easily understood because all have had the experience of interacting with someone whose background led them to do and say things that seemed surprising or unpredictable. When was the last time your mother-in-law visited you and decided to clean house? Culture's consequences are very real, even to lay observers. The elusiveness of culture becomes apparent when one attempts to define it in a theoretical sense. The difficulty is not so much centered on what to *include* in such a definition, but rather what to *exclude*. For example, is the way my mother-in-law cleans house part of her personality, or a product of her culture, or both? And how would one answer the question? If she cleans house differently than I, how can it be a cultural difference if we are both white, English-speaking, Anglo-Saxon, Protestant, American mothers of the early years of the twenty-first century? The vagueness of culture's boundaries are echoed in the all-encompassing but pithy definitions of culture to be found in the social science literature: for example, culture is the "human-made part of the environment" (Herskovits, 1955), culture is "the software of the mind" (Hofstede, 1991), culture is "a set of schedules of reinforcement" (Skinner, 1981), culture is "any interpersonally shared system of meanings, perceptions, and values" (*Millennium*, 1993). Things do not become any clearer as one moves to more detailed definitions of culture. The following five have been chosen not for their uniqueness as definitions of culture, but for their typicality in the theoretical literature on culture:

1. "I use the term culture to mean an organized body of rules concerning the ways in which individuals in a population should communicate with another, think about themselves and their environments, and behave toward one another and towards objects in their environments" (LeVine, 1973).
2. "Culture consists in patterned ways of thinking, feeling and reaction, acquired and transmitted mainly by symbols, constituting the distinctive achievements of human groups, including their embodiments in artifacts; the essential core of culture consists of traditional (i.e., historically derived and selected) ideas and especially their attached values" (Kluckhohn, 1951).

3. "Culture is a set of human-made objective and subjective elements that in the past have increased the probability of survival and resulted in satisfaction for the participants in an ecological niche, and thus became shared among those who could communicate with each other because they had a common language and they lived in the same time and place" (Triandis, 1994).

4. "Culture [consists] of learned systems of meaning, communicated by means of natural language and other symbol systems, having representational, directive, and affective functions, and capable of creating cultural entities and particular sense of reality. Through these systems of meaning, groups of people adapt to their environment and structure interpersonal activities" (d'Andrade, 1984).

5. "[Culture is] an historically transmitted pattern of meanings embodied in symbols, a system of inherited conceptions expressed in symbolic form by means of which men communicate, perpetuate, and develop their knowledge about and attitudes towards life" (Geertz, 1973).

With definitions like these, it is not hard to see why culture became "the explanation of last resort" for a field such as International Relations, which was heavily influenced by behavioralism. What "crucial experiment" could be constructed capable of falsifying the hypothesis that culture affects what nations do in the international arena? Indeed, all human activity—including foreign policy—becomes both a product of and a component of culture. The seamlessness of culture rendered problematic early behavioralist attempts to separate and then relink in causal fashion the independent variable of culture and the dependent variable of national policy; we call these early attempts of the 1940s and 1950s the "national character studies." If the German national character could be described as "methodical," their policy would evince the same characteristic; ditto for the "stoic" Russians and the "xenophobic" Japanese.

National character studies were vulnerable to criticism on several grounds: methodological, theoretical, and moral. For example, the methodologies used predisposed one toward potentially tautological inferences: if a sample group perceived Germans as methodical, this proved significant psychological inducement to perceive whatever Germans did as methodical. Likewise, on theoretical grounds, the fact that individual variation within national groups always exceeded variation between national groups on any given characteristic was very troubling. Last, national character studies seemed a natural bedfellow of the "racial psychology" studies, whose worst excesses contributed a "scholarly" rationale for genocidal Nazi policies.

However, the twenty-first century brings with it a substantially new context than students of culture possessed in the 1940s. For one, the world after 9/11 now takes cultural differences very seriously as a potent source of foreign policy behavior. Second, the study of culture has matured substantially over the last six or seven decades. And so we begin to see a small interface between the study of culture and the study of foreign policy developing in International Relations (and specifically FPA). Let's look first at the evolution of the study of culture.

The Study of Culture

The study of culture has had a fascinating genesis, worthy of many book-length treatments in its own right. From the thought of Emile Durkheim, Max Weber, Talcott Parsons, Margaret Mead, and others through the hiatus of such thought in the 1960s to the renaissance of the study of culture in the 1980s is an intellectual journey well worth taking. Let us concentrate on the noteworthy themes of the renaissance period for their possible applicability to the development of a culture/foreign policy research agenda.

Though definitions of culture continue to be very inclusive of the human experience, there appears to be a subtle trifurcation in the conceptualization of culture in recent works. There are scholars who emphasize culture as *the organization of meaning*; there are others for whom culture remains primarily *value preferences*; and a third group of scholars conceptualizes culture as *templates of human strategy*. Of course, a natural reaction is to assert that culture includes all three elements, and indeed, it is futile to impose a hard-and-fast distinction between the different conceptions. However, as we have seen, the more inclusive view of culture is the least useful in a research sense. The particular emphasis of the three groups of scholars has allowed each to ask (and answer) more concrete questions about the consequences of culture than was possible in earlier periods. Indeed, a close look at the longer definitions presented earlier will reveal the following emphases:

Culture as the organization of meaning. If culture is a system of shared meaning, how is it constructed, perpetuated, and modified? Also, how does one system of shared meaning compare to another system, and what are the ramifications of interaction between two very different ontologies? Because meanings are shared through interpersonal expression, the study of such expression, whether it be art, writing, film, conversation, and so forth, is often the focus of such analysis. The classic work in this category would be Clifford Geertz's *The Interpretation of Cultures* (1973). Geertz insisted that a structural-functional explanation of, say, a Balinese cockfight, would miss the more holistic *meaning* the cockfight held for the community. In what way can an outsider become privy to meaning within a society? Alluding to the Whorfian hypothesis (Whorf, 1956) that language itself colors thinking, many researchers look to language use as a key. One approach, for example, is to analyze public discourse on issues of high controversy. Luker (1984), for example, is able to trace the contorted evolution of public moral discourse on abortion, and discovers that the meaning of *abortion* has seesawed back and forth over the centuries, and depended in large part upon which authorities were accepted as having highest legitimacy in the society at the time. Others have asked how it is that scientists come to regard a finding as "important" or even "scientific" in the first place (see, for example, Root-Bernstein, 1989; Pickering, 1984). Comparisons of the meanings of certain phenomena in one culture as versus those in another have uncovered some startling differences (see Triandis, 1994, 97–99; Bleiker, 1993). Nor need we be confined to analyzing verbal communication: nonverbal messages can construct and share meaning, as well. Of course, differences in nonverbal communication can derail otherwise normal interactions: one oft-cited example is the propensity of the Japanese to smile when being reprimanded (see Argyle, 1975).

Culture as value preferences. This view of culture follows the lead of Weber, Parsons, and others in suggesting that culture tells us what to want, to prefer, to desire, and thus *to value*. Such motivations prompt certain predictable behaviors—"syndromes"—in cultures. To the extent that culture has been studied in modern political science and International Relations, this is the primary approach taken (Almond and Verba's 1963 *The Civic Culture: Political Attitudes and Democracy in Five Nations* would be the classic example). Geert Hofstede's seminal study (1980) dimensionalizes cultures according to their affinity for five factors: individualism/collectivism, high/low gender differences, degree of uncertainty avoidance, power distance (low/high), and long-term/short-term orientation (Hofstede scores for about fifty countries can be found at www.geert-hofstede.com). Hofstede was able to show a nonrandom geographic pattern of cultures with respect to such values. The immense literature on organizational behavior in different cultures starts primarily from a Hofstede-type theoretical basis (see McDaniels and Gregory, 1991; Tse et al., 1988). Triandis discerns three cultural dimensions, which may interrelate to form unique cultural proclivities: cultural complexity, cultural "tightness," and individualism (1994, 156–79).

Closer to home, the work of Mary Douglas and Aaron Wildavsky can be placed in this category as well. Wildavsky, for instance (building on the work of Douglas), classifies cultures into four types: fatalist, hierarchist, egalitarian, and individualist. He is able to predict the responses of each type of culture to resource scarcity, nature, change, alliances, and other broad issues (see Wildavsky, 1987; Thompson, Ellis, and Wildavsky, 1990).

Other political scientists have used this approach to focus in on a particular culture (see Pye, 1968; Solomon, 1971).

There is also a growing research effort in the comparative study of ethical systems. Continuing the approach of Max Weber in his pioneering work on the ethics of Protestantism, Hinduism, and Confucianism (Weber, 1930, 1951a, 1951b, 1963), a new generation of scholars compares traditions of moral reasoning in dealing with common ethical problems (see Green, 1978; Little and Twiss, 1978; Chidester, 1987; Carman and Juergensmeyer, 1990). For example, what are the differences in the Christian just war tradition and the Islamic just war tradition? Such differences in moral reasoning based on culture may skew traditional assumptions of rational choice theory (see, for example, Sen, 1982, 1987). They may also lead to distinctive patterns of economic development, with some cultures possessing a distinct advantage simply because of their culture (see Kahn, 1993). There may even be implications for conflict: in a famous study, Nisbett and Cohen (1996) assert that white males from the American South are more likely to become physically violent when provoked because of their ancestors' deep roots in Scotland as pig farmers.

Culture as templates for human strategy. One group of scholars argues that the values espoused by members of a culture are not sufficient to explain actual behavior by those members. Often, there is great slippage between professed ends and the actual use of means. These scholars assert that the more important explanatory variable is the capability advantages bestowed by one's culture. One will play the game one's culture has conditioned one to play *well*. Indeed, Ann Swidler goes so far as to say: "Action is not determined by one's values. Rather, action *and* values are organized to take advantage of cultural competences. . . . (W)hat endures is the way action is organized, not its ends. . . . [P]eople will come to value ends for which their cultural equipment is well suited" (1986, 275, 276, 277). What culture provides its members is a repertoire or palette of adaptive responses from which members build off-the-shelf strategies of action. What matters is not the whole of culture, but rather "chunks" of "prefabricated" cultural response. We may not be able to predict choice and construction of a particular response by a particular member of the culture, but we can know *what is on the shelf* ready and available to be used or not. As Linton argues, "(i)ndividuals tend to imitate the culture patterns of their society when confronted by a new situation, then to take thought as the situation is repeated and try to adjust these patterns to their individual needs" (1945, 104). A related approach is taken by the "dramaturgical school," in which culture provides scripts and personae that are reenacted and subtly modified over time within a society (see Wuthnow, 1987; Kurtz, 1986).

It is in this area of cultural research that we also find efforts linking cultural background with information-processing proclivities. Studies from many fields have pointed out that rationality itself may mean different things in different cultures (see, for example, Motokawa, 1989). Douglas and Wildavsky, for instance (1982), discovered that fatalistic cultures do not engage in probabilistic thinking, and thus perceive risk taking (a subfield of rational choice study) in a very different fashion from nonfatalistic cultures. Ehrenhaus (1983) argues that culture may predispose a person to certain types of explanations and certain types of attribution and inferencing. This, in turn, makes certain errors in reasoning (Type I or Type II errors) more prevalent in some cultures than in others.

THE INTERFACE

As noted previously, there does exist a small interface between the study of culture and the study of foreign policy. To illuminate this interface literature, I have tried to make a distinction between foreign policy studies with little or no attention paid to cultural factors, cultural studies of particular nations ("country studies," "area studies") with no specific implications for foreign policy, and cultural studies of particular nations or regions with identifiable implications for foreign policy research. Only the last category of research is included. However, the other two categories of research are potential sources of theoretical and empirical insight that should not be overlooked.

As we review the interface literature, we will pay particular attention to the creation and modification of methodologies capable of asking and answering questions concerning the culture/foreign policy nexus.

Shared systems of meaning in foreign policy and foreign policymaking. Rather than accepting preferences and beliefs in International Relations at face value, a new generation of scholars asks how they were formed. In effect deconstructing statements of international reality, these scholars untangle the threads that culminated in the articulation of such statements. Many of the threads would fall under the first category of culture definitions: shared, evolving meanings conditioned by historical precedent and contemporary experience. We see and believe and desire what our horizons of the moment permit us to see and believe and desire—but these horizons are constantly shifting.

One lesson for the culture/foreign policy research agenda to be derived from postmodernist critique is that it may be fruitless to search for an exclusively *political* culture. The notion that political science studies some subset of culture called *political culture* is long-standing (see Almond and Verba, 1963; Inglehart, 1988). Yet, at least from a cursory reading of recent American politics, it is almost impossible not to see the political horizons shift their shape according to trends in broader societal culture, and vice versa.

(How would Bill Clinton's horizons have been different if Doonesbury had chosen a box of Wheaties instead of a floating waffle as his symbol?)

Definitions of political culture are virtually indistinguishable from definitions of general culture. Here's one: *political* culture is all of the discourses, values, and implicit rules that express and shape *political* action and intentions, determine the claims groups may and may not make upon one another, and ultimately provide a logic of *political* action. Cross out every *political*: "Culture is all of the discourses, values, and implicit rules that express and shape actions and intentions." Sounds familiar, doesn't it? It sounds like our earlier all-encompassing definitions of culture. The postmodern critique suggests that things *political* can be deconstructed and shown to have their roots in broad systems of shared meaning. To snip the overtly political elements of culture from their roots is to cut the researcher off from the wellsprings and source of change and permutation of political horizons. After all, another definition of culture is "common ways of dealing with social problems" (Triandis, 1994, 17). Dealing with social problems (or, dressed up in political science jargon, "value allocation processes in situations of conflict over scarce resources") *is* the study of politics. Nor should we forget the important feminist contribution on this score: the personal is the political.

However, it is in politics that cultural conversations become most explicit: What ends should the nation pursue? Using what means? Foreign policy is arguably at the very high end on a continuum of conversational explicitness (though it may not seem so from the receiving end!). Foreign policy is first, *a formal* affair because second, foreign policy concerns relations with *outgroups*. Outgroups serve simultaneously as a source of national identity (we're not like them) and as a threat to national identity (we must resist becoming like them). Thus we are led to theorize that the relationship between a culture and the acts it performs in the international arena must be fairly strong. Vertzberger sums up the conundrum this way:

> It is extremely difficult to positively prove the causal links, direct and indirect, between societal-cultural variables and foreign-policy-related information processing. The difficulty in directly observing societal-cultural effects, however, does not prove the opposite, that is, that societal-cultural influences are minor or negligible. I believe that the influences are important, even though they are not always tangible and easily observable" (1990, 261).

If one were to search for systems of shared meaning in foreign policy and foreign policymaking, how would one go about it, methodologically speaking? How would one tap into postmodernist insights to clarify the connection between culture and foreign policy? Let's examine five research efforts: Sylvan, Majeski, and Milliken (1991); Boynton (1991); Lotz (1997); Banerjee (1991, 1997); and Tunander (1989). All four projects seek to uncover the meaning, the basis, and the rules of political discourse in concrete circumstances (see also Chan, 1993, and Alker et al., 1991). Sylvan, Majeski, and Milliken's, Lotz's and Boynton's are within-nation studies, and Banerjee's and Tunander's are between-nation studies.

Sylvan and his coauthors examine the mountains of material generated by the national security establishment with reference to the conduct of the Vietnam War. Sylvan, Majeski, and Milliken ask the origins of war policy recommendations in this material. When did a statement become a "bona fide" recommendation? How did it fit into the flow of recommendations and counter-recommendations? How did persuasion occur? On what doxa was the entire discourse based? Sylvan's group schematically maps the river of recommendations in order to answer such questions. They see their work as a *cultural* investigation:

> our emphasis is cultural: how, within a particular foreign policy community, certain statements are fitted together into a comprehensible recommendation. . . . [Our model] must of necessity take into account the construal within a particular culture of certain statements as arguments, evidence, conclusions, and so forth. . . . [O]ur concern is with how, for a given bureaucratic and political culture, various statements are taxonomically related to each other so as jointly to compose a bona fide policy recommendation (327–28).

Boynton uses the official record of hearings of congressional committees to investigate how committee members make sense of current events and policies. By viewing the questions and responses in the hearings as an unfolding narrative, Boynton is able to chart how "meaning" crystallizes for each committee member, and how they attempt to share that meaning with other members and with those who are testifying. Boynton posits the concept of "interpretive triple" as a way to understand how connections between facts are made through plausible interpretations. Boynton is then able to illuminate how plausibility is granted to an interpretation—in effect, ascertaining which interpretations are plausible within the cultural context created by the hearings. Boynton (1996) extends those ideas to political ad campaigns—how can we understand why some ads are successful and some are not? As Boynton puts it, "In presidential elections, citizens turn their attention to politics and candidates turn their attention to citizens. The interaction is constructing political culture; some constructions of the world of international affairs are reaffirmed and new understandings develop." Political ads, then, are a source of continuing cultural dialogue within the nation.

Hellmut Lotz is interested in how politicians make use of the heroic myths citizens hold about their countries to mobilize support or diminish opposition to new policy initiatives by the government. His case study concerns the controversy over the ratification of the North American Free Trade Agreement (NAFTA) with Mexico. The public was deeply divided, and opposition was spearheaded by Ross Perot, who warned of a "giant sucking sound" if NAFTA were to be ratified—which sucking would pull jobs from the United States into Mexico. Then vice president Al Gore was tapped to debate Perot live on national television in November 1993. Before the debate, almost 30 percent of the electorate was undecided about NAFTA extension to Mexico, with the remainder almost evenly divided between supporters and opponents. In polls taken after the debate, 57 percent of the American public favored ratification. How could one debate have so moved the undecideds? Lotz analyzes the heroic myths of the United States and uncovers both well-known elements, such as the American dream and populism, as well as two variants of the myth of American exceptionalism: world leadership versus isolationism. He content analyzes the debate for the invocation of these myths. What he discovers is that the debate involving elements of populism was a wash, because both Gore and Perot were upper-class elites. Perot, as a billionaire businessman, could not speak to the issue of whether NAFTA was designed to benefit big business. However, their invocation of the other three myths differed substantially: Gore emphasized the American dream and American leadership for the world. Perot emphasized the need for America to remain isolated and protected from the rest of the world because of America's perceived vulnerability. Lotz points to Gore's summation, "This is a choice between the politics of fear and the politics of hope. It's a choice between the past and the future. It's a choice between pessimism and optimism. . . . We're not scared." Gore tapped into what Americans want to believe about themselves (strong, leaders, optimistic), and Perot tapped into issues that Americans do not want to believe about themselves (vulnerable, scared, pessimistic). No wonder the response to the debate was so dramatic: Gore had skillfully manipulated the core self-identity myths of Americans.

Banerjee extends the notion of communication as constructing culture (or shared meaning) to interstate relations. Each state's "psychocultural structure contains a variety of action rules, encoded in the language of acts, which trigger themselves when certain acts are perceived" (1997, 319). The language of acts, or social scripts, persists because "(a) subject perceives an historical structure as a chain of recurring instances of the same script. The perceived script defines the situation for the subject. Over time, the script becomes 'the way things are', reified as a natural or traditional order" (318; this concept of "scripts" is in distinction to cultural scripts already in place; see next section for the dramaturgical approach, which utilizes historically established scripts within a society). This natural order of things can be conceptualized as *internation culture*, which can be as recognizable and predictable as national culture (see also Solomon, 1992 on this point). Banerjee applies his analysis to relations between India and Pakistan, as they emerged from the rhetoric of Gandhi, Nehru, and Jinnah in the early years following independence from Great Britain. Nehru felt that the "other" facing the peoples of the Indian subcontinent was Great Britain, and that the people's greatest victory would come when sectarian divisions were overcome and the people united to overthrow their colonial masters. But for Jinnah, the "other" being faced was Hinduism, with its emphasis on caste inequality and impurity of non-Hindus. For Jinnah, Great Britain symbolized positive attributes, such as reliance on religion and support for the abolition of social inequalities. Indeed, "Pakistan" itself means "land of the pure." Banerjee points out how these founding understandings contributed to differences in foreign policy, not only one nation toward the other, but also in their interactions with other states. For example, India was part of the nonaligned movement, opposed to the machinations of East and West. But Pakistan was only too willing to align itself with great powers in order to stand as an equal vis à vis India.

Tunander offers an innovative semiotic explanation of U.S.–Soviet naval moves in the North Atlantic as "signs" in a complex conversation taking place between the two nations (Tunander, 1989, 169–80). Taking off from Derrida's "the missile is a missive," Tunander sees these naval maneuvers as part of the body language of states. In Tunander's view, the Navy is the principal character in a hyperreal drama: the Navy "speaks about his mad brother" (cruise missiles) and "plays with the key to the lion's cage" (strategic bombers and intercontinental ballistic missiles [ICBMs]) (174). Episteme (science) and doxa (opinion) merge in a strange game of shifting perceptions.

Differences in values and preferences in foreign policy and foreign policymaking. Much of the work concerning cultural effects on international negotiation examines the effects on such negotiations of cultural differences in value preferences (see Cohen, 1991). For example, because the government of the People's Republic of China (PRC) must base its legitimacy on its superior virtue and morality (in line with Confucian culture), it must explicitly pass moral judgment on the conduct of other nations. In order to assert moral claim to advantage in negotiation, a negative moral judgment must presage serious negotiation with another nation. From the Western point of view, this is the last thing a nation would do before entering into serious negotiations. It is permissible to talk about the unfairness of the status quo before negotiation, but a negative moral judgment of another nation's actions would more likely presage a Western nation's *disengagement* from serious negotiation (see Shih, 1993). The Western approach, too, derives from its unique Judeo-Christian values. Similar to the study of values in international negotiation is the study of values with reference to strategy. In the 1980s, a body of literature on "comparative strategic culture" developed to explain persistent differences between the United States and the USSR on military strategy (see Booth, 1979; Gray, 1986). Why did the Americans eschew strategic and civil defense in favor of mutually assured destruction (MAD), while the Soviets embraced defense to the point of adopting a war-fighting strategy contradictory to MAD? Scholars of strategic culture pointed to cultural and historical differences predisposing each nation to the choice it actually made, simultaneously noting the inevitable anxiety these choices would cause in the other nation.

Studies in Foreign Policy Analysis paralleling the "cultural syndrome" studies in other disciplines also exist. In its broadest sense, the idea of "national role conception" (K. J. Holsti, 1970) describes a national syndrome with respect to the nation's external relations (in its more specific application, national role conception studies resemble more the dramaturgical-style studies of the next section). A nation's leaders rise in part because they articulate a vision of the nation's role in world affairs that corresponds to deep cultural beliefs about the nation. In the rhetoric and action of these leaders, one may discern the nature of this role. Holsti's labels for such roles include "bridge," "isolate," "mediator," "bastion of the revolution," "defender of the faith," "regional leader," and so forth. Holsti and others (see Wish, 1980; Walker, 1987; Seeger, 1992; Breuning, 1992 and 1997) could then investigate the degree of concordance between expected role behavior/rhetoric and actual behavior/rhetoric. Breuning, for instance (1997), was able to trace differences in the assistance-giving behavior of Belgium and the Netherlands to differences in the two nations' national role conceptions, despite the nations' ostensible similarities in most other respects.

The next step in this line of inquiry is studies that trace in more detail how certain cultures come to conceive of their nation's roles in particular ways. Sampson (1987) and Sampson and Walker (1987) are two such attempts. Specifically, Sampson and Walker, in contrasting Japan and France, assert that cultural norms of dealing with subordinates and superordinates in organizational settings within the nations will be applied by those nations when dealing with subordinates and superordinates in the international arena. Sampson and Walker compare Japan and France on their reaction to and emphasis on group harmony, indebtedness, concern/dependency on others, a superior's empathy for an inferior, collaboration and consultation, and sense of responsibility owed within an organization. They find that Japan's and France's profound differences on these values result in equally profound, but now predictable and understandable, differences in national role conceptions.

Zurovchak (1997) also investigates this issue of culture organizing the structure of bureaucracies. A natural historical experiment was afforded him as he studied the construction of the foreign ministries of the Czech Republic and Slovakia after the disintegration of Czechoslovakia. Using the Hofstede rankings mentioned previously, he is able to show that Czech culture and Slovak culture have some important differences. His research question then became, would those differences influence the structure and function of the two newly created foreign ministries? He found that there were in fact interesting differences. The Slovak ministry was much more hierarchically organized; in contrast, the organization chart for the Czech ministry did not even indicate lines of authority! In addition, the functioning of the two ministries was also different: for example, "going over someone's head" organizationally to discuss a problem was forbidden in the Slovak ministry, but was encouraged in the Czech ministry. The gender compositions of the two ministries were also different.

Wilkening (1999) offers a divergent approach to the above-mentioned works. His work spans conceptualization of culture as a system of meaning and a set of value preferences. He discusses the tremendous attention paid to the issue of acid rain among the Japanese, in contrast to their neighbors who also experience acid rain. Wilkening's research is a tale of how environmental activists were able to awaken the Japanese public by use of deeply held, shared meanings, and also how the resultant widespread citizen involvement in the issue of acid rain propelled Japanese government leaders to take a more aggressive stance internationally on acid rain. According to Wilkening, shared meanings about the importance of rain as a source of fresh water in Japan, as well as the importance of growing things, such as plants and forests, tap into core beliefs about national identity. Specific types of plants, particularly short-lived beautiful flowers, occupy a privileged spot in the Japanese imagination. Environmental activists used these cultural elements to construct a grassroots campaign where citizens would grow morning glories, and then observe whether the flowers changed color in response to the acidity of the rain. Housewives, schoolchildren, office workers, gardeners, and Japanese from many different walks of life planted morning glories and were sending in reports on color changes. Haiku contests on the theme of acid rain were organized. News broadcasts began to feature changes in morning glory color from various parts of Japan. As the population was mobilized on the issue of acid rain as a threat to the strongly held value preference of maintaining purity of rain and plant life, this provided a basis for enterprising Japanese politicians to capitalize on public concern and move more aggressively in the international arena for agreements to limit the output of acid rain from other countries in the region.

Prefabricated templates of action in foreign policy and foreign policymaking. In Foreign Policy Analysis, the work of Leites (1951), George

(1969), Walker (1977), and others on "the operational code" comes closest to this conceptualization of culture. Defining an operational code involves identifying core beliefs of a leader or group, as well as preferred means and style of pursuing goals. It is this last half of the operational code definition that assists us in determining what templates of action may exist within a nation with respect to foreign policy. For example, in elucidating the "Bolshevik" operational code, one finds some explicit maxims on political action: a) one cannot "muddle through" because in every situation there is just one correct policy, and even minor mistakes can be disastrous; b) don't calculate the probability of succeeding as a precursor to determining what your goal will be; c) maximize one's gains rather than satisfice, but avoid adventuristic actions where the outcomes are either maximum payoff or maximum loss; d) push to the limit, pursue one's opponent even if he or she lets up, but be prepared to engage in strategic retreat rather than suffer large losses in strength; e) rather than limit objectives, limit the means you use to achieve your objectives so as to prevent a strong reaction from the enemy; f) use rude and violent language to heighten your enemy's estimate of your strength and resolve (all adapted from George, 1969). George is then able to demonstrate how these maxims for action were followed by the Soviet Union in its relationship with the United States. (Social Science Automation has recently automated the Verbs in Context System [VICS], an operational code text interpreter; see Young and Schafer, 1998.)

Such "action maxims" can affect broader aspects of cognitive processing, as well. Ball (1992) asserts that Asian culture predisposes one to take a more long-term perspective than other cultures: he quotes Sukarno saying, "We, the Indonesian people, have learned not to think in centimeters or meters, not in hours or days We have learned to think in continents and decades" (5). M. G. Hermann has found evidence that certain cultures are more likely to exhibit certain aspects of decisionmaking and interpersonal style than others; for example, she found that Middle Eastern leaders were much more distrustful of others than leaders from other cultures (1979), and therefore more likely to discount discrepant information. Furthermore, certain types of leaders are predisposed toward specific styles of foreign policymaking (structure of decision groups, method of resolving disagreement, etc.), and the prevalence of certain types of leaders varies according to region and culture (see M. Hermann, 1987). Gaenslen (1989) persuasively shows that cultures reliant on consensual decisionmaking may not be as open to dissonant information—even from reliable sources—as cultures in which majority vote is sufficient for decisionmaking. Yaacov Vertzberger asserts that certain cultures may predispose one to abstractive as versus associative reasoning, and to universalistic as versus case particularistic reasoning (1990).

As noted earlier, the more specific approach to "national role conception" provides an interesting parallel to the dramaturgical approach to culture. In Foreign Policy Analysis, the work of Chih-yu Shih (1993), Lloyd Etheredge (1992), and others falls into this category (see also Esherick and Wasserstrom, 1990; Katzenstein, 1997). Shih and Katzenstein both feel that Chinese foreign policy behavior corresponds to relatively specific scripts of action inherited from exemplary episodes in that nation's history. The reenactment of such scripts allows Chinese foreign policy to be *meaningful to the Chinese themselves*. According to Shih, "the Chinese style of organizing world politics is more dramatic than realist. . . . Every drama can and will be repeated till the demise of the moral regime" (Shih, 1993, 201 and 197). Shih then analyzes several Chinese scripts, the knowledge of which allows for the reconciliation of otherwise contradictory Chinese foreign policies.

Katzenstein argues that a Chinese script virtually unknown to Westerners, but forefront in the minds of Chinese on both sides of the strait, will be the template for eventual resolution of Taiwan's anomalous status (1997). Etheredge, in his study of American national security policy, persuasively argues that such policy is incomprehensible without an understanding of important American dramatic requirements. "(A)ll power relationships are a dramatic art, and one creates and manages power as an exercise in applied psychology, shaping a dramatic presence that, in the minds of others, becomes their experience of reality" (1992, 62). The logic of being impressive imposes theatrical requirements far different from those of strict rationality, "like a *Star Wars* drama of good versus evil and a battle for control of the universe" (67). To try to understand American nuclear strategy without a knowledge of the impression the United States was trying to make with its strategy would be to conclude the United States was acting irrationally. It was not acting irrationally, but it was acting—a very specific role for both internal and external audience consumption.

Hudson (1999) attempts to develop a methodology whereby action scripts for nation-states can be identified. Rather than rely on writings or speeches of elites, she develops a scenario-based survey designed to elicit whether there are shared understandings about appropriate responses to a variety of foreign policy situations in which the nation may find itself. Seven scenarios are postulated: involvement in UN peacekeeping operations in less-developed nations; threatened closure of strategically important shipping lanes by hostile powers in the region; terrorist kidnappings of one's own citizens in a foreign land with demands for ransom and policy changes as conditions for the hostages' release; the acquisition of a nuclear arsenal with IRBM capability by a hostile rogue regime; the violent disintegration of a neighboring state with significant refugee migration to one's own state; a showdown over trade issues with another nation; and a situation where military takeover of territory of one's own nation is threatened. A list of possible state responses was given and respondents were asked to suggest which options their nation would probably consider and which options their nation would not consider. Respondents from the United States, Russia, and Japan were involved. They were also asked which options each of the other two cultures would probably consider and which options the other cultures would not consider. In general, Russian responses were the most heterogeneous, and Japanese responses were the most homogeneous. The favored response of Japanese citizens was to not use force unilaterally and to petition for assistance from and cooperate with relevant intergovernmental organizations (IGOs). For the United States, in situations with clear ramifications for national security, the favored response was unilateral military action coupled with economic punishment. Russian responses were so heterogeneous that few generalizable patterns emerged, except for consensus that events in Ukraine were of special concern. Americans and Japanese were pretty confident what the other would probably do or not do in a situation, but neither was confident about probable Russian response in these situations. There were some noteworthy mistakes, though. Americans incorrectly perceived that Japan would never negotiate with terrorists. This is the American policy, but Japan does negotiate with terrorists. This exercise shows the prima facie validity of searching for national action templates. For some nations, such as Japan, consensus on appropriate response may be quite predictive of government behavior. For other nations, the ability to predict government response on the basis of shared action templates would be altered in greater measure by situational variables.

THOUGHTS ON MOVING AHEAD

"Cultural analysis" means different things to scholars even within the same field of IR, and even within FPA itself. However, some approaches may be less fruitful than others. For example, the understanding of cultural analysis employed currently in the security studies subfield of IR is that culture is an approach that serves as an intellectual rival to the dominant paradigm of explanation—power politics. Cultural variables are seen as useful only insofar as they explain that which cannot be explained by actor-general power calculations. Culture is seen as a synonym for continuity in nation-state foreign policy—qualities both persistent and particularistic. The broad, general direction of culture within a society is noted in this style of analysis. Culture has become, if you will, a static residual in this view.

However, from an FPA standpoint, cultural trends are useful only insofar as they can be harnessed to the task of understanding and projecting near term foreign policy choice. In this context, it may be at least as important to explore cultural change as cultural continuity. In an overarching sense, what is paramount is an exploration of culture as a political instrument. Explanations on the basis of power and explanations on the basis of culture are therefore not mutually exclusive. In this view, culture is not a reified concept, but a dynamic force and an element of political power competition. As Wilkening puts it, "culture in and of itself is *not* a cause of anything in international relations or any other area of human activity. It is in the 'who draws what ideas' and the 'how the ideas are employed' aspects [of cultural analysis] that causes of events can be found" (Wilkening, 1999, 8).

Indeed, rather than explain, say, Chinese behavior in the Spratly Islands by recourse to the thought of Hsun Tzu, perhaps we ought to ask which faction in Chinese politics is picking which elements from Chinese culture to promote their policy agenda on the Spratlys? And then ask who opposes this agenda, using which *other* elements of Chinese culture. By tracking which cultural "story" becomes ascendant through the rough-and-tumble of power politics and the persuasiveness of the story to broader elements of society, we can then ask what obeisance must then be paid to the cultural elements that compose it—regardless of risk, rational choice, and power politics considerations.

In other words, the choice of cultural ideas to promote a particular political agenda entails constraint. One of the key points of usefulness about cultural analysis is its ability to tell the analyst what would be considered impossible in the FP of the country. Rational choice and Realpolitik cannot exclude options on the basis of cultural impossibility—only an understanding of the other's culture can do that. At the same time, cultural analysis should be able to tell you what types of options will be favored, ceteris paribus. Well-known and well-practiced options, preferably tied in to the nation's heroic history, will be preferred over less well-known and less familiar options or options with traumatic track records—even if an objective cost-benefit analysis of the two options would suggest otherwise.

This view of culture—as dynamic and as a political instrument—provides policy relevance. But it does more than that. It suggests that cultural analysis and power politics analysis are not mutually exclusive theoretical rivals. A culture is important *because* of power politics. And culture itself confers a preferred structure and process *to* power politics. How power is conceived of and employed *is an element of culture.* Those who concentrate on foreign policy decisionmaking (FPDM) are less likely to see these approaches as theoretical rivals, and more likely to see them as inextricably related.

This view of culture argues for certain desiderata in the analytical sphere:

1. Comparative analysis: Only comparatively do differences in culture and the effects of those differences become apparent. Such comparison can be done between cultures or between subnational interpretations of the same culture.

2. Subnational analysis: If one is interested in FPDM, it may not be very profitable to study culture at the level of the regime (except under rare circumstances, such as a totalitarian microculture). One must look at power nodes within the society, and ask their link to and use of culture. Without subnational analysis, one is left with culture as only a force of continuity. Culture as a force for change becomes elusive.

3. Discourse analysis: To see culture being wielded as an instrument of power in society, one must trace the discourse between power nodes. When they disagree over policy direction, to what myths, stories, heroic historical elements, contemporary cultural memes, or other elements do they refer? What are the alternative or rival stories? Which become ascendant? This is not to say that no other methodological approach may be used, but rather to admit that probably all meaningful methodologies in this area will ultimately rest on an examination of cultural understandings, which are most observable when made tangible in discourse.

4. Horizon analysis: This is an analysis of the constraints and incentives bestowed by the cultural "story" being advocated. What horizon of possibility will each competing story produce? What becomes impossible to do if this story is advocated? What becomes more likely?

5. Interaction analysis: If nation X, with story A currently ascendant, faces a conflict of interest with nation Y, wherein story J is currently ascendant, how will they interact? What will be the points of conflict? Who can compromise on what issues? Who cannot compromise on what issues? Which strategies will be more likely to be employed on each side? Does either party have culturally permissible contingency plans in the event of failure? Or are contingency plans on some issues forbidden?

One recent piece that takes us furthest in these directions is that of Andrea Grove and Neal Carter (1999). Their article incorporates each of the five desiderata mentioned above. They compare the 1984–1986 discourse of Gerry Adams and John Hume, political rivals vying for control over the evolution of the Northern Ireland conflict, with special reference to the Catholic minority. These years were chosen for they bookend the 1985 Anglo-Irish Agreement (AIA). Before the agreement, Adams's political support was on the upswing; after 1985, it would be Hume who was ascendant. Grove and Carter first identify which strategy for identity formation each man used to mobilize support for his position. Hume's strategy was one of inclusion and healing of the rift among the peoples on the island of Ireland; Adams's was much more exclusive and focused on ousting the British and opposing the Protestants. This comparison allows for an analysis of the horizons of policy possibility for each man and the groups that follow them. Grove and Carter are able to map out the maneuvering room Adams and Hume left themselves by adhering to their particular story of the conflict. The AIA vindicated Hume's strategy, leaving Adams in a pickle. Rather than emulating Hume's approach, however, Adams actually accentuated his preferred strategy, becoming even more exclusive and resorting to significantly more historical references in an attempt to turn the electorate by the strategy of storytelling.

Even more boldly, Grove and Carter go on to suggest how the pressure and influence of third parties, such as the United States, possessing their own story of the Northern Ireland conflict, could either succeed or fail depending on the state of the internal debate between Adams and Hume. Grove and Carter state:

> If observers [i.e., third-party nations—ed.] follow leaders' portrayals of out-groups over time, they may observe changes in the degrees of threat posed by particular outgroups, or changes in the relevant outgroups altogether. In this way, foreign policy decision-makers may learn when there are crucial times in which the country can intervene, suggest negotiation, offer incentives for cooperation, or take other methods that often depend on timing (27).

Grove and Carter point out that U.S. government-directed increased investment in Ireland following the AIA was an important boost to the Hume position of negotiated settlement, and was timed very well. The European Community's encouragement of an Irish voice also helped Hume to persuade the Catholic minority that if it abstained from violence, influential third parties would eventually pressure the British to leave. Grove and Carter's work points to new horizons in the study of culture and foreign policy.

In conclusion, then, the study of how culture and identity affect foreign policy, though only in its early years, has the potential to offer much to both theorists and policymaker alike. We hope to see more scholars, and younger scholars, continuing to pursue this approach to FPA into the future.

NOTE

Portions of this essay are used by permission from previously published works, to wit, Martin Sampson and Valerie Hudson, "Editors' Introduction," *Political Psychology*, 20(4) (December 1999), Special Issue on Culture and Foreign Policy Analysis, 667–77; and Valerie M. Hudson, "Culture and Foreign Policy: Developing a Research Agenda," in *Culture and Foreign Policy*, edited by Valerie M. Hudson, Boulder, CO: Rienner, 1997, 1–26.

5

Domestic Politics and Opposition

If war is the continuation of politics by other means, pace Clausewitz, then it is certainly also the case that many times foreign policy is simply the continuation of domestic politics by other means. While we have explored in chapter 3 the politics of groups small and large within the executive branch of government, here we explore the political contestation present in the larger society and how it affects foreign policy.

In all human collectives, large and small, there exists both a diversity of viewpoint and an unequal distribution of power. These characteristics lend themselves to an unsurprising result: power struggles. Power struggles are simply endemic to the human condition. Even if there were only two human beings left on the planet, there would probably still be a power struggle, overt or implicit. And even in the most controlling totalitarian state, there would still be power struggles. Such struggles are surely mediated by the personality of the top leaders involved, but they nevertheless exist (Hermann and Preston, 1994).

However, it is also fair to say, with Helen Milner, that "Although many scholars have recognized the interdependence of domestic and international politics, few have developed explicit theories of this interaction. . . . No counterpart exists to Waltz's *Theory of International Politics* for the role of domestic factors" (1997, 2, 234; however, see Bueno de Mesquita et al., 2003, for a heroic attempt in the rational choice tradition). While it is true that International Relations' only quasi-law-like generalization concerns the linkage between domestic political system and foreign policy (i.e., the democratic peace thesis—the assertion that democracies tend not to fight one another [see chapter 1]), that is about as far as we have gotten since the end of World War II. The content of this chapter is a testament to that lamentable theoretical state of affairs, even within Foreign Policy Analysis (FPA).

THE DOMESTIC POLITY: CHARACTERISTICS
AND INSTITUTIONS

Robert Dahl points out that the nature of the regime itself—that is, its degree of inclusiveness and public contestation—may predispose the nation to particular syndromes of domestic politics (1973). For example, he felt that hegemonies fell prey to the syndrome of regarding all opposition as disloyal, thereby ensuring that all opposition will be disloyal. For mixed regimes with constraints on either inclusiveness or public contestation, Dahl felt a cycle of liberalization and repression would ensue because the government would desire to lower barriers to participation but simultaneously be afraid of runaway opposition. Polyarchies, in Dahl's view, are prone to polarization and segmentation as the political process ensures that no one's preferences are satisfied.

Thus, the nature of the regime itself, with all its particular strengths and weaknesses and predispositions, must be made a central part of any analysis of the domestic roots of foreign policy. Milner (1997) asks three central questions of any domestic political context: How different are the players' policy preferences? How distributed is information domestically? In what fashion is power distributed by domestic political institutions? This last question invites us to examine how institutions are not only structures, but shape processes. Institutions created a weighting of the varied preferences held by domestic actors, for example. Institutions also create means by which the polity addresses a particular agenda of problems. Institutions may construct checks and obstacles to the enactment of preferences: veto power, super-majorities necessary for certain types of legislative action, confirmation and investigational hearings, requirements for judicial review, the system of budgeting, and so forth.

This web of contingency, molded by the institutional context, can have direct and indirect effects on foreign policy. U.S. presidents need two-thirds of the Senate to ratify a treaty, and U.S. negotiators can use this fact to persuade their foreign counterparts that additional compromise may be necessary if the treaty has any chance of being ratified. Negotiators from multiparty systems can argue that their coalition government will fall from a vote of no confidence if additional concessions are not forthcoming, and intimate that their successors will be even more intransigent. But this game is not only the executive's to play; key senators can parlay their support on one international issue to the president's position on another issue, with the threat that Congress may cut funding for a particular foreign policy initiative in budgetary meetings. Furthermore, national culture can make the views of ordinary citizens count more than those of legislators; nations such as Switzerland, for example, rely heavily on national referenda to decide important national issues.

The institutional context can also be circumvented. A famous example occurred in the Iran–Contra scandal during the Reagan administration. When Congress used its powers to pass the Boland Amendment, which stopped funding to the Contras in Nicaragua, the staff of the National Security Council undertook an elaborate scheme to sell Iran spare parts for American weapons systems by funneling them through Israel. Money from those sales, completely off official records, was then directed to the Contras.

Foreign policy can also become election fodder, as it did for Lyndon B. Johnson in regards to the Vietnam War and for George W. Bush concerning the invasion of Iraq and the war on terrorism. Though the American public is easy to embarrass concerning its abysmal lack of knowledge about the world, American citizens do not lack for opinions about major international issues. Foreign policymakers often lament the "CNN effect" that jerks the public's attention from one foreign cataclysm to another, driving short-term foreign policy initiatives (Hill, 2003). Electoral accountability for foreign policy fiascoes may constrain choice of foreign policy behavior by the government.

ACTORS IN DOMESTIC POLITICS

Despite its importance, the regime, with its accompanying political institutions, is but one actor in a larger social play. To explore how societal power struggles affect foreign policy, we must start by identifying potential actors who may take part. Students are generally able to form usable classification schemes of actors in domestic politics, based solely on their personal knowledge of their nation. Potential actor types might include:

- the executive branch of government
- the legislative branch
- the judicial branch
- political parties, their factions and wings
- businesses and business coalitions
- political action groups
- domestic interest groups
- the media
- unions
- state governments
- powerful/influential individuals, such as the Senate majority leader, former presidents, etc.
- epistemic communities, such as environmental scientists
- religious groups
- criminal and terrorist forces (domestic)

Of course there are also nondomestic actors whose actions circumscribe and influence the range of play in domestic politics:

- other nation-states
- treaty alliances
- multinational corporations
- international nongovernmental organizations
- intergovernmental organizations
- transgovernmental coalitions
- foreign media
- foreign powerful/influential individuals
- foreign epistemic communities
- foreign courts
- foreign criminal and terrorist forces

Robert Putnam (1988) has likened the movements of all these players to simultaneous play on two linked game boards: the game board of domestic politics and the game board of international politics. What is happening in international politics cannot fail to have an effect on domestic politics. And the exigencies and outputs of domestic politics will certainly have an effect on international politics. In fact, the line between the two boards can become noticeably indistinct in certain cases. Nevertheless, foreign actors do not have the power to make policy decisions for any sovereign national regime. That is why in discussing the relationship between domestic politics and foreign policy, we are primarily interested in the domestic game board for its effects on the regime's moves on the foreign game board. However, once moves on the domestic game board are understood, the effects produced by moves on the foreign game board can then be postulated.

One useful way of organizing a discussion of actors is to examine them along several dimensions. A first dimension for consideration could be proximity to the foreign policy decisionmaking (FPDM) positions, indicating the relative weight accorded the preferences of each actor in the political system concerning foreign policy. So, for example we could array some of the aforementioned actors along a scale of proximity in this type of fashion:

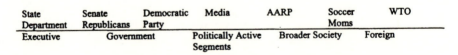

State Department	Senate Republicans	Democratic Party	Media	AARP	Soccer Moms	WTO
Executive	Government		Politically Active Segments	Broader Society	Foreign	

⇐ Greater Proximity to Governmental Decisionmaking

Figure 5.1   The Proximity to FPDM of Domestic Political Actors

The State Department arguably is more proximate to foreign policy decisionmaking power than other members of the larger government, such as the Senate Republicans. In turn, the Senate Republicans are more proximate than politically active segments of society such as the Democratic Party, or the media, or the American Association of Retired Persons (AARP). The politically active segments of society in turn are more proximate than elements of the broader society, such as soccer moms. And foreign actors are the least proximate, though they may be more powerful and influential than, say, soccer moms.

A second dimension worth examining is how cohesive or fragmented each of the identified actors is. Joe Hagan has developed the variable of regime fragmentation, in which he classifies regimes according to the degree to which a regime is plagued by divisions (1993). For example, his scale classifies as least fragmented (or most cohesive) those that are dominated by a single leader, followed by those dominated by a single group, then those dominated by single groups with established factions, then those regimes in which the ruling party shares power with minority parties, and classifies as most fragmented those regimes that are a coalition of autonomous political groups with no clear dominant group. Hagan finds that the more fragmented the regime, the more constraints it faces in foreign policy, which results in more ambiguous, less commitful, and more passive behavior for accountable regimes. Milner, too, finds that divided regimes are less likely to be able to cooperate internationally (1997). But Hagan finds these constraints provoke the opposite type of behavior for less-accountable regimes, such as dictatorships.

We can use a scale of cohesiveness to examine not only the regime in question, but also the other domestic actors in which we are interested, as one indicator of the relative power of these groups vis à vis one another. (See figure 5.2.)

We can now place our actors in two dimensions, noting not only proximity but now also cohesiveness/fragmentation. From the regime's perspective, the more proximate and the more cohesive an actor is, the more powerful the actor could become on the domestic game board.

We would also be interested to understand the number of people represented by the actor in question. An accounting of size would also be an indicator of how much influence a given actor might bring to bear on a particular issue of foreign policy. Since we can't create three dimensions on a two-dimensional page, let us alter the size of the marker to denote relative size.

Size, proximity, and cohesiveness are not enough, however, to determine relative influence of an actor on the domestic board game. We must also determine the degree of difference in viewpoint between the domestic actor and the regime. The greater the difference in viewpoint, the greater the degree of competition over the issue at hand. Such differences in viewpoint

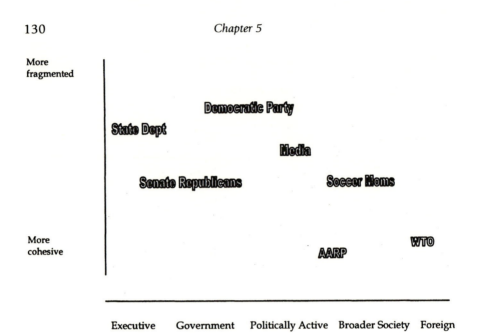

Figure 5.2 Multidimensional Decisionmaking

could be assessed in some generalized ideological fashion, or it could be evaluated on a particular issue (domestic or foreign); in this hypothetical example we will take the foreign policy issue of the war in Iraq. We will assess degree of difference in viewpoint between the regime and the actors we have postulated and denote difference as a function of shading: the darker the shading, the greater the difference.

Finally, we will also be interested to know how active a particular actor has been on a given foreign policy issue. Large, powerful actors can also be completely disinterested in a given issue, and that should be noted. We will denote activity by shadowing those actors that have been active on the issue of the war in Iraq.

Putting these five dimensions together, we produce the chart depicted in fig. 5.3.

Thus, in this hypothetical example, only three of the seven identified actors are active on the issue of the war in Iraq: the State Department, the media, and the Democratic Party. Most of those active are also actors with strongly differing viewpoints from the regime. The Senate Republicans, though fairly proximate and generally supportive of the regime, are nonetheless not mobilized on this issue. Other actors, less proximate but fairly large, are not very active on this issue as well, such as the AARP or soccer moms. The World Trade Organization (WTO) as a body, of course, takes no position on the war in Iraq itself, though individual member states may. Therefore, the domestic game board concerning the war on Iraq in this

More
Fragmented

Democratic Party

State Dept

Media

Senate Republicans

Soccer Moms

WTO

More
Cohesive

AARP

| Executive | Government | Politically Active | Broader Society | Foreign |

Figure 5.3 Proximity, Fragmentation, Size, Degree of Difference in Viewpoint, and Activity of Domestic Political Actors

illustration would include the regime, the State Department, the Democratic Party, and the media at a minimum in this example. It is possible the uninvolved actors in the diagram could be approached by the involved actors to become involved, but unless mobilized in some fashion, the uninvolved actors are likely to play a smaller role in contestation over a particular issue.

Thus far we have concentrated on the actors involved: the regime with its particular characteristics, institutions, strengths, and weaknesses; and the various actors on the domestic game board examined for attributes such as proximity, cohesiveness, size, difference in viewpoint, and level of activity on an issue. However, an examination of actors is not enough. We must also discuss strategy.

REGIME STRATEGY ON THE
DOMESTIC GAME BOARD

The study of strategy in domestic politics could occupy many lifetimes. There are an infinite variety of ways to shape the direction of nation-state foreign policy, none guaranteed to work and none completely fated for futility. Influence attempts in domestic politics are so fundamentally *contingent* on everything else that is happening at the same time that outcomes are notoriously unpredictable. And what appears a handicap in one venue (for example, two-thirds Senate majority needed for treaty ratification) may prove an ace in another venue. ("Sorry, that will never make it through the Senate; we need to move further toward my preferred position.") Furthermore, seeming acts of fate intervene: the Navy hangs a banner "Mission Accomplished" above the president as he gives a speech; a key senator switches parties midcareer; seniority places a particular congressman in charge of a key subcommittee; scandal forces a union leader to resign; gasoline prices rise above $3.00 per gallon.

Douglas Van Belle classifies regime approaches based on two political motivations: the desire to prevent harm to one's political career, and the desire to enhance one's standing in the political arena. He discriminates between various approaches based on degree of public approval in the event the approach is successful, and in the event the approach is a failure. The chart below allows us to visualize the types of approaches that could be taken.

While Van Belle focuses on risk in relation to motivation to characterize

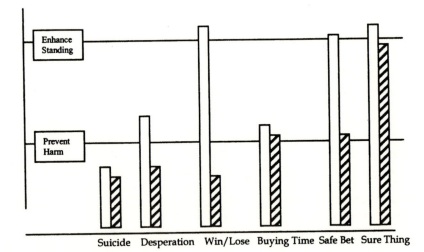

☑ Public Approval if Successful
☐ Public Approval if Failure

Figure 5.4   Best and Worst Case Scenarios of Various Regime Strategies (adapted from Van Belle, *Limits*, 1993, 160)

types of regime strategies, it is also possible to look at actual means employed by regimes to prevail in the face of opposition. Despite the volatility of domestic politics, certain basic strategies for securing one's desired ends in the face of opposition can be identified. These four are: ignore, direct tactics, indirect tactics, and compromise. These strategies are not mutually exclusive, and some are used simultaneously while others are used sequentially. Let's take each in turn, taking the viewpoint of a regime reacting to opposition regarding its policies—which would be the focus of standard FPA. It would of course be possible to study the strategies of other actors on the game board, but FPA places primacy on regime strategy given its focus on foreign policy decisionmaking, which is effected by the regime.

The fine art of ignoring or refusing to engage the opposition is one worth cultivating. Sometimes a regime may lend credibility to an otherwise impotent opposition by regime reaction. It is also difficult for the media to promote a story when one side refuses to acknowledge or react to its opposition. Ignoring as a tactic can also be perilous; such an approach may backfire if the regime appears ignorant of what is happening in the world or to have abdicated its responsibilities as a result. Ignoring may also leave fora of discussion to one's opposition, which may persuade enough other actors on the domestic game board to become involved that an impotent opposition may morph into a potent one.

Direct tactics are those that provide tangible rewards and punishments to groups or individuals of the opposition. Punishment of opposition actors can range from simple harassment to imprisonment and execution. Even the most open democracies possess means whereby the regime may punish those who take a stand against it: IRS audits, investigative journalism sparked by regime leaks to journalists sympathetic to the regime, support for the opponents of one's opponents, and so forth. In other, less open societies, one can simply be "disappeared." However, it is also possible to provide tangible rewards for those in opposition who consent to be co-opted by the regime. Sometimes the best way to sow confusion in the ranks of the opposition is to find a power struggle within that opposition and co-opt one side. Rewards can include access to policymakers, public compliments, positions of authority, or even out-and-out bribery of one form or another. Of course, direct tactics can also prove counterproductive. The Argentine military junta's era of disappearances solved its domestic opposition problems in the short term, but determined its overthrow in the medium term. And the recent oil-for-food scandal shows us how common bribery is even at the international level, but also reminds us how short-lived can be the political careers of both those being bribed and those doing the bribing.

Indirect tactics are numerous in kind, but all share the same objective: to gather enough support on the issue at hand or on other issues that there is no need to change policy direction in response to opposition. The most commonly used tactic is to out-persuade the opposition. Using well-crafted rhetoric and settings such as interviews, speeches, town hall meetings, and press conferences, the regime may simply take its case to the citizens of the nation and highlight the virtues of its approach versus the failings of the opposition's approach. At a higher level of escalation, this campaign of persuasion can also include subtle or not-so-subtle denunciation of the motives or methods of the opposition itself.

A second indirect tactic is to form alliances with other groups within the society to support the regime's position in exchange for some type of consideration. In open societies, this tends to result in regime lobbying of influential senators, in regime access for journalists willing to paint the regime in a flattering light, in regime approbation for the research of certain scholars, and so forth. In less open societies, the types of alliances formed may be less savory, where criminal bosses and regional warlords are given special dispensations in exchange for their support of the regime. A variant of this tactic is to seek the support of foreign groups or entities for the regime. This foreign support might range from simple rhetorical flourishes to actual material support in a military campaign.

A third indirect tactic is to somehow deflect the attention of the nation away from the struggle between the regime and its opposition to a new focus that promises to rally increased support for the government. Several variants of this approach exist. The regime could restructure its government, casting off unpopular members or inviting in new, popular ones. The regime could engage in tough talk with traditional adversaries, as was evident recently when China accused Japan of overlooking the war crimes the latter committed against the former, provoking large anti-Japanese street protests in China. The regime could even engage in dramatic international action to deflect attention away from the woes of the homeland, such as when the Argentine junta invaded the Falkland Islands.

A final category of regime strategy is that of compromise. Many regimes, even in open societies, find compromise fairly painful. Nevertheless, compromise may be necessary even when the regime is simultaneously using other strategies, as well. Often a regime will build some "wiggle room" into its policies, allowing space for minor compromise so as to appear to have engaged and defused the opposition's claims. Minor reversals of policy to appear accommodating may be themselves reversed later. For example, early in the Iraq War, when the insurgency was beginning to sour the American mood, the Bush administration decided against an assault against the Sunni town of Fallujah where insurgents were dug in. This was an accommodation designed to show domestic audiences that the administration was sensitive to Sunni concerns and unwilling to undertake tactics that would lead to a spike in American deaths. About a year later, when Fallujah fighters had basically taken over the town and had been fingered as responsible for many American deaths, the administration changed course and launched an all-out offensive against Fallujah to show domestic audiences that the United States was doing all it could to pacify the country in preparation for a new Iraqi government to take control, and that it would not stand for insurgent strikes against its soldiers. Though the military lamented that the strike should never have been called off the first time around, it was the domestic political need to show a face of accommodation and responsiveness that led to this series of policy reversals.

Minor accommodation is one thing; very rarely do regimes survive major compromise intact. The necessity of making wholesale changes to policy—changes advocated by the opposition—usually signals that the regime is weak enough to be voted out of office, or in less open societies, to be overthrown. The Ukrainian Orange Revolution is a case in point, where "official" vote results were overthrown by a combination of court action and grassroots demonstrations. Even though a new election was held, which saved some face for the incumbent government, it was clear that the incumbent regime had already lost its power to control events.

STRATEGY AND FOREIGN POLICY

The effects of domestic political competition on foreign policy will vary according to the strategy chosen by the regime to carry on that competition. Some strategies will likely have little or no effect on regime foreign policy; others will have substantial effects.

If the regime chooses to ignore the opposition, there will likely be few foreign policy effects seen. Directly punishing the opposition may also entail few effects unless the punishment campaign is of such a scale that it so drains the regime of resources or support that it must lower its foreign

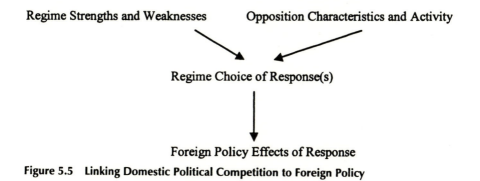

Figure 5.5   Linking Domestic Political Competition to Foreign Policy

policy activity profile. Co-opting or bribing elements of the opposition, if successful, should actually embolden the regime, allowing it to maintain its foreign policy intact or perhaps even pursuing that direction to a new level.

Certain indirect tactics will have greater effects on foreign policy than others, and much will be contingent on the actual situational context. Attempts to out-persuade the opposition based on a message of "stay the course" should see only minor cosmetic and/or reversible changes to foreign policy, if foreign policy is the issue engaged by the opposition. Indeed, the very occasion of the persuasion attempt may be the only concession made to the opposition. Colin Powell's presentation to the UN on the grave and growing threat of Saddam Hussein's weapons of mass destruction (WMD) capabilities was arguably more for domestic consumption than foreign consumption. The United States did not in the end seek a UN resolution authorizing the use of force to deal with what the United States viewed as material breaches of the cease-fire resolution that ended the first Iraq war.

Drumming up new sources of support by offering some type of quid pro quo may or may not affect foreign policy—it largely depends on the interests of the group being courted. If their interests do not lie in foreign policy, then the foreign policy direction of the regime should remain unchanged. But there are some groups whose interests would necessitate some foreign policy consideration. For example, in the U.S. context, wooing the support of Armenian Americans will entail public recognition of the Armenian genocide of the early twentieth century. Jewish Americans are interested in U.S. foreign policy toward Israel. The Federation of American Scientists is opposed to national missile defense. The AFL-CIO is upset over outsourcing of labor to less developed countries.

Of course, gathering new international support may very well have foreign policy ramifications. When President Bush reached out to countries to join his antiterrorism campaign, that meant simultaneously muting criticism of how Russia was handling Chechnya and South Ossetia, and how China was handling minority issues in Xinjiang. The war on terror has also hobbled the administration's ability to say very much at all that was critical of Pakistani president Musharraf.

Deflecting the attention of the public away from the domestic game board typically does involve foreign policy directly. The reason for this is that the expected payoffs may be substantially higher than deflecting to some other issue on the domestic game board, such as a restructuring of government personnel. In regard to U.S. foreign policy, the Cold War created conditions whereby "politics stopped at the water's edge," meaning that there was a largely bipartisan consensus on foreign policy designed to show the Soviet bloc that the United States was strong, united, and possessed of a determined will. But as the globe becomes ever more interdependent in the post–Cold War system, domestic political consensus on foreign policy has become a fairly exceptional phenomenon. Nevertheless, issues involving a direct security threat to a nation, or direct insults to a nation's honor or pride, are still capable of producing greater national consensus and higher approval ratings for leaders. Scholars call this the "rally 'round the flag" effect. There is no quicker, surer way of obtaining an immediate boost in domestic support than to do something dramatic on the world stage. The boost may be short-lived, to be sure, but it will still occur. Being the first president to visit the People's Republic of China did not save Richard M. Nixon from impeachment hearings, but it helped divert the public's attention from his domestic woes in the short term. George W. Bush's approval ratings significantly increased after the March 2003 announcement that American troops were landing in Iraq, despite the fact that the public was deeply divided over the wisdom of that course.

Compromise, of course, can have minor or major effects on foreign policy, depending on the situational context. President Bush can call further Israeli settlement activity in the West Bank "unhelpful" in an attempt to show that he is not out of step with the world of nations, but there appear to be few consequences for U.S.–Israeli policy from this statement. As noted previously, major compromises on foreign policy are not usually won by domestic opposition forces; such are usually only the result of intense foreign opposition. Sometimes formal acceptance of an international regime, such as the WTO, may strengthen the hand of leaders who must counter powerful organized interests: having to submit to WTO arbitration on an issue provides a natural face-saving way for the regime to duck a possible domestic political battle. However, even the presence of significant foreign opposition may play a confounding role on the domestic game board, where domestic audiences might think less of their government if it acquiesced to foreign opinion. Domestic opposition may succeed in thwarting regime foreign policy, such as Senate refusal to ratify a treaty such as the Comprehensive Test Ban Treaty (though the president can counter by abiding by the terms of the treaty via executive agreement and executive orders), but domestic opposition is not usually capable of extracting a major compromise or reversal of foreign policy. Even when major changes in U.S. foreign policy have occurred as a result of domestic changes or opposition, the change is usually enacted in the course of a change in administration. We will see this play out in an examination of how domestic politics affected the course of U.S. involvement in Vietnam.

Case: U.S. Involvement in Vietnam

Historian John Stoessinger notes that American involvement in Vietnam came full circle from the end of World War II to the fall of Saigon in 1975

(2001). Though there were some very important changes in the world system during that time, it is also true that the story of the Vietnamese War would be incomplete without a treatment of the domestic political conditions within the United States during this period. The following account is based upon Stoessinger's analysis.

When the Japanese invaded the colonial territories of French Indochina (modern Laos, Cambodia, and Vietnam), they faced an already established indigenous insurgency. Whereas these insurgents had once fought the French, they now turned their attention to the Japanese invaders. The most proactive and successful of the various insurgent groups were those associated with the Viet peoples, and particularly those under the leadership of Ho Chi Minh. Ho had sought assistance from both the West and the East; he was both an admirer of the American Constitution as well as a recipient of training by the Soviet Union. By all accounts, Ho's forces inflicted substantial damage on the Japanese, making the Vietnamese partners with the Allied forces.

Ho felt, not without justification, that the valor of his troops would entitle the Viet people to regain their homeland as a free people, putting an end to French colonial rule. He had good reason to feel this way: Franklin Delano Roosevelt had remarked on several occasions that the French were not entitled to recolonize the territories they had lost during World War II, and in particular singled out French Indochina as an example. It was no secret that FDR despised the French, and was said to have vastly preferred the company of Josef Stalin to that of Charles de Gaulle.

However, post-VE Day exigencies forced Roosevelt, and then his successor Truman, to trade permission to take back their colonies for French cooperation in the Western alliance after the war. Roosevelt did, in a sense, sell out the Vietnamese people for what he thought was a more important objective. But when the French attempted to return to Indochina, the Viet insurgency was renewed and intensified. There was a French Vietnam War long before any American involvement.

Our tale of the effect of domestic politics on U.S. policy toward Vietnam starts with Harry Truman, who became president after the death of Roosevelt. Truman also had no love for the French, and refused to aid the French in their attempt to retake French Indochina. Stoessinger points out that Truman even demanded that the British remove American-made propellers from British aircraft being sold to the French for use in that region. But as the Iron Curtain descended in Europe, and as China "fell" to the Communists, the American people began to sense the great struggle between East and West that was to become the Cold War. One of the domestic political ramifications of this new interpretation of world events was to ask how the East could have made such gains. The loss of China seemed particularly ominous. Was the U.S. government somehow at fault for Eastern success?

This inward-looking gaze was capitalized upon by Senator Joseph McCarthy, whose political ambitions were furthered by hearings to ferret out those within government and even within the broader elite that were Communist sympathizers—"pinkos." Though in historical retrospect there were indeed members of government who turned out to be Soviet spies, the broader carnage wrought by McCarthy would shape the political landscape for decades to come. The Democratic Party—the party of FDR— would be tarred with the brush of being "soft" on Communism. Republicans like McCarthy, and others such as Richard M. Nixon, who assisted him at the hearings, would be viewed by the public as being tough anticommunists. Many of the "China Hands," the Asian experts in the State Department, were purged, and replaced by analysts with firm anticommunist credentials who had previously analyzed the Soviet Union and its neighboring bloc states in Europe.

Truman reacted to these threatening moves on the domestic game board with efforts to show how he, and the Democratic Party more generally, could be as tough against communism as any Republican. By the end of Truman's administration, he was funding approximately one-third of the French war effort in Indochina, approximately $300 million.

The Democrats were voted out of office, however, and the new Republican administration of Dwight Eisenhower came into office. Though Eisenhower was more concerned with matters such as the Korean War and the precarious position of Berlin, the French continued to reap the benefits of fighting what they characterized as a procommunist insurgency. By 1954, Eisenhower found himself paying over one-half of the French war effort, amounting to then about $1 billion. Unfortunately, the French were not winning, and with the fall of the fortress at Dienbienphu, the French decided they had had enough. The Geneva Accords were signed, creating the three countries of Laos, Cambodia, and Vietnam, demarcating the Seventeenth Parallel as the line to either side of which the troops of the two sides would be massed, and setting out a timetable for troop withdrawal and for elections slated for 1956 that would be supervised by the United Nations.

The Geneva Accords put Eisenhower in a tough spot domestically. In a sense, even though the French wanted out, this was unacceptable from an American domestic political standpoint. Though Eisenhower would not send troops to Vietnam because of the domestic political mood, simultaneously he could not afford to be accused of "losing" Vietnam on his watch because of consequences for the domestic game board. Eisenhower felt sure that Ho Chi Minh would win any election held in 1956.

So there must not be any election. The means by which Eisenhower accomplished this, without any significant military involvement, were really quite remarkable. He formed SEATO, the Southeast Asian Treaty

Organization, in 1954. SEATO was a standard collective security treaty, pledging each member to come to the other's aid if attacked. One of the signatories was a nation that did not exist—South Vietnam. This nation then declared that since it had not been a party to the Geneva Accords, it would not be bound by them. There would be no election in Vietnam in 1956. The Republican Party, including President Eisenhower and Vice President Richard M. Nixon, would not lose Vietnam on their watch.

The 1960 campaign was both close and bitterly fought. The Democratic nominee for president, John F. Kennedy, was attacked by the Republican nominee, Richard M. Nixon, for being too young, too Catholic, and too Democrat. In other words, Kennedy was painted as being simply not tough enough to stand up to the communist threat. Though Kennedy was in fact elected, he was dogged by suspicions that he really wasn't up to the task of confronting the Russians. He was tested in Berlin, after an abysmal showing at the Bay of Pigs. He was tested again in the Cuban missile crisis.

Though Kennedy was not inclined to send troops to Vietnam, he did escalate U.S. involvement by sending units of the brand new Special Forces, as well as advisors and massive levels of aid, to South Vietnam. One of his advisors, Kenneth O'Donnell, believed that Kennedy's true aim was to exit Vietnam, but that he could only do so after he had been reelected. O'Donnell writes:

"In the spring of 1963, Mike Mansfield again criticized our military involvement in Vietnam, this time in front of the congressional leadership at a White House breakfast, much to the President's annoyance and embarrassment. Leaving the breakfast table the President seized my arm and said, 'Get Mike and have him come into my office.' I sat in on part of their discussion. The President told Mansfield that he had been having serious second thoughts about Mansfield's argument and he now agreed with the senator's thinking on the need for a complete military withdrawal from Vietnam.

"'But I can't do it until 1965—after I'm reelected,' Kennedy told Mansfield.

"President Kennedy felt, and Mansfield agreed with him, that if he announced a total withdrawal of American military personnel from Vietnam before the 1964 election, there would be a wild conservative outcry against returning him to the Presidency for a second term.

"After Mansfield left the office, the President told me that he had made up his mind that after his reelection he would take the risk of unpopularity and make a complete withdrawal of American forces from Vietnam. 'In 1965, I'll be damned everywhere as a Communist appeaser. But I don't care. If I tried to pull out completely now, we would have another Joe McCarthy red scare on our hands, but I can do it after I'm reelected. So we had better make damned sure that I am reelected'" (Halperin, 1974, 70 note 15).

Well, he probably would have been reelected, but he was assassinated instead, and his vice president, Lyndon B. Johnson became his successor. The newly declassified tape recordings made by Johnson in the Oval Office paint the picture of a man who knows that Vietnam is not a conflict he can win, but also that it is a conflict he cannot lose. "The biggest damn mess I ever saw. . . . I don't think it is worth fighting for, and I don't think we can get out," Johnson says in the spring of 1964. On another tape he refers to a sergeant that he works with and says, "Thinking of sending that father of those six kids in there and what the hell we're going to get out of his doing it—it just makes the chills run up my back." The man he is talking to, Senator Richard B. Russell, responds, "It does me, too. We're in the quicksands up to our neck, and I just don't know what the hell to do about it." Johnson then replies, "They'd impeach a President, though, that would run out, wouldn't they?" (Baker, 1997, A19).

Johnson's decisions were also framed by his electoral possibilities. He could not leave Vietnam. But it was also apparent that he could not defeat the enemy. One of the Pentagon Papers noted that 70 percent of the United States' goals in Vietnam were to "avoid a humiliating US defeat." However, the mood in America was turning against the war. After the Tet Offensive, Walter Cronkite went to Vietnam and reported that the war was not progressing, but that we were slipping further into a stalemate. Johnson reportedly said after that broadcast, "If I've lost Walter Cronkite, I've lost middle class America" (Baker, 1997, A19). Johnson pulled out of the presidential campaign.

The winner of the election, Richard M. Nixon, promised the land "peace with honor." This is the formula that had eluded his predecessors. But he could not have achieved "peace" without a felicitous coincidence of international, domestic, and personal factors. First, a new era of "détente" with communist nations was beginning. Nixon would be the first U.S. president to visit the PRC, and several important new treaties, such as the Anti-Ballistic Missile Treaty, were signed with the Soviets. Second, America was tired of the Vietnam War and wanted a leader who could extricate them without wounding American pride. Third, Nixon himself possessed certain characteristics that allowed him to get away with "Vietnamizing" the war without dire domestic political repercussions. He was a Republican; he was an old Cold Warrior that had once sat at the sides of McCarthy and Eisenhower. If "only Nixon could go to China," as reportedly the Vulcans say, then "only Nixon could get us out of Vietnam." It was a fascinating constellation of planets, especially on the domestic political game board, that aligned in the early 1970s.

The peace accord signed by the Americans in 1973 actually looked quite a bit like the 1954 Geneva Accords signed by the French. Stoessinger's comment that the United States came "full circle" on Vietnam is not far from the mark. It was an odyssey that took well over twenty years to accomplish, and though many factors were in play, it is hard to overestimate the effect of domestic political considerations on the decisions of the five presidents from Truman to Nixon with regard to Vietnam.

6

The Levels of National Attributes and International System: Effects on Foreign Policy

To this point, we have examined what is considered to be the core of Foreign Policy Analysis (FPA): explanations involving psychological factors, small and large group effects, culture and social discourse, and domestic politics. In a way, these could be described as micro-level theories of foreign policy decisionmaking. In this chapter, we examine forces at a higher level of abstraction, that is, more of a macro-level approach to understanding foreign policy.

Notice that in shifting to a more macro level of analysis, the analyst is also forced to shift from foreign policy *decisionmaking* (FPDM) to foreign *policy*. If we consider the metaphor of foreign policy as a drama, then the actual humans and human collectives involved in FPDM are the actors, and the core of Foreign Policy Analysis provides situational motivations, understandings, and processes. But this drama is taking place on a stage, and that stage sets some parameters to any drama enacted upon it. Certain types of actions by human actors become more or less likely depending upon the layout of the stage and its props. So while more proximate causes of foreign policy decisionmaking are to be found in FPA's core, there is no doubt that analysts must also look to less proximate causes that nevertheless "set the stage" for foreign policy decisions.

Moving to this more macro level of analysis also moves us closer to more conventional traditions of International Relations (IR) theory. Nevertheless, it is also true that theorists working at this level of abstraction are often not interested in creating theories of foreign policy. That is, a foreign policy analyst must often make the connection between, for example, system-level theories of international relations and foreign policy, because the theorist in question may not make that connection himself or herself. Despite this requirement for additional labor, a foreign policy analyst would be remiss in dismissing these macro-level theories. To reach its potential, FPA must examine all levels of analysis for possible impact on foreign policy choice.

However, it is also true that many of the variables at these more macro-levels are fairly stable over the course of a particular foreign policy decision-making episode. The international system may not have changed at all over those two weeks in October 1962 during the Cuban missile crisis. Neither did the national attributes of either the United States or the Soviet Union. Neither did the United Nations system. So the primary explanatory mode of using macro-level variables in FPA is, generally speaking, not to posit how change in these variables led to changes in foreign policy direction. Rather, the mode of explanation is to show how the particular value of these macro-level variables leads to a probability distribution over certain types of foreign policy choices, and that this probability distribution does affect foreign policy decisionmaking in a particular context. It was not a viable option for Kennedy to acquiesce in the Soviet emplacement of intermediate-range ballistic missiles (IRBMs) in Cuba, given the tight bipolar Cold War system of 1962, the military capabilities of the United States, the geographical proximity of Cuba to the United States, and the impotence of the United Nations system. None of those variables changed during the Cuban missile crisis, but their values affected decisionmaking during that crisis just as surely as did the personalities of the ExCom members. Those personalities were more proximate to the decisions made, to be sure, but the "stage" defined many of the parameters of choice.

NATIONAL ATTRIBUTES AND FOREIGN POLICY

We will first examine how attributes of the nation-state may affect foreign policy direction. National attributes often include elements of what we would consider to be the power of the nation-state: natural resources, geography, population characteristics, size, and so forth. Of course, national attributes are typically relative: France is a large nation in Europe, but it is not one of the largest nations in the world.

Size. Size may affect both nation-state goals as well as decisionmaking processes. For example, alignment with a neighboring large state may be an attractive foreign policy direction for a small state. Of course, if a small state happens to find itself between two large states that are in conflict, a position of neutrality might also appear desirable. Small states are usually unable to either reward or punish other states, and thus may find themselves honing diplomatic skills of persuasion or protest. Small states, particularly those that are also relatively poor, may have a small bureaucracy and few embass-ies, which may hamper the scope of foreign policy. Before Baby Doc Duva-lier was overthrown in Haiti, UN officials would have to fill out the paperwork on behalf of the Haitian bureaucracy so that Haiti could receive UN economic assistance.

Large states, on the other hand, are more likely to be active in foreign policy. Often, the foreign policy aims of a large state will increase as addi-tional capabilities are developed. In fact, large nations have a tendency to become more assertive in foreign affairs as their capabilities grow. Large nations are harder to defeat in war, but may also be more difficult to unite. Larger nations also have a higher probability of possessing important natu-ral resources, simply on the basis of landmass.

Natural Resources. Natural resources, or the lack thereof, may also play a role in foreign policy. For example, the burgeoning energy needs of China, whose major energy resource is inefficient coal, has led that nation to become the patron of countries whose oil is not already contracted to the West and Japan. This has recently led China to let it be known that it will veto any attempt to bring the Darfur crisis in the Sudan to a vote on action by the UN Security Council. Sudan has contracted its oil to the Chi-nese. It also led China into a bidding war with Japan over a new pipeline to bring Russian natural gas southward. India also has gigantic new energy needs, which has led it to court countries such as Iran and Turkmenistan. A new "Great Game" appears to be coalescing around Caspian Sea oil, turn-ing otherwise weak nations such as Azerbaijan into international "players." The politics of oil, who has it and who doesn't, fuels quite a lot of what goes on in international relations today.

But oil is not the only natural resource that has affected foreign policy. One of the reasons that the United States was loathe to repudiate the white regime in South Africa during the Cold War was that South Africa possessed the only major holdings outside of the Soviet Union of several important minerals needed for advanced weapons technology. Likewise, the otherwise undesirable Western Sahara region has also been the subject of interna-tional dispute because of its extensive phosphate deposits. Natural uranium deposits can also affect foreign policy, as those with such natural deposits may either use them to develop their own indigenous nuclear weapons pro-duction, or may sell them on the market to countries that desire such a capability. Niger was approached by Saddam Hussein to sell Iraq "yellow-cake," a processed form of uranium. Some analysts believe that Libya invaded and for a time occupied certain northern portions of Chad that contained natural uranium deposits.

Sometimes it is not only oil or minerals that constitute natural resources, but also arable land and agricultural capability. Certain nations have been given the nickname of "breadbasket," due to their abundant fertile land

and prosperous agriculture. Though complimentary, the designation of "breadbasket" may have unfortunate foreign policy consequences as aggressive nations without such bounty may be tempted to incorporate their territory by force. Ukraine was an agricultural prize for the Soviet Union (though it later did much to destroy the agriculture of that area), and Cambodia was an agricultural prize for Vietnam. Furthermore, soil erosion and desertification and other types of environmental degradation may become national security concerns for affected nations. For example, many nations bordering the Sahara are losing arable land to that encroaching desert. Other countries that are islands in the seas worry that their arable land—and perhaps their entire nation—will be swallowed by the sea as a result of global warming.

Water is becoming an increasingly important natural resource. Fresh water from major rivers and aquifers can be the lifeblood of many countries, especially those in desert and near-desert climes, and is becoming an issue to fight over. Peace between the Palestinians and Israelis depends as much upon their ability to come to an agreement over their shared aquifers as it does over issues of nationalism. Turkey has built the Ataturk Dam, which controls the downstream flow of many of the area's most important rivers. The Turks have even said that if their neighbors, such as Syria, give them any trouble, they will dam up the flow of water to those nations.

Geography. The particulars of geography can also drive foreign policy. Of course, geography plays a role in natural resources. If you occupy volcanic islands in the middle of an ocean, you are going to have energy problems in an economy based on fossil fuel. Basalt doesn't contain such fuel, and you will have to seek it elsewhere, as Japan must. But geography also has effects independent of natural resources.

Access to ports, waterways, and strategically important land features is an aspect of geography with great import for foreign affairs. Why do people keep invading Afghanistan? Afghanistan has very little worth coveting. But what it does have is a land pathway from the Middle East to Asia. Similarly, the Golan Heights and Kashmir are flashpoints because they are the high ground between countries that have traditionally been enemies. Who controls the high ground controls peace or war between the two nations. Highlands may also be important for their water resources. The Indus River, which is vital to the survival of Pakistan, flows through Kashmir, and two very important tributaries to the Indus (Chenab and Sutleg rivers) have their headwaters in Kashmir. Similarly, in the Golan Heights, the Jordan River flows along its border and two very important tributaries to the Jordan (Dan and Banyas rivers) are located directly in the heights. In fact, Syrians building a dam on the Dan River prompted an Israeli strike to destroy Syria's ability to control the water resources of this region.

Access to the sea is another important facet of geopolitics. Many land-locked countries fall prey to their neighbors with coastline, who then may exert disproportionate influence over their economy. But even countries with abundant ports can have difficulties: Russia has also pushed outward in an effort to gain warm-water ports. Their natural ports are frozen six months out of the year. "Choke points" along the SLOCs (sea lines of communication) of the world's oceans and seas are often guarded by the navies of those countries dependent on globalized trade. One example is the Strait of Hormuz at the mouth of the Persian Gulf, which provides such a natural choke point for stopping oil shipments that Jimmy Carter made protection of free passage through the strait a "vital" national interest, meaning the United States would defend free passage by force if necessary.

The borders of a nation may also have foreign policy implications. Some scholars have argued that nations with more borders tend to be involved in more regional wars than nations with few borders, arguing that proximity may become the catalyst for conflict. A cursory comparison of the borders of the United States and Russia do leave one with the impression that the geography of Russia's borders augurs for increased levels of cross-border and near-border conflicts compared to those of the United States. And, truly the travails of Russia's "near abroad," as the Russians term it, has been a long-standing security vulnerability both in contemporary times as well as historically. Borders drawn with more reference to a map than to realities on the ground may also have profound foreign policy effects. It is difficult to imagine how the East and West Pakistan of 1948 could ever have survived as a single country, despite a common religious heritage. Many borders drawn by colonial powers in Africa are similarly troublesome; tribes were divided by these borders; long-standing enemies were placed within the same borders; accessibility to ports was dependent on the outcome of struggles between colonial powers; borders crossed linguistic lines, and so forth. A striking example is the situation of Senegal and Gambia. Senegal completely surrounds small Gambia, and the people are of the same ethnic grouping. But Gambia's main port and the land inward from it was claimed by England, whereas Senegal and the ports on either side of Gambia's port were claimed by the French. For years the peoples of these two countries have been trying to merge into "Senegambia," but the legacy of the two different colonial languages, English and French, have stymied them. In the Middle East, the politics of the creation of Kuwait by the colonial powers has always irritated Iraqis, while the question of how a state called Palestine can be built from two noncontiguous areas of land, the Gaza Strip and the West Bank, preoccupies the minds of those who yearn for a Palestinian homeland.

Demographics. The characteristics of a nation's population may also have foreign policy repercussions. Nazli Choucri and Robert North developed the concept of "lateral pressure," meaning that nations with high population growth rates become hard-pressed to satisfy the needs of their citizens without pressure to obtain these resources from abroad, through trade, migration, colonization, or conflict (1975). In the twenty-first century, one might also need to develop a theory concerning the inverse of lateral pressure; perhaps the "lateral vacuum." Many of the richest nations of the world now have birthrates significantly below replacement levels. These nations are depopulating, particularly in Europe (including both eastern and western Europe) and Japan. Issues of migration from high growth rate poor countries to negative growth rate rich countries are now beginning to dominate the domestic politics of many developed nations, with clear foreign policy consequences. Will Turkey be admitted to the European Union? Will the Russian Far East become ethnically Chinese? How will the balance of power in East Asia be affected as Japan dies out?

However, there is more to population than simply rates of growth or decline. Other variables come into play as well, including age distribution of the population, gender distribution of the population, wealth distribution within the population, ethnic/linguistic/religious fractionalization of the population, and education and health of the population, among many others. For example, both India and China have similar-sized populations. Nevertheless, China is considered more of a contender for superpower status, and part of that assessment is based on population characteristics. China's population, speaking in the aggregate, has a higher life expectancy and higher literacy rates (particularly among women) than India. It is also less fractionalized by ethnic and religious differences.

But China and India do share some population challenges that may affect their foreign policy: their gender distribution is extremely abnormal, as is Pakistan's. Because of entrenched son preference in these lands, coupled with other variables, such as the one-child policy pursued from 1978 on in China, in each successive birth cohort since the 1980s there have been increasingly more boy babies born than girl babies. China's birth sex ratio is now officially 118, though there are probably at least 121 boy babies born for every 100 girl babies born. India's birth sex ratio is officially about 113, but in some locales can reach over 150 boy babies born for every 100 girl babies. When these young men grow up, 12–15 percent of them will not be able to marry and form families of their own. Historically, the presence of a sizeable number of "bare branches" (young men, typically at the lower end of the socioeconomic spectrum who are surplus to the number of females in society) has led to severe domestic instability (Hudson and Den Boer, 2004). Governments do become aware of the problem, and are tempted to co-opt these young men into the armed forces and send them away from population centers of their own country. Governments also may be forced into a more authoritarian mode to cope with the social disruption caused by the bare branches. In sum, abnormal gender distribution within a population may be an aggravating factor in international affairs, and in contemporary times may have ramifications for conflicts such as those involving Kashmir and Taiwan.

In the age of HIV/AIDs and drug-resistant tuberculosis and malaria, the overall disease burden of a population is another important national attribute. Approximately 40 percent of Botswana's population is infected with the HIV virus, predominantly among the young adult population whose labor typically supports both the elderly and the young of society. This heavy disease burden saps a nation of economic and social strength. International migration flows and human trafficking also profoundly affect both the nations from which people come and the nations to which people go. For example, the Philippine government has set a limit on how many nurses may take foreign employment. The government knows that if it lifted its cap, Filipino society would lose nearly all its nurses to employment in more developed nations, with disastrous consequences for the Philippines.

Political System. The type of political system governing the nation-state may also have consequences for foreign policy. One of the few regularities identified by International Relations is the "democratic peace." It has been observed that democracies typically do not fight other democracies. Of course, there are exceptions—the War of 1812, for instance. Furthermore, the political system must be a "true" democracy, not a "pseudo-democracy," such as Iraq under Saddam Hussein where in the final election before the invasion of 2003 Hussein garnered 97 percent of the popular vote (and the other 3 percent, if identified, probably met an ill fate). There are many explanations for why the democratic peace exists: some feel that the transparency of democracy leads to increased empathy between democratic nations; others feel that voters punish politicians who would wantonly enter conflict; still others believe there is a common cultural outlook among democratic peoples that prevents the emergence of much conflict; others feel that it is the relatively high status of women in democracy that causes the democratic peace phenomenon. Interestingly, researchers have found that there is no effect on the amount of conflict between democracies and nondemocracies. Democracies fight nondemocracies at least as much as other nondemocracies do (Bremer, 1993; Dixon, 1993; Merrit and Zinnes, 1991).

Military Capabilities. A nation-state's level of military capabilities is an important national attribute with obvious import on foreign policy. Superiority in arms can often lead to a foreign policy stance of "coercive diplomacy," where one can press for one's own advantage more aggressively than otherwise. Some have argued that the military superiority of the United States, which spends more on defense each year than the rest of the entire world combined, leads it to lean more heavily on military instruments of power than necessary to achieve its aims. Military capabilities can also sub-stitute for international support; the United States invaded Iraq without the support of the United Nations or the international community more broadly. Israel is able to ignore many United Nations resolutions condemn-ing its actions because of its military capabilities (not to mention the sup-port of militarily empowered allies, such as the United States).

Weapons of mass destruction belong in a category all their own. Though the capability to produce chemical weapons is no longer considered ex-ceptional—pretty much any nation with industrial capability can produce them, and chemical weapons do not offer much strategic value if both par-ties have them (for example, in the Iran–Iraq War)—nuclear weapons and biological weapons are still hallmarks of military strength. Most biological agents are easy to produce, but weaponizing them requires a significant level of technology. However, biological weapons are considered a marker of "rogue" regimes, as most established powers have eliminated their Cold War stockpiles and signed the Biological Weapons Convention. Nuclear weapons, on the other hand, still confer cachet. Nations with nuclear weap-ons are nations to be reckoned with in a military and diplomatic sense, even if they are poor as dirt, as is North Korea. The possession of nuclear weapons can profoundly alter foreign policy situations. The 1998 detona-tions of thermonuclear weapons by India and Pakistan frames the Kashmir situation in a very new light, inviting the intervention of third parties to ensure that the world's first nuclear war does not take place on the Indian subcontinent. In the Middle East, if Iran succeeds in developing nuclear weapons, the politics of that region will be fundamentally altered.

Economic Capabilities. Students of international politics have long looked at the relative wealth of nations as a variable in understanding their behavior. In earlier years, scholars would speak of the First World (Western developed nations), the Second World (Eastern bloc command econo-mies), the Third World (underdeveloped nations), and the Fourth World (nations at the lowest levels of development). In the globalized economy of the twenty-first century, patterns of economic dependence and interde-pendence must be traced to understand the effect that economic forces have on foreign policy.

Of course, there are some rather simplistic popular theories in this area that pin the ultimate motivation of all foreign policy to monetary gain. We have all heard theories that ultimately ascribe the U.S. invasion of Iraq to the pursuit of Halliburton's financial interests. But surely the motivation to invade Iraq was multifactorial, and if consideration of Halliburton's ledgers were an issue, it was but one issue among many others and likely not the most proximate. There are other theories that assert that rich countries get what they want in foreign affairs. But surely the United States is a case in point where that is not always the outcome. The United States fought the

World Trade Organization (WTO) on steel tariffs, lost, and acquiesced in dismantling those tariffs. The United States did not receive backing from the UN Security Council to invade Iraq. It is fair to say that the whole premise of FPA is a fundamental rejection of more simplistic theories of economic determinism.

Nevertheless, foreign policy analysts would be remiss in overlooking economic capabilities and economic interactions as a source of foreign policy. And in the area of global economics, it is wise to remember that some of the most important actors are not nation-states, but also multinational corporations and intergovernmental bodies such as the WTO. Even subnational units, such as states and provinces within nation-state boundaries, can be impressive global economic actors. We will return to this subject when we explore the international system's effects on foreign policy.

How do economic capabilities affect foreign policy? One aspect to examine is dependence; that is, nonreciprocal needs for the economic inputs of others. Economic dependence is easily seen in the economies of certain less-developed countries. A dependent economy is usually characterized by reliance on the export of a single or a small set of commodities (as versus manufactured goods). Unless the export is a scarce resource possessed by few countries, it is likely such an economy will not become rich through such exports. Rather, the disadvantage of the relatively low price of commodities may be compounded by fluctuating prices, which make government financial planning for future years difficult. The one-sidedness of such an economy also makes it vulnerable to shortages of items needed for the society to function. For example, some West African nations heavily dependent on the export of cocoa have to import food to feed their people, even though their economy is geared toward agricultural production. Such vulnerable economies are also in a subservient position to nation-states that consume their goods; if relations sour, trade may be used as a weapon, which would be a hardship for the more dependent country. Trade dependence may create foreign policy compliance.

Even producers of relatively scarce goods, such as oil, have their own challenges. Both cartel members and nonmembers must cooperate in an intricate dance that allows them to sell their resource at a price that not only is beneficial for them and prevents price defections but also does not create incentives for their consumers to look elsewhere for oil or oil substitutes. If the United States were to invest in a type of intensive "Manhattan Project," as has been recently recommended to develop energy alternatives to fossil fuels, what would happen to nations such as Russia and Saudi Arabia, which are so dependent on oil income to keep their governments afloat?

One of the most interesting historical cases in which economics skewed international relations was that of Cabinda during the latter half of the

Cold War. Cabinda is an oil-rich province of Angola that is not completely contiguous with most of Angolan territory. Angola during this time period was ruled by a Marxist government allied with the USSR, and faced an anticommunist insurgency called UNITA that was predictably backed by the American government. However, Western oil companies, including Chevron, an American company, were invited by the Angolan government to set up refineries in Cabinda, which arrangement provided a nice source of hard currency for the communist government. These oil installations became an important target of attack for UNITA, meaning that American-backed insurgents were attacking the holdings of Western, even American, companies. But the plot thickens. The Angolan government asked for military troops from communist Cuba to help protect Chevron and the other companies from U.S.-backed UNITA insurgents! Castro's agreement to send troops became a major escalation of the Cold War during the 1980s.

The new globalized economy introduces its own wrinkles into the linkage between economic relations and foreign relations. For example, the United States is the largest debtor nation in the world, and copes with this debt by the issuance of Treasury bills. The largest holder of these Treasury bills is the People's Republic of China (PRC). This creates a situation in which the United States must be concerned about whether the PRC will continue to buy T-bills at the same rate, or whether at some point the PRC would "dump" these T-bills. Either way, this gives the PRC an abnormal degree of leverage in the U.S. economy and, by extension, has reverberations for broader Sino–U.S. relations (including issues such as support for Taiwan).

Another example is the "Asian flu" of 1997. Speculation in the Thai currency caused its stock market to collapse, triggering collapses and near-collapses not only in the Asian region, but also around the world. Though the U.S. stock market only experienced a serious downturn, Mexico's economy was so affected that the United States had to step in with economic assistance to avoid a crash there that would certainly have wreaked havoc in the American market. Still another example of the new wrinkles added by the global economy is the political controversy over the outsourcing of labor. American companies can become more profitable by hiring workers in India and other countries to do the work of their American employees at a fraction of the cost. Radiologists in India may read your X-rays, or answer your technical support questions concerning your computer, or take your order from a catalog. However, such outsourcing also places a burden on American society, as increasing amounts of social welfare funding is necessary to pick up the pieces for the American workers whose jobs have been outsourced. Political discourse in the United States teeters between the rhetoric of free trade and the rhetoric of fair trade, with enormous implications for foreign relations.

Globalization, then, has introduced new types of economic dependence, interdependence, and even capabilities. The new globalized economy has also introduced a spectrum of new players, but we will address that dimension as we turn to the effects of the international system on foreign policy.

THE INTERNATIONAL SYSTEM
AND FOREIGN POLICY

The international system is arguably the highest level of abstraction in the study of international politics. Rather than examine nation-states, or dyadic relationships between nation-states, the system level of analysis looks more abstractly at the nature of the system composed of all the nation-states.

One example could be the neorealist notion of anarchy in the international system. Briefly put, the system of states does not have a real governing body with the ability to enforce state compliance. This anarchy produces a variety of dysfunctional behaviors, such as the security dilemma in which my attempts to become more secure may actually lead me to become less secure over time as other nations react to my growing capabilities. Cooperation becomes very difficult, because there is no foundation of enforced law upon which trust may be granted. Powerful nations must always be balanced by other nations or coalitions of nations. Smaller powers must find a way to protect themselves, often by aligning with larger powers. Altruism in world affairs is, in essence, punished, as self-restraint upon the part of one nation in, for example, fishing so as not to deplete global stocks, may not be matched by self-restraint by other nations. Systems-level thinking is thus not focused on foreign policy per se, but rather on the context in which foreign policy is made. Yet it is quite possible to imagine how a particular system might have tangible effects on foreign policy, as we have just seen with the concept of international system anarchy.

In thinking about systems theory, it appears that some types of systems theory are more teleological in nature than others. That is, some types of systems theory speak to the question of how systems change over time, either in some sort of repeated cycle or on a linear path to a particular telos. Other, probably more conventional, types of systems theory posit system permutations, but do not necessarily address the issue of transition itself. We will begin with the latter.

System Attributes and Their Effect on Foreign Policy. Scholars have typologized systems according to a number of attributes. We could examine the number of actors in a system, the distribution of power across those actors, the number of major powers or poles within a system, the degree of adherence to these poles through formal or informal alliance mechanisms, the presence/absence and strength of supranational organizations, the number of contested issues in the system, and so forth. It would be possible to take each attribute in turn and hypothesize about the effect of its value on foreign policy. For example, Maurice East posits that the greater the number and type of issues contested in the international system, the greater the level of bargaining behavior in foreign policy and the lower the level of ideological intransigence (1978).

This manner of hypothesizing from system attributes to foreign policy is useful, but also noteworthy for what it cannot tell us. Will all nations in the system react similarly to the issue attribute? Or will nations react differentially according to the particular permutations of both system *and* national attributes? Is the hypothesis so general that no specific effects on, say, the foreign policy of Kenya can be derived from it? Or is it a starting point for analysts to factor in the particular circumstances, attributes, personalities, politics of Kenya? Despite the difficulty in pinning down exactly how the foreign policy analyst is to use system-level variables, it is also difficult to deny that the task must be attempted. Consider U.S. foreign policy in 1935 versus 1945. Or 1955 versus 1989. Or 1989 versus 1992. System clearly makes a difference in foreign policy. The trick is how to track it and use it.

One approach is to create the typology, as above, and then derive general principles of foreign policy behavior from it. One such exercise was performed by Morton Kaplan (1957 and 1972). Kaplan's typology included both real-world systems and hypothetical systems, the latter included to show that the derivation of behavioral generalizations from system-level variables could be posted counterfactually.

The two real-world systems emphasized in Kaplan's were the classic balance of power system in Europe from 1815 to 1914, and the loose bipolar system of the mid- to late Cold War period. Kaplan felt that the "equilibrium rules" that allowed this type of system, requiring a minimum of five actors, to persist were the following:

1) increase capabilities, but negotiate rather than fight;
2) fight rather than fail to increase capabilities;
3) stop fighting rather than eliminate an essential actor;
4) oppose any coalition or single actor that tends to assume a position of predominance within the system;
5) constrain actors who subscribe to supranational organizational principles;
6) permit defeated essential actors to reenter the system as acceptable role partners, or act to bring previously inessential actors within an essential actor classification; treat all essential actors as acceptable role partners.

Of course, if the rules changed, the system would change as well. However, assuming the rules are in the self-interest of the actors leads to continuation of the system for at least a while, and in this case almost a century.

Kaplan believed that several behavioral tendencies would emerge in a system with this structure and these rules. Alliances would tend to be specific and of short duration, shifting according to advantage (not ideology) even in the midst of conflict. Wars would be fairly limited in their objectives. International law would emphasize the rules of war, and such rules would have force over the actors in the system.

Contrast this with Kaplan's outline of the loose bipolar system. This system can have any number of actors, but among them are two actors whose power capabilities dwarf those of all other actors in the system. Two blocs developed, but unlike the "tight bipolar" variant of this system where all other system actors are aligned with one or the other pole, in the loose bipolar system there are bloc members, nonmembers, and intergovernmental and supranational organizations. Kaplan puts forth twelve rules for this type of system, but we will mention only an illustrative subset here:

1) all blocs subscribing to hierarchical or mixed hierarchical integrating principles are to eliminate the rival bloc;
2) all such blocs are to negotiate rather than fight; to fight minor wars rather than major wars, and to fight major wars rather than to fail to eliminate the rival bloc or allow the rival bloc to attain a position of preponderant strength;
3) all bloc actors are to increase their capabilities relative to those of the opposing bloc;
4) all bloc members are to subordinate the objectives of universal actors (i.e., supranational actors such as the United Nations) to the objectives of their bloc in the event of gross conflict between these objectives, but to subordinate the objectives of the rival bloc to those of the universal actor;
5) non-bloc member nations are to act to reduce the danger of war between the bloc actors, and are to refuse to support the policies of one bloc actor as against the other except in their roles as members of a universal actor;
6) bloc actors are to attempt to extend bloc membership to nonmembers, but are to tolerate nonmembership if the alternative is to force a nonmember into the rival bloc.

With these system rules, foreign policy behavior will have different tendencies compared to the classic balance of power system described above. Alliances are now long-term and based primarily on bloc ideology. If there were no nuclear weapons, war would probably be unlimited, but given possession by both blocs of nuclear weapons, wars tend to be less frequent than in the balance of power system. International law is fairly impotent in this type of system, as the opposing blocs do whatever they feel they must to stop the ascension of the other bloc.

This contrast between the behavioral tendencies of a loose bipolar system and those of the classic balance of power system are an excellent way of demonstrating the profound effect of the system "backdrop" to foreign policy. At least with reference to three foreign policy behaviors—nature and duration of alliances, war frequency and aims, strength of international legal conventions—the behavioral tendencies are opposite in these two systems.

Kaplan also discusses several hypothetical systems, of which we will discuss three: the universal system, the hierarchical system, and the unit veto system. The universal system would be a system in which a body such as the United Nations did have the power to enforce the will of its members against recalcitrant nations. The universal system's primary actor would be a benign federation of the world's nations. Kaplan hypothesizes that after an initial period of testing the will and capabilities of the federation, war would pretty much cease to exist. The hypothetical hierarchical system is most likely a less benign version of the universal system, where a particular nation has achieved world dominance and rules through force. Kaplan posits that this could result in even greater stability than the federated system, depending upon the manner in which the ruling nation exercised its authority. A third type of system, the unit veto system, would be one in which a significant number of nations possess first-strike nuclear capabilities. There would be no need for alliances in such a system. The propensity for war would be significantly dampened as most nations pursued a hedgehog policy of relative isolationism, but if war did break out in such a system, nuclear-capable third-party involvement might escalate the war to global proportions.

One of the trickiest aspects of using system theory is that the most important changes to the system—that is, transition from a system with one set of attributes to a system with a different set of attributes—are not usually predictable on the basis of system-level variables alone. The foreign policy analyst understands this intuitively, because while some may tend to reify or anthropomorphize systems, systems are simply aggregations of international actors such as states, and these actors in turn are simply aggregations of humans. "Systems are us," and theories of system change at some point must find agents of system change—and those agents are ultimately human beings acting singly or in groups. Enter FPA.

Nevertheless, it is possible to find some systems theories that have a sort of teleological cast to them, in that the theory posits predictable system transition. We will examine two such theories.

Concepts of System Transition and Transition's Effect on Foreign Policy. In this section, we will examine the "long cycle" theory of George Modelski, who posits a regular and cyclical set of system transitions, and we will also look at classic Marxist theory that propounds more of a forward-moving spiral movement of the international system culminating in an end state with no further transition (Modelski, 1981, 63–83).

Modelski puts forth the idea that the international system goes through a 120-year cycle, with each cycle opening by the accession to a preponderance of power of a particular system actor, usually in the context of a major war involving all contenders to power. Since 1500, Modelski suggests that Portugal, the Netherlands, Great Britain (twice in succession), and the United States have held this position. According to Modelski, for a time the position of each seems strong and unassailable, and the great power acts in the common good. In the next phase, there begins to be a creeping decay and dispersion of power brought about by the erosion of this power monopoly by rising rivals. Finally, a multipolar system emerges as power is dispersed more and more to other poles within the system. But this multipolar system will gradually move toward open conflict, and once again through the mechanism of a great war, a new predominant power will emerge and the cycle will begin all over again.

The four phases of the cycle, then, are 1. Global War (and emergence of the new great power), 2. World Power, 3. Delegitimization of the World Power, and 4. Deconcentration of Power to Other Actors. Each of these stages lasts for approximately thirty years. Also, the wax and wane of world power is not only tied to military capabilities, but economic capabilities as well, as seen in the timeline in table 6.1:

Table 6.1   Modelski's Long Cycles (adapted from Modelski, 1981)

Years	Phase	Military Buildups	World Economy
1763–1792	Deconcentration	Rising	Expanding
1792–1815	Global War	Depleting	Scarcity
1815–1848	World Power	Rising	Expanding
1848–1873	Delegitimation	Depleting	Scarcity
1874–1913	Deconcentration	Rising	Expanding
1913–1946	Global War	Depleting	Scarcity
1946–1973	World Power	Rising	Expanding
1973–2001	Delegitimation	Depleting	Scarcity
2001–2030?	Deconcentration	Rising	Expanding
2030–2060?	Global War	Depleting	Scarcity

The long cycle theory posits, then, that the political, military, and economic processes of the international system are actually coordinated movements of one underlying deep structure. Waves of political problems and innovations coincide with periods of economic scarcity and bring the reordering of political and military structures and the rise of powerful new system actors. Foreign policy predispositions may be derived from the phase of the cycle in which the world finds itself. As this textbook is written, according to long cycle theory we are in a dangerous period of deconcentration, where the world power of the United States will be increasingly challenged by rivals. The United States will react by attempting to hold onto its preponderance of power, but may have to face a crucial contest for world power in approximately the year 2030. Modelski provides not only phase-related system attributes, but a way to track and foresee system transitions that will alter foreign policy tendencies.

The classic Marxist view of the history of the international system differs somewhat from the long cycle theory in that instead of the cycles merely repeating themselves, history is more of a forward-moving spiral, in which cycles of the dialectic, though similar in form, propel us toward an "end of history," a final transition that will end the dialectic itself.

The engine of history, including what we now call the international system, is the force of dialectical materialism. Since we are not philosophers, suffice it to say that the "materialism" part of this phrase refers to the fact that Marx felt that all social phenomena were ultimately rooted in the material. That is to say, land, natural resources, labor, and the means by which these things were organized to produce the goods and services of society were the underpinning of all else that occurred socially. So philosophy, the arts, religion, the form of government, and everything else would be derivative of the forces of material production. For example, in the developed world the social science we call economics tells us that capitalism is the most efficient type of organization of production, and that the self-interest of individualism is the foundation of all good within a society. Marxists would explain this materially; scholarly economics is merely an apologist for the forces of production that underlie it and make it possible.

The forces of materialism work dialectically—at least until the end of history. All history, according to Marx, is the history of class struggle. In every epoch of history there are haves and have-nots whose interests are opposed. This struggle of thesis and antithesis will give rise to new social forms and structures. Thus perhaps in earlier epochs the struggle was between masters and slaves, but in the Middle Ages this dialectic morphed into a struggle between lords and serfs, and in the modern era of capitalism we have a struggle between the bourgeoisie and the proletariat. The players and structures and modes of production may change, but the dialectic repeats itself over the course of history.

However, the era of capitalism is different than all preceding eras, according to Marx. Under "ripe" capitalism, the disparity between the rich and the poor is so great, and the percentage of the population that is the proletariat is so large, that a possibility comes into being that did not exist before. If the proletariat does revolt (due to misery under the bourgeoisie, consciousness-raising by Marxists, and the inherent self-contradictions of capitalism), given that they are 99 percent or so of the population of the world, it is possible that what will result is not a new class struggle, but instead the abolition of class itself. There would no longer be haves and have-nots. As a result, the dialectic would end, and history would end since history is but the tale of dialectical class struggle. As the proletariat rose in rebellion in certain parts of the world, they would establish a classless dictatorship of the proletariat. As workers in other parts of the world began to rise up, first socialism and then finally the end state of communism would be brought about. In the final state of communism, which would be global, there would be no rich and no poor. There would be no nation-states. It would be "from each according to his abilities and to each according to his needs." There could only be peace at the end of history.

This interesting view of history had a few problems. Marx wrote *The Communist Manifesto* in the mid-1800s and felt the global proletarian revolution would be imminent. It wasn't, of course, and not only that, the large capitalist nation-states seemed to grow ever stronger while the proletariat not only failed to rise up, they also were patriotic and fought for their nation-states in what Marx viewed as capitalist conflicts. One of the contributions of Vladimir Ilyich Lenin was to posit the means by which capitalism was staving off its self-destruction. This contribution was viewed as so valuable by Marxists that communist theory became known as Marxism-Leninism. And it is Lenin's theory of imperialism that gives us the most pertinent link to foreign policy behavior.

Lenin's *Imperialism: The Highest Stage of Capitalism* was written while he was still in exile in Zurich in 1916. The following year, of course, the Bolshevik Revolution in Russia, aided by Kaiser Wilhelm returning Lenin to his homeland to weaken one of his World War I opponents, was the communists' first important victory. This victory would produce a worldwide communist movement, insurgencies in noncommunist nation-states, and a large bloc of communist nations, and lead to a protracted and very expensive Cold War between the Soviet Union and the United States.

Lenin's thesis was that the self-contradictions of capitalism would have led to imminent revolution if capitalists had been confined to the resources, labor, and markets of their own finite states. However, powerful capitalist states could stave off those contradictions by going abroad in search of new territories. These new territories, which would be colonized, would provide the colonizer's capitalists with very cheap land, natural resources, and labor, and also offer new markets and consumers for their products. The

homeland's economy could be rationalized in this fashion and not suc-
cumb to the cancers of capitalism.

The mechanism by which this would come about would be the increasingly monopolistic nature of a nation's major businesses. These monopo-
lies would produce companies with unheard-of levels of financial power.
These large financial pools would enable companies to begin to take over
the banks of the nation. Thus, the leadership of banks and industry would
become intertwined. This new economic power would allow for gradual
subsumption of the powers of government, as government leaders would
be increasingly drawn from the ranks of this financial elite and also be
increasingly beholden for revenue to this financial superstratum. The interests of the government then begin to mimic the interests of the financial
elite. This allows the financial elite to use the government and its capabilities as a tool to achieve their objectives.

And, as noted, one of their prime objectives becomes colonization of
new territories. Thus the capabilities of the government are put to good use
fielding soldiers, bureaucrats, engineers, and administrators to go out and
subdue and make useful these new lands.

Unfortunately, there is not one colonizing nation. Several advanced capitalist nations are vying for new territories. When colonization first begins,
there is plenty and enough to go around. As colonization reaches a satura-
tion point, the only way to obtain new territories is to obtain them from
others by force of arms. Lenin postulated that several recent wars, including
the Spanish–American War of 1898, the Anglo–Boer War of 1899–1902,
and World War I (1914–1917), were actually wars of imperialism. The
interests of the nation were superseded by the interests of the financial elite,
to a devastating loss of life by the proletariat, but to impressive financial
gains by the capitalists.

However, Lenin felt that the era of imperialism would bring with it the
eventual downfall of capitalism in these advanced countries through over-
reach and depletion of the nations' wealth and manpower in these intermi-
nable wars. Furthermore, the monopoly stage of capitalism itself is stagnant,
preferring to squash new technologies rather than adapt and progress.
Monopoly capitalism creates a class of what Lenin called "coupon clippers,"
who were incredibly wealthy but utterly idle and incapable human beings.
He felt that émigrés from colonized nations would become the vital force of
these advanced capitalist nations, and that over time the oppressed would
become much stronger in a military sense than the idle rich. If this happened, the dictatorship of the proletariat was only a Marxist away.

When imperialism did not destroy capitalism on time and colonies were
freed by their colonizers, other Marxist philosophers stepped in with neo-
imperialist theories. Imperialism is redefined as structural violence, and not
necessarily actual violence as perpetrated by government military forces.

Thus, we can see a transnational class struggle evolve, where in rich nations there are haves and have-nots, but in poor nations there are also haves and have-nots. The haves of the developed world and the haves of the underdeveloped world collude to keep the poorer nations in thrall to the richer ones. In fact, it is much cheaper to "economically colonize" a nation than it is to militarily colonize a nation. Economic imperialism would denote all the many ways and means that richer nations possess to keep poorer nations dependent upon them. For example, American fruit companies so dominated the economies of several Central American nations that these became known as "banana republics," basically appendages to the United States. The terms of trade problem, where commodities are generally less valuable on the world market than manufactured goods, would be another example of structural violence against poorer nations. Agricultural subsidies by rich nations to their farmers would be a third example of the means by which the system is stacked against poorer nations.

Some have argued that there is also a more "hands-off" type of imperialism that is even more effective and less costly than military or economic imperialism (Galtung, 1971). This would be cultural imperialism, where a nation's people are seduced into developing preferences for goods and services that the rich producers wish to sell them. So even in the poorest slums of Africa, Asia, and Latin America, residents want to watch movies made in rich countries, drink the soda pop that people in rich nations do, wear the jeans that people in rich nations wear, and so forth. If people in poor nations are acculturated to want what the corporations of the rich nations sell, there is no need for strong-armed physical or economic imperialism. The structure of desire itself will ensure dependence, as it does for the working class in rich nations.

Behavioral tendencies in foreign policy can be derived from Marxist-Leninist theory, as it can with any systems theory. As we have seen, this will be fairly broad-brush derivations. Elites in rich nations will collude with those in colonized (or neocolonized) countries. The international economy will be structured so as to favor the interests of the rich nations. Advanced countries will primarily not wage war against one another (at least not yet), but rather within the territories of less developed nations, especially those with valuable natural resources.

In sum, then, system attributes and transitions should not be overlooked by the foreign policy analyst. There are discernible predispositions, general tendencies, and parameters of foreign policy behavior that can be derived from system-level theory. Nevertheless, variables at lower levels of abstraction are likely to be more proximate causes of foreign policy behavior. The analyst must decide if a particular nation, with its own set of decisionmaking idiosyncrasies, is likely to follow these behavioral derivations or be an exception. And, in the final analysis, the ultimate source of persistence or transition of an international system lies with human decisionmakers.

Wendt gives an excellent example of this (1999). Given a system attribute of "anarchy," where there is no supranatural authority, what will transpire in an international system? One could imagine an anarchic system where there is absolutely no trust and state parties take advantage of one another to the extent possible, even involving the use of force. But one could also imagine an anarchic system where similar values and priorities lead nations to cooperate, and the use of force virtually disappears. Simply consider the difference between the Europe of 1914 and the Europe of 2005. As Wendt puts it, "anarchy is what states make of it." The same can be said of any other conceivable system attribute. The final result of any system attribute is, in the end, whatever the human beings that make foreign policy decisions decide it will be. True, system attributes tend to create a web of incentives and disincentives, but psychological experiments show us that any such web can be circumvented by actors who have higher priorities than the values addressed by that web. The same could also be said of national attributes. Consider how the Dutch dealt with an unfortunate geography: they created a way to clear land below the level of the sea adjacent to that land, and became one of the world's greatest maritime powers in an earlier century. In the final analysis, though both national and systemic attributes are important to consider in FPA, there is a stronger force to be reckoned with—the force of human ideas, creativity, and will.

III

PUTTING IT ALL TOGETHER, OR NOT

7

Theoretical Integration in Foreign Policy Analysis: Promise and Frustration

Foreign Policy Analysis theory, as we have seen in this textbook, is rich, detailed, multilevel, multidisciplinary, and centered on foreign policy decisionmaking (FPDM) as it is performed by human beings. There is a catch. You may have noticed this textbook's chapters examined theory at each of several levels: personalities of decisionmakers, small group effects, large group effects, culture, domestic politics, national attributes, systemic influences. That is because it is fairly straightforward to examine each separate level of analysis. But the true promise of Foreign Policy Analysis (FPA) must be theoretical *integration*: the integration of theory across these several levels to develop a more complete perspective on foreign policy decisionmaking. Such an integration fosters several goals.

First, theoretical integration permits scholars to assess the interrelationship among factors at different levels of analysis. In a theoretical sense, this is quite important. Examining only variables at different levels of analysis is a bit like figuring out a chemical reaction taking place in a vacuum. In the real world, variables at different levels of abstraction are somehow interacting. New concepts, new propositions, and new generalizations may arise from attempting theoretical integration. Theory improves.

Second, explanation improves. The integration of theory demands that one assess the scope conditions under which variables at certain levels of analysis prove more important in an explanatory sense than variables at other levels of analysis. There may also be interaction effects, where variable 1 by itself might augur for X behavior, variable 2 by itself might also augur for X behavior, but variable 1 and 2 together might augur for Y as a behavioral predisposition. Analysts begin to gain a more nuanced and hopefully more accurate perspective on the use of FPA variables to explain a particular decisionmaking episode.

Third, estimation improves. For foreign policy analysts working in a professional setting where FPA is used to gauge likely behavior of other nation-states over time, only theoretical integration will permit coherent estimation. If an analyst is tasked with figuring out what the North Korean regime will do in response to a new U.S. policy initiative, it is possible to combine in ad hoc fashion the variables at different levels of analysis in one's mind and come up with a rough projection. But surely that integration process is inferior to one in which the interrelationships between these variables have been made explicit, have been worked out in some detail, and have been probed for validity and reliability by subjecting them to historical and counterfactual testing.

For all these reasons, theoretical integration is an imperative for FPA. Nevertheless, there are many obstacles to integration. Let us mention a few at the start, and then return to this issue after we have examined some actual integration efforts.

OBSTACLES TO THEORETICAL INTEGRATION
IN FOREIGN POLICY ANALYSIS

The first obstacle to theoretical integration is that FPA data is impressive in its quantity and diversity. A full FPA along the lines described in this textbook usually synthesizes a vast quantity of information. And that information may be at various levels of measurement precision: categorical or nominal, ordinal or ranked, interval, or ratio level. Whatever means are devised to perform theoretical integration must be able to manipulate and integrate large amounts of often ill-fitting data.

A second obstacle is that foreign policy decisionmaking is dynamic and full of contingencies and creative agency. Social science methods, generally speaking, are not well equipped to handle dynamic systems, especially those defined at lower levels of measurement precision. Furthermore, data must be tracked almost continuously to identify contingency points. For example, at a critical meeting of the COMOR (Committee on Overhead Reconnaissance) group during the Cuban missile crisis, the director of central intelligence (DCI), John McCone, was absent because he was on his honeymoon. Had he been present, the outcome of that meeting, which was to have the U-2s fly only around Cuba's periphery, might have been different because of his strong feelings on the matter. It was not until early October that McCone in COMOR meetings finally won the right to make overland U-2 flights of Cuba, which flights discovered the Soviet missile construction there. If he had not been on his honeymoon during the latter part of September, he might have gotten those overland flights two weeks earlier. In addition to these types of contingencies, the analyst in quest of theoretical integration must also take into account the possibility of human creativity. Human creative agency may produce forces that cannot be modeled; it may produce outcomes that have never been seen before. No social science model could ever possibly capture the entire horizon of foreign policy decisionmaking.

A third obstacle is that some data is likely to be missing. Whether because the regime is highly secretive or for some other reason difficult to obtain information about, or because the analytic task must be performed in real time where situations are changing rapidly, it is quite often the case that some data points will not be available to the analyst. This means that theoretical integration as a scholarly endeavor is likely to proceed on the basis of extremely well-documented historical cases where most data points are accessible—and that it may be difficult to apply such integrated theory in cases where key data points are unobtainable.

A fourth obstacle is the question of what the explanatory or applied output of theoretical integration in FPA would look like. Does it look like a probability distribution? If so, a distribution over what? "Types" of foreign policy behavior or choice? How are such "types" defined, and at what level of abstraction? Or perhaps the output looks like a contingency diagram, or a series of if-then statements? Perhaps the output is a set of statements concerning the generalized predispositions of a particular regime at a particular point in time? Perhaps the output is an actual point prediction? The methods chosen to implement the integration and the purposes for which the analyst desires integration will all affect the output of this endeavor.

We will now examine several types of existing integration efforts.

ROSENAU'S PRE-THEORIES

Rosenau's 1964 "Pre-theories" article, discussed in chapter 1, is not only noteworthy for its significance as one of the founding articles of FPA, but also for its precocious attempt at theoretical integration. After all, the field did not really even exist in 1964, and Rosenau was looking forward to the day when integration would be at the top of every foreign policy analyst's agenda! In that early article, Rosenau points out:

> To identify factors is not to trace their influence. To uncover processes that affect external behavior is not to explain how and why they are operative under certain circumstances and not under others. To recognize that foreign policy is shaped by internal as well as external factors is not to comprehend how the

two intermix or to indicate the conditions under which one predominates over the other (1964/66, 98).

Rosenau does not stop with a call for integration. He tries his hand at it in an exercise that he labels "pre-theorizing," by which he means a philosophy of integration. He takes as his departure the metaphor of Mendelian genetics, with its distinction between genotype and phenotype. One of Mendel's remarkable achievements was to demonstrate that genotype determined phenotype, and that two similar phenotypes might have different underlying genetics. Rosenau posited that there was a genotype of nations, and that this underlying genotype would tell us about the relative importance of variables at different levels of analysis in FPA.

To demonstrate how this approach to integration would work, Rosenau needed to choose "genotypic" variables as well as names for the "clusters" of variables to be found at different levels of analysis. The genotypic variables Rosenau chose were size, wealth, and political system, all dichotomized (large/small; developed/underdeveloped; open/closed). The cluster of explanatory variables whose importance he will rank according to genotype are individual-level variables (e.g., personalities of leaders), role variables (e.g., national role conception), governmental variables (e.g., domestic politics), societal variables (e.g., national attributes and more cultural variables such as level of national unity), and systemic variables (e.g., bipolar, multipolar, etc.).

Rosenau presents a diagram to illustrate how integration might take place. A revised version of that diagram appears below:

Table 7.1   Rosenau's Pre-Theory (adapted from Rosenau, 1964)

Large				*Small*			
Developed		*Underdeveloped*		*Developed*		*Underdeveloped*	
Open	*Closed*	*Open*	*Closed*	*Open*	*Closed*	*Open*	*Closed*
Role	Role	Indiv	Indiv	Role	Role	Indiv	Indiv
Soc	Indiv	Role	Role	Sys	Sys	Sys	Sys
Gov	Gov	Soc	Gov	Soc	Indiv	Role	Role
Sys	Sys	Sys	Sys	Gov	Gov	Soc	Gov
Indiv	Soc	Gov	Soc	Indiv	Soc	Gov	Soc
USA 1964	USSR 1964	India 1964	PRC 1964	Netherlands 1964	Czecho-slovakia 1964	Kenya 1964	Ghana 1964

We can immediately notice a few generalizations that Rosenau is making. The individual-level variables have the least significance for developed/

open states, and the most significance for underdeveloped states. Role variables are most important for developed states, but are never lower than third rank for any genotype of nations. Systemic effects are much more important for small states than for large states. Governmental variables are never higher than third rank for any type of nation and are least important for underdeveloped/open nations. Societal-level variables are least important for closed nations. And so on.

Rosenau also felt that it was important to measure the degree to which the internal and external environments of nations were meshed, and posited another variable of "penetration." Furthermore, he felt that these rankings might differ according to the specific issue area involved.

It was an ambitious beginning, and it is easy to be critical in hindsight. The importance of Rosenau's contribution is hard to overstate. And yet we must admit that Rosenau's pre-theory still does not give us the necessary scope conditions or an understanding of the integration of these variables that Rosenau himself held up as benchmarks for success.

BRECHER AND WILKENFELD: THE QUESTION OF QUANTITATIVE VERSUS QUALITATIVE INTEGRATION

Michael Brecher and Jonathan Wilkenfeld worked together on several projects involving crisis and crisis behavior. They also each attempted to offer a vision of FPA theoretical integration. What is striking is that these two collaborators offered very different methodological approaches to integration. Brecher's instantiation of theoretical integration was to be accomplished through qualitative historical case study. Wilkenfeld's instantiation was through multiple regression methodology.

Brecher's *The Foreign Policy System of Israel* (1972) remains a classic of FPA. Through exhaustive historical case studies and content analysis, Brecher integrates an examination of many different FPDM variables. Brecher develops a framework that shows the interrelationship between several clusters of input and output variables. He posits two important environments for decisionmaking: the operational environment and the psychological environment.

The operational environment refers to the set of potentially important factors that arguably set the parameters for FPDM. In Brecher's framework the operational environment consists of two parts: the external and internal. In the external realm, relationships and issues are variously placed at the global level, issue- or geography-based subsystem level, and/or bilateral level. The internal sector of the operational environment examines attributes of the state and the polity, such as military capability, economic capability, political structure, interest groups, and competing elites. Information about the operational environment is conveyed to the decisionmaking elite through a variety of means, including firsthand knowledge, media reports, and contacts with members of society.

This information is then filtered through the psychological environment of the decisionmakers. This environment is also characterized by two aspects: elite images and the attitudinal prism. Elite images refers to the interpretation elites have placed upon the information communicated to them about the operational environment. As Brecher notes, perception of reality might not correspond to reality, but the perceptions held by elites may be much more formative of foreign policy than objective measures of the operational environment. The attitudinal prism refers to the attitudes generally held in society concerning their identity and history, which also color elite beliefs and attitudes.

Brecher's framework then addresses the formulation of decisions, typologized into several categories for ease in determining which parts of the operational and psychological environments are most pertinent, and also the implementation thereof. Feedback loops help update the system. Overall, Brecher's framework for integration resembles the diagram in fig. 7.1.

Brecher's framework helps us order our integration effort, pointing out clusters of variables and suggesting how they might interrelate. Issues of scope conditions or rules of integration are left unspecified. Like Rosenau's effort, though much more specified and accompanied by case studies of how such integration can be accomplished, Brecher's framework is more of a pre-theory of philosophical approach to integration.

Jonathan Wilkenfeld, a sometime collaborator with Brecher, offers a vastly different approach to integration, with his coauthors Gerald Hopple, Paul Rossa, and Stephen Andriole, in the book *Foreign Policy Behavior: The Interstate Behavior Analysis* [IBA] *Model* (1980). Wilkenfeld and colleagues articulate a very detailed model, with independent, intervening, and dependent variables.

Independent variables would include clusters such as psychological, political, societal, interstate, and global. Subclusters would include variables such as:

1. Psychological Component
    —psychodynamic factors
    —personality traits
    —belief systems
2. Political Component
    —formal institutional factors
    —linkage mechanisms
    —political system aggregate descriptors

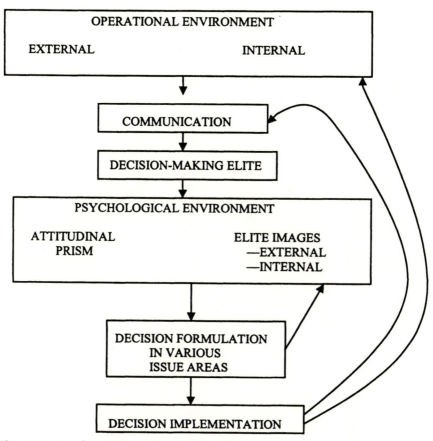

Figure 7.1   Brecher's Vision of Integration (adapted from Brecher, 1972)

3. Societal Component
    —national culture
    —societal aggregate descriptors
    —social structure
    —domestic conflict
4. Interstate Component
    —action/reaction patterns
    —dependency/interdependency relationships
5. Global Component
    —global system aggregate descriptors
    —status-rank conditions
    —subsystemic phenomena
    —textural factors

The intervening variables are a classification of state types. The two main characteristics examined are state capabilities and governmental structure. Capabilities involve size (area, population, gross national product), military power (military manpower, defense expenditures, defense expenditures per capita), and resource base (percentage of energy consumed that is domestically produced). Governmental structure involves political development (number of parties, power distribution, local government autonomy), political structure (selection of executive, legislative effectiveness, selection of legislators), and political stability (coups, constitutional changes, major cabinet changes, executive changes). Wilkenfeld and his colleagues perform a Q-sort factor analysis to come up with a fivefold typology of states as Western, closed, large developing, unstable, or poor.

Their classification of the dependent variable is also quite involved. Though they desire to create a six-dimensional classification for foreign policy behavior (spatial, temporal, relational, situational, substantial, and behavioral), given data collection constraints they are forced to perform a factor analysis on World Event/Interaction Survey (WEIS)-coded data. This produces three factors: constructive diplomatic behavior, nonmilitary conflict behavior, and force.

Thus, the integrative framework looks like this:

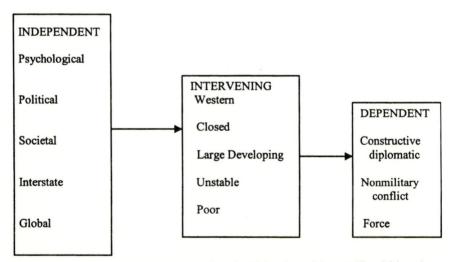

Figure 7.2   The Interstate Behavior Analysis Model (adapted from Wilkenfeld et al., 1980)

Unlike Brecher, the approach to implementing this integrative framework is quantitative. Using partial least squares regression, Wilkenfeld and his colleagues give us the partial correlation coefficients between each rectangle above, and also the correlations for the independent variables given different values of the intervening variables. These coefficients are to tell us the "relative potency" of each variable and variable cluster as it relates to accounting for the variance in the three types of foreign policy behavior. Results are explained in discourse such as the following excerpt:

> Several noteworthy findings emerge. First, the overall model explains 94 percent of the variance in foreign policy behavior. In terms of the three behavioral dimensions, it explains 74 percent of the variance in constructive diplomatic behavior, 61 percent of the variance in nonmilitary conflict, and 50 percent of the variance in force. Clearly the model does quite well in explaining foreign policy behavior, although the more routine actions, particularly of a diplomatic nature, are better explained than the force and conflict acts (Wilkenfeld et al., 1980, 197).

It should be clear from the above quotation why, though certainly an integrative effort, the IBA project was eventually abandoned. Relative potency testing is well and good, but does not address the more important questions of FPA theoretical integration. Wilkenfeld and his coauthors state, "No attempt has been made to develop more sophisticated causal models, building upon the results of the relative potency tests. Such models should now begin to stress the complex types of interrelationships among the clusters of determinants, as well as a variety of mediated relationships between the determinants of foreign policy and its various behavioral manifestations" (Wilkenfeld et al., 1980, 243).

Two of the coauthors on this project, Stephen Andriole and Gerald Hopple, also worked on the EWAMS (Early Warning and Monitoring System) project for the Defense Advanced Research Projects Agency (DARPA) in the late 1970s and early 1980s, as mentioned in chapter 1. EWAMS also used events data, in this case to monitor and predict the use of force.

RULE-BASED PRODUCTION SYSTEMS

During the late 1980 and early 1990s, advances in computer technology and artificial intelligence allowed foreign policy analysts to play with new means of implementing integration. One of the most oft-experimented with approach of this time period was that of rule-based production systems.

A rule-based production system is simply a group of interrelated "if-then" statements. A simple example could be used to describe how, say, actions upon waking up in the morning are produced:

This very simple diagram explicates the rules that a person is using to produce behavior. "If" the alarm clock rings, "then" turn off the alarm

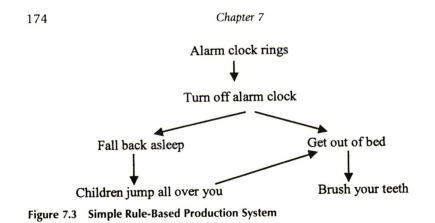

Figure 7.3   Simple Rule-Based Production System

clock. At the second tier, note that we can make a probability distribution if we so desire: "If have turned off the alarm clock, then 10 percent of the time fall back asleep/90 percent of the time get out of bed." Notice that we have also specified two different routes to brushing your teeth: you could fall back asleep, have your kids jump all over you, and then brush your teeth. Or you could turn off your alarm clock, get out of bed, and brush your teeth. If we wanted to, we could include a numeric variable: "If snowfall greater than three inches, then go back to bed." Notice we could also make this into a computer program:

```
If Ring = 0 then Sleep = 1;
If Ring = 1 then OutofBed = 1;
If OutofBed = 1 then Brush = 1
```

In other words, a rule-based production system is one of the most flexible instruments for theoretical integration one could imagine. If you can conceive of a specific relationship between any two variables—regardless of their form or level of measurement precision—you can make a rule-based production system. And if you can make a rule-based production system, you can simulate, by programming a computer, the entity you are investigating. Some of the most intriguing early rule-based production systems in FPA were of individuals, such as the system JFK, or of states, such as the system CHINA_WATCHER, or more general decisionmaker systems, such as POLI or EVIN (Tanaka, 1984; Thorson and Sylvan, 1982; Taber, 1997).

"Situational Predisposition" (SP) was the name of the rule-based production system I created many years ago (Hudson, 1987). The aim was to create a very simple system based on few variables that would produce predictions of foreign policy behavior. Assessing the accuracy of the simple system would allow me to say under what conditions you did not need all of the detail of a full-fledged FPA-style analysis and under what conditions you did. An overview of what I had to do to create that system will explain both the promise and the downside of using rule-based production systems.

SP used the Comparative Research on the Events of Nations (CREON) event data set as its dependent variable. CREON used four main dimensions to describe events: affect (positive/negative), level of commitment (words/deeds), instrumentality (diplomatic/economic/military), and target (identity of the "direct object" of the event). The goal would be to "postdict": that is, using the independent variables of the SP framework, I would create "postdictions" as to what should have happened in the actual historical event. I could then compare these postdictions with the CREON events and determine if the SP system had been accurate or not.

But first I had to create the rule-based production system, and explicating the steps of this creation will be instructive as to the pros and cons of this approach. The independent variables were situational role, type of situation (derived from situational roles), prior affect between the acting nation and the other role occupants, capabilities of the acting nation relative to the other role occupants, and salience of the other role occupants for the acting nation. There were three basic situational roles: actor, source, and subject—with the latter two roles defined from the perspective of the acting nation.

In any foreign policy situation, there is a problem that is the occasion for decision. The acting nation (or actor) whose behavior we want to explore must decide which entity or entities has caused the problem—that is, who occupies the role of "source." The actor must also decide what entity or entities are directly affected by the problem caused by the source—that is, who occupies the role of "subject." Thus we can see that different types of situations are defined by the identification of the other role occupants by the actor. So, for example:

Actor X / Source Y / Subject X: In this type of situation, Y has directly caused a problem for the actor. The task facing the actor is to somehow stop Y, if possible.

Actor X / Source Y / Subject Z: In this type of situation, Y has directly caused a problem for Z, and X must decide if it wants to get involved and if so, to what degree and on whose behalf.

There turn out to be five main types of situation defined in terms of role occupants. However, in order to get from situation to behavior, more information is necessary. The actor must assess its relationship to the other role occupants. This relationship is defined in terms of some very simple questions: Do I like them or not? (prior affect). Are they stronger than I am or not? (relative capabilities). Are they in some way especially important to me or not? (salience). Consider the same situation with two very different permutations of the relationship variables:

Actor X / Source Y / Subject X: Prior affect to Y is negative; X is much stronger than Y, Y is not salient to X.

Actor X / Source Y / Subject X: Prior affect to Y is positive; Y is much stronger than X; Y is salient to X.

In the first case, we can make the prediction that X will aggressively, perhaps even forcefully, attempt to stop Y from continuing to create a problem situation for X. However, in the second case, we would predict that X will attempt to entreat with Y, as a much stronger and important friend, to recognize the problem Y is causing for it and persuade it to stop. Same situation, two very different behavioral predictions.

After collecting all of the data, the most important task facing me was to create the "if-then" statements that would lead from each permutation of independent variables to a prediction on the dependent variables. Though I thought I had created a very simple model, I ended up having to posit 191 "if-then" statements to create a complete system. Actually, it was not the sheer number of statements that was the problem. This brain-wracking exercise demanded that I understand how each of the variables interacted with one another and how those differences in interaction would lead to differences in behavior. Sometimes that task seemed almost impossible, but it did force me to create three levels of rules: isolation rules, meta-rules, and interaction rules.

Isolation rules are rules about how one particular variable will influence behavior without regard to what the other variables' values are. Without isolation rules, no other level of rule is possible. So, for example, one example of an isolation rule is: If the SOURCE possesses a significant CAPABILITY ADVANTAGE over the ACTOR, the actor will most likely respond by using DIPLOMATIC INSTRUMENTS and will NOT use HIGH COMMITMENT.

What is being posited is that when relative capabilities do not favor the actor, regardless of what else is going on in the situation, that variable will have impact on two dimensions of behavior: instrumentality and level of commitment.

But isolation rules aren't enough. You have to figure out how these variables will interact with one another. A first step in this direction is the positing of "meta-rules," or rules about rules. In the SP system, meta-rules took one of several forms: ignore/precedence rules, additive/augment rules, can-cel/dampen rules. An ignore/precedence rule might be, If SITUATION is ASSISTANCE CONSIDERATION, PRIOR AFFECT takes PRECEDENCE over all other relational variables. An additive/augment rule might be, If SITUA-TION is CONFRONTATION and SOURCE and actor have NEGATIVE prior affect, when SOURCE is WEAKER than ACTOR, this will augment the effect of prior affect. A cancel/dampen rule would be the reverse: If SITUATION is CONFRONTATION and SOURCE and ACTOR have NEGATIVE prior affect, when SOURCE is much STRONGER than ACTOR, the effect of prior affect will be dampened.

Now all of these intermediate rules are but precursors, then, to the final rules that must specify a production for each possible permutation of vari-able values. So a final interaction rule might look like: In a CONFRONTA-TION SITUATION, if PRIOR AFFECT between the ACTOR and the SOURCE has been NEGATIVE, and the SOURCE is SALIENT for the ACTOR, and the actor's relative capabilities are GREATER THAN those of the source, the likely behavior attribute values for the actor will be HIGH NEGATIVE AFFECT, MODERATE COMMITMENT, DIPLOMATIC INSTRUMENTS, with the SOURCE as TARGET.

This exercise brings to light some of the upsides of rule-based production systems, but also some of the downsides. First off, the very methodology forced me to specify how FPA variables were to be integrated. And the form of the integration was completely up to me; I was not stuck using mathe-matically based relationships such as addition and multiplication, for example. Second, the system was complete. Every possibility had to be examined—or the computer program would not run. Third, I could com-bine all sorts of variables together: nominal and interval level variables could easily be combined in one rule. And instead of looking at relative potencies, I could actually say something about accuracy of postdiction (in case you are interested, I discovered that in about 30 percent of the 6,605 cases examined, SP was sufficient to accurately predict the resulting foreign policy behavior).

However, there were some definite downsides. This was a small model, very un-FPA-like, and I had not only 191 final rules, but also multitudinous isolation rules and meta-rules to boot. The exercise forced me to go beyond what I knew simply to accomodate the exponential growth of permuta-tions. In a way, the dependent variables were overdetermined by the com-plexity of the rules, and the rule maker was overwhelmed in the attempt to find differences in the dependent variables based upon all the permutations of the independent variables. This method of integration is almost too strong compared to the current specificity of the theories that are to be inte-grated.

CREON EFFORTS

No discussion of integration would be complete without an examination of the most ambitious integration project in FPA history: the CREON attempt, which in chapter 1 was called CREON II because it was actually a second attempt at integration (the first was more along the lines of the IBA Project discussed previously). Before we look at CREON II per se, it is worthwhile to examine a preliminary integration exercise undertaken by CREON investigators with regard to decisions taken in 1972 and 1973 by the Soviet Union concerning the sale of advanced weaponry to Egypt. CREON II would continue some of the same themes as this earlier integration exercise.

The effort in question, by Philip Stewart, a country expert on the Soviet Union; Margaret Hermann, a political psychologist; and Charles Hermann, who studies group processes in decisionmaking, asks why the Soviet Union refused to send this weaponry to Egypt in 1972, but then reversed themselves and sent it in 1973 (Stewart, Hermann, and Hermann, 1989). This is an interesting case because at the time the article was written, the Soviet Union still stood and was a closed regime about which little information was publicly available. Could this team use unclassified information to answer this question?

The strategy of attack was also noteworthy. First, the country expert, Stewart, was asked to determine what type of decision group the Soviet Politburo was at this particular time period. Stewart decided it had an oligarchic power structure, where some members mattered more than others. Stewart identified the strongest members of the Politburo as being Brezhnev, Kosygin, Podgorny, and Suslov.

Stewart then handed off the baton to Margaret Hermann, whose task was to inform the team about the background, expertise, preferences, and strength of preferences of the members of the Politburo. She examined the background of each man, noting whether they were generalists or careerists and from which parts of the bureaucracy they had arisen, in an attempt to determine the strength and nature of their organizational affiliation. She also content analyzed their speeches to decide how important Middle East issues were to each man, what their stance was and how strongly they held it, and whether they were generally sensitive or insensitive in a cognitive sense to the world around them. She discovered that there was only one member of the Politburo who had any strong feelings about the Egyptian situation, and that was Marshal Grechko.

Margaret Hermann then passed the baton to Charles Hermann, who on the basis of the information he had been provided classified each man according to whether he was an advocate or a particular position, a cue taker who would generally follow the direction in which the majority were moving, or a broker whose support was necessary before any advocate could succeed and whose opinions could be swayed by advocates. Hermann then created what he calls a "decision tree," but which we are already familiar with as a rule-based production system, to help him decide what position each man would take in group deliberations. Here, for example, is the branch of the decision tree for Grechko:

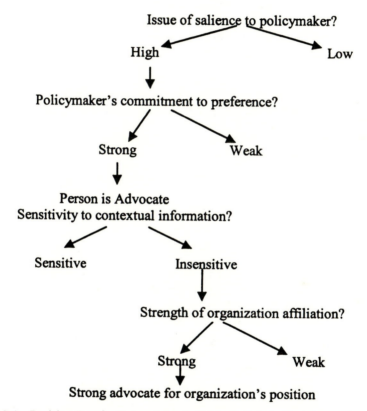

Figure 7.4 Decision Tree for Determining Individual's Role in Decisionmaking (adapted from Stewart et al., 1989)

Hermann then traced the change in group dynamics over the period from 1972 to 1973, noting that in 1973 Kosygin, a sensitive cue taker, moves to support Grechko's position due to changes in Anwar Sadat's foreign policy orientation. Suslov, a broker, supports this move. Brezhnev, normally a broker, acquiesced. Thus Stewart, Hermann, and Hermann are not only able to show why the Politburo changed its position on this issue, but how exactly that change came about.

This earlier effort contains some of the same elements as the later, larger CREON II project. First, foreign policy analysts are working hand in hand with country experts, using information from country experts as inputs to the model, and asking country experts to comment upon the workings of the model itself. Second, the central element of this analysis becomes the actual decision unit—the actual individual or group who will make the decision. Third, there is a series of successive "cuts" at the analysis, with each specialist making a contribution upon which other team members in other specialities can build.

The CREON II model was also centered on decision units. The overall CREON model at its most abstract level had this form:

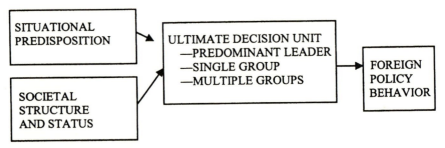

Figure 7.5   CREON II Model

We've already met situational predisposition; here it becomes an input to the central element of ultimate decision unit. (Societal structure and status was never created.) Foreign policy behavior is going to be operationalized along the lines discussed with situational predisposition. The most important contribution, however, is the set of rules that will integrate theories pertinent to the decisionmaking of the ultimate decision unit.

The ultimate decision unit can take one of three basic forms, with variants. The predominant leader decision unit is where a single leader has the power to decide, on his or her own if desired, what the foreign policy behavior of the nation will be. There are two variants of this type: the leader insensitive to contextual information, and the leader sensitive to contextual information. This will be determined by psychological analysis of the leader's personality. The single group decision unit's variants revolve around the nature of the loyalties of group members as well as the nature of the decision rules. There can be groups where the loyalty is to the group itself; groups where loyalties are to entities outside of the group and where a majority is required for decision; and groups where loyalties are again outside of the group but where unanimity is required for decision. Multiple autonomous groups are fairly infrequent, but they do occur, as in the case of military juntas. Here the variants depend upon whether the groups have established means of working with one another, especially in the case of conflict of opinion about the desired course of action. Variants include: multiple groups where unanimity is required for action; multiple groups where there is an established process of working majority decisionmaking; and multiple groups where there is no real established process for decision.

Determinaton of the type of ultimate decision unit carries with it theoretical implications for the most relevant FPA theories to examine to understand what this type of group is likely to decide. The CREON researchers developed the following chart:

Table 7.2   Ultimate Decision Unit Variants and Accompanying Theory in the CREON II Model (Hermann, Hermann, and Hagan, 1987)

Type of Decision Unit	Variant	Type of Theory Exemplified
Predominant Leader	Insensitive	Character Determined; Top-Down Cognitive Processing
	Sensitive	Bottom-Up Processing; Situation-Determined
Single Group	Loyalty to Group	Group Concurrence (Groupthink)
	Working Majority	Coalition Formation
	Unanimity	Bureaucratic Politics
Multiple Groups	Unanimity	Bargaining/Negotiation
	Established Rules	Minimum Winning Coalition
	No Rules	Oversized Coalition Formation

This was a real contribution: by putting type of decision unit at the heart of the analysis, one could highlight the insights of theories most pertinent to that particular type of decision unit. However, it still wasn't enough. You still couldn't get to foreign policy behavior specification from a chart like this. So the CREON II researchers came up with the decision trees needed to put this integration together in a way that could lead to behavioral projections. Figure 7.6 shows just one tree, for one variant of the single group decision unit.

You can see in this chart that the authors have used the theories of coalition formation to try and decide what questions they should be asking about this group. Behavioral predictions are given, but they are at a fairly abstract level, such as "lopsided compromise." Such charts will not really mean much until they are put into action. So CREON II decided to do just that. They asked country experts to develop case studies of the different variants of decision units. Then the applicable decision tree would be used by the country expert, with the expert providing the answers to the ques-

SINGLE GROUP ULTIMATE DECISION UNIT, LIMITED LOYALTY
WITHOUT REQUIREMENT FOR UNANIMITY

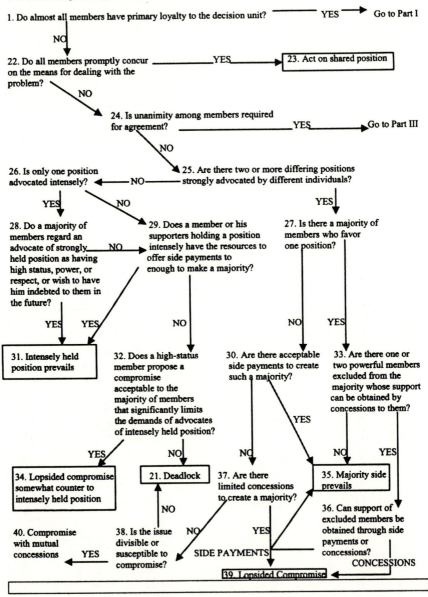

**Figure 7.6　One Part of the Single Group Decision Tree in the CREON II Model
(adapted from Hermann, Hermann, and Hagan, 1987)**

tions in the tree, and the expert would look to see if the tree led to a behavioral projection that matched the real outcome. Then the country expert would be asked to provide feedback about the approach, and also the particular tree used. It was an immensely ambitious undertaking. There is no other integrative effort in FPA that even comes close to what CREON II attempted (Hermann, 2001).

Nevertheless, this integration effort also had some significant shortcomings, which probably limit its ability to be seen as a final solution to the problem of FPA integration. The country experts who were asked to use the decision trees came back with some important feedback. First, the idea of "occasion for decision," that is, the foreign policy problem that allows one to start moving down the branches of the trees, is a bit messier than that assumed by the tree framework. For example, most important foreign policy decisions are not made in one sitting; they may be drawn out affairs in which a mix of decision units may be involved. Indeed, one suggestion is that decision units may need to be understood more as a dependent variable than as a starting input variable. Furthermore, the actual occasion for decision might have layers of predecession, where policymakers have dealt with this same situation or same entities before. Memory of these antecedent occasions for decision are an important input into any particular occasion for decision, but there is no current way of making these memories part of the decision trees. The trees appear to treat the occasion for decision as a tabula rasa, rather than as sequences of linked decisions.

The CREON II integration also does not consider issues of implementation, which we have seen in previous chapters may have considerable impact on the foreign policy behavior produced. The boxed outcomes of the decision trees are also fairly broadly defined, leaving one to wonder what degree of falsification an output such as "lopsided compromise" or "paper over differences" may afford the researcher.

The country experts also found that they themselves were at a loss to answer every question in the decision tree. The data requirements to use these trees are so high that some of the experts resorted to informed guessing. Furthermore, the questions in the tree had to be answered in fairly definitive fashion, whereas in the real situation being explained it is possible that the members of the decision unit itself might have suffered from a sense of uncertainty. In some cases, the fact that the decision unit-based integration effort did not include variables such as culture was to be lamented. One expert, commenting on the use of the trees to examine a foreign policy decision in Sweden, noted that cultural norms of consensus and consensus building made the decision less one of political bargaining and more one of joint problem solving. But such a distinction could not be made in the existing trees.

CONCLUSION

Even as the field of Foreign Policy Analysis was first being formed, the goal of theoretical integration was put forward as an essential task. And yet that objective cannot yet be said to have been reached, despite the many ambitious efforts to do so. At the same time, such theoretical integration cannot be impossible. After all, foreign policy decisionmakers act every day. Somehow they are, in a sense, integrating variables at many different levels of analysis in order to make a decision. If decisionmakers are able to do this implicitly, surely it could be modeled explicitly by foreign policy analysts. Some researchers have even experimented with "think aloud" protocols, asking decisionmakers to verbalize what they are thinking of as they make a decision. But what we are finding is that we are only barely beginning to understand the capabilities and complexity of human reasoning. The new wave of neuroscientific studies that visually map what the brain is doing during thought and emotion are only scratching the surface of what we will uncover in the next several decades. Is it possible that the task of theoretical integration in FPA must await the findings from this new exploration of the human mind? Are we missing necessary elements of theory, methodology, and perhaps even technology? Theoretical integration in FPA must be possible, but it remains a promise unfulfilled for the time being.

8

The Future of Foreign Policy Analysis—and You

The beginning of the twenty-first century was a propitious time for Foreign Policy Analysis (FPA): the field gained its own journal, sponsored by the International Studies Association, entitled, aptly enough, *Foreign Policy Analysis*. There is no longer any doubt that the field, so long on the periphery of International Relations, is becoming more theoretically important. This trend has been bolstered by recent advances in neuroscience that have led social scientists in many fields to become intensely interested in the functioning of the human brain as it makes decisions and reacts to physical and emotional experiences. Foreign Policy Analysis, even though it has been around since the late 1950s, is poised to become one of the cutting-edge fields of social science in the twenty-first century. At the beginning of this textbook, I mentioned you were lucky if your professor was introducing you to Foreign Policy Analysis. I hope, after reading this book, that you now feel that sense of good fortune. Foreign Policy Analysis is simply a great subfield in which to labor; it is rich, it is diverse, it is deeply meaningful.

But you also know after reading this textbook that much remains to be accomplished. That is still fortunate from your perspective: there is room for a new generation to make important and even dramatic contributions that will move the field forward in an obviously progressive fashion. In this chapter, we will discuss some areas of potential contribution.

LESS DEVELOPED LEVELS OF ANALYSIS

While reading this textbook, you probably noted that some of the levels of analysis were more developed than others. Comparatively speaking, far less research has taken place on, say, cultural effects on foreign policy than on, say, bureaucratic politics and its effect on foreign policy. For example, what is the role of religious belief systems in foreign policy decisionmaking? Such a question has hardly been asked, even in a century that began with the 9/11 terror attacks justified as "holy war." Furthermore, at other levels of analysis, such as the effect of domestic politics on foreign policy, there is much information on the situation of specific countries, such as the United States, but little in the way of cross-national frameworks of analysis.

At other levels of analysis, research has been dominated by scholars uninterested in Foreign Policy Analysis. Specifically, research in international political economy and at the systems level of analysis has not been "translated" in a timely fashion into FPA theoretical frameworks because FPA scholars tend not to work in such subfields.

There is also room to speculate about further levels of analysis in addition to the classic levels enumerated in this textbook. Being older, I can't think of missing levels, but I would not bet against younger scholars imagining new levels of analysis. Transnational communication network analysis, anyone?

SCOPE CONDITIONS

The levels of analysis outlined in this book almost resemble disciplinary boundaries. We know that sometimes such mental boundary markers can inhibit new insights. Specifically, in FPA we have too many propositions with little understanding of relevant scope conditions, because an exploration of scope conditions would require cross-level theorizing. Sometimes it would even require cross-theorizing between sublevels of analysis; sublevels where there is a long-standing division of labor between scholars or schools. But surely FPA cannot advance as a field until the question of scope conditions has been tackled. Think of the kinds of questions we could be wrestling with—

- When is actor-specific detail necessary, and when is actor-general theory sufficient to explain (and perhaps predict) foreign policy choice?
- How are problems recognized as such by a group of foreign policymakers?
- How do various leader personality types shape the structure and process of groups serving them?
- How are group structure and process a function of societal culture?
- What is the interaction between variables at the level of bureaucratic politics and those at the level of domestic politics? Does the domestic

political system shape the bureaucracy, such as in the process of "intelligence reform"?
- Do culture and the nature of the domestic political system help determine what leader personality types rise to power?

In other words, there is still plenty of "propositioning" left for enterprising young FPA scholars.

THE DEPENDENT VARIABLE

It should be painfully clear after reading this textbook that the dependent variable of foreign policy is overdetermined by FPA theory. There is more possible variation in the independent variables than there is possible variation in the dependent variable. But that is not an inevitable state of affairs. It is simply a function of lack of emphasis. We are busier explaining foreign policy than conceptualizing what we mean by it. And, frankly, that was probably fine to this point. But now we face a situation where this lack of attention may stymie our efforts to move forward.

The reason is that we do now want to tackle issues such as scope conditions and integration. We do want to refine our methods and also have greater relevance for policymakers. It seems to me that all of these goals are imperiled when we have insufficient conceptualization of what it is we are explaining.

Now, it is probably wrong to rely on a simple behavioral variable, such as a World Event/Interaction Survey (WEIS) code, to capture what we mean by foreign policy. And we have examined the pitfalls of making broad categorizations of foreign policy, such as "lopsided compromise" in the Comparative Research on the Events of Nations (CREON) II effort. But *some* typology or classification scheme is essential, otherwise our levels of analysis cannot "speak" to one another or to the issue of foreign policy. Perhaps one way to imagine it is to think of tiers or cascades of foreign policy behavior. For example, maybe our theories of leader personality will give us a particular "state" for our leader to be in at a particular time on a particular FP issue, which state we can then use as input to our theories of small group behavior, and so on across each level of analysis.

But the pieces must interlock. We must create our propositions in such a way that this interlocking can take place. And at some point, a characterization of the choice or implementation "output" must be made. It is possible that some new variant of the "events data" approach might be made workable to this end. Clearly, conceptualization of the dependent variable is a place where the new generation of scholars can really make a tangible contribution to FPA.

METHODOLOGY

FPA strains, as do all the social sciences, against the methodological net in which we currently find ourselves. There is a deep and growing methodological discontent. The most "advanced" methods we can use seem an ill fit with the types of questions we would like to pose and to answer in social science. The areas of study justifiably approached through mathematical or statistical analysis and modeling are really quite small: most of reality is simply too complex and too dynamic for our current "cutting-edge" methods. They are inadequate to the task, and increasingly feel so, especially to those in a field such as FPA, which eschews parsimony for its own sake and revels in detail, richness, nuance, and agency. Unfortunately, many continue to use these inappropriate methods, by employing simplifying assumptions that evade the complexity with which the methods cannot cope. They have done so because there are few alternatives that offer falsifiability.

Furthermore, most of these methods derive from a strictly arithmetic view of what can be the form of an interaction, and usually involve a firm quantity-based definition of all elements of understanding. As a result, models involving the analysis of interval or ratio-level variables are substantially more developed than those involving nominal-level variables, which latter category constitutes the bulk of variables examined in FPA. But we know from our own lives that there are plenty of interactions in the world that have no counterpart in continuous-variable operations, nor can we define every concept in terms of quantities.

In a very real way, mathematical and statistical approaches are a tiny and quite restricted subset of what the human brain is able to bring to bear on a subject matter in pursuit of understanding. This is not to say such methods are not useful—they are very useful for the realms for which they were constructed. But they are elementary methods compared to what we already know how to do with our own minds. Humans were built to make sense of complexity. In a sense, the way to move past the methodological discontent in social science is to discover more about how our minds in fact do this. The emerging application of neuroscience techniques to social science questions is one manifestation of the longing for methods that exploit the massive computational capabilities of our own brains (McDermott, 2004, 691–706).

Whatever the new methodologies will be, we can predict some of their characteristics. They will tap the powers of the human mind to see patterns in noisy time streams of phenomena, especially social phenomena. They will mimic the human brain's ability to combine disparate types of data in an integrated fashion. They will probably not be quantity based, nor rooted in arithmetic concepts of relationship. They will be robust in the sense that missing "data" or the addition of new components to a mental model will not derail the method. I look forward to the day when these new methods will exist and I am trying to develop them myself (Hudson, Schrodt, Whitmer, 2004, 2005). And I hope that some of my FPA students are the ones who help to develop them.

INTEGRATION

We can now say more precisely why there is very little integrative work in FPA: not all levels of analysis have been developed adequately, there yet remains much work to be done on scope conditions, we have insufficient conceptualization of our dependent variables, and our methodological "technology" has not caught up with our theories yet. It may be that the work of integration must be performed not by the upcoming generation, but by the generation subsequent.

Yet with all that we do in the meantime, the goal of integration must persist. If it persists, it will inform and improve every other effort we make. If we ignore the issue of integration, we will make it less obtainable by those who come after us.

What should be done in this regard? We have already mentioned some ways to further the goal of integration and keep its possibility alive: first, we must continue to speak of it as a goal to one another and to our students. Second, we must make our propositions "interlockable," that is capable of informing one another. Third, we must concentrate on developing methodologies that facilitate, rather than impede, integration. Fourth, as we refine our conceptualizations of foreign policy, we must keep in mind that they must ultimately be used in an integrative fashion, and choose among conceptualizations with that aim in mind. Fifth, we must never allow level or sublevel boundaries to become reified to the point where they would impede integration. We must continue to read and teach across these sublevel and level boundaries in FPA.

These are first steps. As work on more basic issues, such as scope and methods, advances, new ideas about how to foster integration will surely be developed as well.

REAL INTERDISCIPLINARITY

There is no doubt that FPA is a fundamentally interdisciplinary endeavor. And yet what has struck me over the years is how little other disciplines know of FPA work, and in turn, how little interaction FPA scholars have with scholars in other disciplines. It is true that there are certain organizations, such as the International Society of Political Psychology, where such generalizations are disproven. And there are certain FPA works, such as Janis's *Groupthink*, that are seminal in several disciplines. But ISPP and *Groupthink* are more exceptions than they are the rule. Real cross-training in two or more disciplines, real mastery of the corpus of literature in two or more fields of study—this is highly unusual.

Those who are your professors can tell you why that is the case. There are no institutional incentives in academia to become a hybrid. In fact, there are quite a few disincentives. Disciplinary boundaries make universities tick, with rare exceptions (such as the University of Michigan). Rewards, turf, influence, all of these things accrue to discipline-based departments and discipline-based scholars, by and large. If you are a political scientist, for example, your department may give you more credit for presenting at the American Political Science Association than for presenting at ISPP. And if you were to publish in a psychology journal as a political scientist, your works will not be easily "ranked" in political science.

And yet, FPA cannot most effectively progress by IR scholars "dabbling" in related fields such as psychology and organizational behavior and then trying to add new insight into IR phenomena. We must encourage the new generation of IR scholars to reach for a fuller meaning of interdisciplinarity. This may involve dual degrees, dual methodological training, dual presenting/publishing tracks, and so forth. The established generation of FPA scholars owes it to the younger generation to smooth the way for such exceptional behavior to be made possible, and to be institutionally rewarded. Such a fuller interdisciplinarity will reinvigorate FPA, and be a boon to other disciplines that will have more contact with FPA scholars.

Furthermore, FPA scholars should also apply these desiderata to subdisciplines within political science as well. You may recall that the CREON II project yoked together country experts and FPA generalists in its integration efforts. And FPA scholars have had sizeable interaction with American politics specialists as they have investigated the intricacies of American foreign policymaking. Inter-subdisciplinarity is a worthy goal, as well.

CRITICAL INSIGHTS

Since the end of the Cold War, a variety of new types of criticism have developed within the social sciences, including IR. We have been greatly informed by postmodernist criticism that lays bare underlying assumptions based on class, power, gender, and race. We have begun to see how a significant proportion of what passes for "common sense" in IR theory is not common at all, and thus not sensical, either. We create and recreate the world as we study it, and that study is not value-free, nor is it neutral among values.

However, it is fair to say that FPA theory, because of its comparative marginalization within IR over the last several decades, has not intersected very much with critical theory. Surely the next generation of FPA scholars will not only see critical theory interface with FPA, but hopefully they will be a part of bringing such an interface to pass. For example, most theories of decisionmaking in FPA are gender-blind, asserting that propositions about personality and choice hold equally well for males as well as females. Certainly assumptions such as these are ripe for deconstruction within FPA, and we look forward to the time when FPA will experience such scrutiny.

POLICYMAKING

Because of its very nature, FPA has had more impact on actual policymaking institutions than has most mainstream IR theory. As George puts it:

> Practitioners find it difficult to make use of academic approaches such as structural realist theory and game theory, which assume that all state actors are alike and can be expected to behave in the same way in given situations, and which rest on the simple, uncomplicated assumption that states can be regarded as rational unitary actors. On the contrary, practitioners believe they need to work with actor-specific models that grasp the different internal structures and behavioral patterns of each state and leader with which they must deal (1993, 9).

We have referred to scholars such as Jerrold Post, who have brought FPA-type theories and methods to the U.S. national security establishment. Of course, Post was formerly an employee of that establishment, but other scholars, such as Margaret G. Hermann, have also worked with these institutions from their positions as academics.

This is a good thing, for both parties. First, it encourages government agencies to use more rigorous theoretical frameworks for analysis, and also offers them more advanced methods to be used in analysis. Second, it encourages FPA scholars to remain "on-task," that is, to develop propositions and concepts that can be operationalized and used in real-life, unfolding, dynamic situations. Third, this type of interaction forces FPA scholars to consider integration more explicitly: you can't make a projection or prediction unless your framework has been constructed to make integration possible. Fourth, such interaction allows for testing—projections, estimates, and predictions can be falsified over time as international events unfold. Given that most FPA scholars in academia must be satisfied with investigating historical cases due to high data requirements, such real-time falsification opportunities are especially significant.

In sum, then, greater interaction between FPA scholars and their country's foreign policymaking and analysis institutions is worth fostering. The FPA community might consider developing postdoctoral and senior fellowships within policymaking bodies that would encourage such interaction to a greater extent than exist today.

EVALUATION

Is there a normative aspect to FPA? After reading this textbook, I hope what you are asking is, rather, Why isn't there more of a normative aspect to FPA? After all, in studying decisionmaking by humans acting singly and in groups with regards to foreign policy, evaluation of a nation's foreign policymaking should be a natural possibility. True, FPA can no more tell you what is in the national interest than realism can, but it can judge the quality of the decisionmaking that is taking place. And insofar as citizens may have some say in who makes foreign policy, and insofar as the modern world contains weapons of mass and undiscriminating destruction, issues of quality are not moot. Indeed, some FPA scholars have an explicitly normative agenda: James David Barber, a preeminent political psychologist, writes in the preface to his book *The Presidential Character: Predicting Performance in the White House,*

> I address this book to the next generation, in the hope there will be one. The shape of the rising future will be significantly framed by the Presidents we elect. Far from all-powerful, the President is the most powerful politician in the world. In the nuclear age, we had better find Presidents who can and will protect the national interest—in survival and in the advancement of the values which make survival worthwhile. All we have to go one, as we seek out a President to crown, is what he or she has been, assessed in the light of conditions as they are. And to judge among contenders for the Presidency, we need to know how others like them have performed in that office. Thus predicting performance in the White House is no parlor game; it is nothing less than putting your brains to work to save your life (1985, vii).

Barber then goes about the task of deciphering an at-a-distance assessment of presidential personality type, and then suggests which personality types we should favor as presidents, and which we should strenuously avoid.

Irving Janis, in his classic book *Groupthink*, also has an ethical imperative behind his studies:

All along, I have assumed that many people are inadvertently victimized when war-and-peace decisions are dominated by groupthink, that many lives are unintentionally sacrificed as a result of ill-conceived nationalistic policies. In the back of my mind has been the expectation (and hope) that improving the efficiency of policy-making groups will increase the chances that they will fulfill their humanitarian goals along with their other goals (1982, 274).

Janis's book lays out the disastrous consequences of groupthink, and then gives concrete advice on how to avoid groupthink; advice clearly aimed directly at foreign policymakers. One pair of cases, the Bay of Pigs and the Cuban missile crisis, serves to show how a leader who lived to regret a groupthink decision was able to carefully circumvent any tendency toward groupthink in a subsequent decision. In addition to its explanatory significance, Janis's work clearly has normative implications as well.

John Vasquez, in his ambitious *Evaluating U.S. Foreign Policy* (1986), sees a very unique role for FPA research in this area:

In a sense, what we need (be) is a Ralph Nader for foreign policy. As academics, we need to instill in policymakers and policy advocates a respect for the truth and a fear that distortions will be exposed. In this regard it is important that our scholarship be impeccable. Eventually the foreign-policy-attentive public(s) will come to respect our integrity and trust our information. It is important that the truth of information distributed by the government and private policy advocates be assessed. This is not only because the truth is a value in and of itself, but because distortions of this sort are probably one of the reasons why foreign policy so often results in disasters or in wars many people do not want (1986, 12).

Though FPA's potential as a tool for foreign policy evaluation has yet to be fully exploited, I believe that potential to be very great. It would be gratifying if some of the rising generation in FPA placed evaluation higher on the list of priorities for the field.

PEDAGOGY

Last but not least, the future of FPA is tied to the teaching of FPA, not only at the graduate level, but also at the advanced undergraduate level, as well. In fact, my impetus for writing this textbook—and let's face it, writing a textbook is about as much fun as eating chalk—was to broaden the opportunities for professors to introduce FPA to their students. The future of the field depends upon our ability to expose a rising generation to the "vision" of social science provided by FPA. That vision, with its emphasis on human decisionmakers, interdisciplinarity, new nonarithmetic methodologies, multiple levels of analysis, integration, and so forth, is very different from many other subfields of study, especially in contemporary IR. As explained in the first chapter, if FPA did not exist, it would have to be invented. It is the longhand version of social science as applied to IR phenomena. And FPA is dedicated, among other things, to the "seeing" of human agency, human accountability, and human creativity. FPA is a subfield whose significance will only rise in the coming decades.

But it can't reach its potential if students are never taught it exists. More than all the other desiderata just mentioned, what FPA needs is a strong new generation of scholars. And so, as unglamorous as it sounds, the most important thing that the current generation of FPA scholars can do is teach FPA, every year, year in and year out. And if some of you students who read this textbook go on to make a research career in FPA, teaching FPA to an even younger generation is what you owe those who mentored you.

FPA has a bright future—in you.

Bibliography

Achen, C. H. (1975) "Mass Political Attitudes and the Survey Response," *American Political Science Review*, 69:1218–31.

Alker, Hayward, Gavan Duffy, Roger Hurwitz, and John Mallery (1991) "Text Modeling for International Politics: A Tourist's Guide to RELATUS" in *Artificial Intelligence and International Politics*, edited by Valerie M. Hudson, Boulder, CO: Westview, 97–126.

Allison, Graham T., and Morton H. Halperin (1972) "Bureaucratic Politics: A Paradigm and Some Policy Implications," *World Politics*, 24:40–79.

Allison, Graham T., and Philip Zelikow (1999) *Essence of Decision: Explaining the Cuban Missile Crisis* 2nd edition, New York: Longman.

Almond, Gabriel A. (1950) *The American People and Foreign Policy*, New York: Praeger.

Almond, Gabriel A., and Sidney Verba (1963) *The Civic Culture: Political Attitudes and Democracy in Five Nations*, Princeton, NJ: Princeton University Press.

Anderson, Paul (1987) "What Do Decision Makers Do When They Make a Foreign Policy Decision? The Implications for the Study of Comparative Foreign Policy," in *New Directions in the Study of Foreign Policy*, edited by C. F. Hermann, C. W. Kegley, and J. N. Rosenau, Boston: Allen & Unwin, 285–308.

Andriole, S. J., and G. W. Hopple (1981) "The Rise and Fall of Events Data: Thoughts on an Incomplete Journey from Basic Research to Applied Use in the U.S. Department of Defense," U.S. Department of Defense, Washington, DC, unpublished paper.

Appleby, R. Scott (1994) *Religious Fundamentalisms and Global Conflict*, New York: Foreign Policy Association.

Argyle, M. (1975) *Bodily Communication*, New York: International Universities Press.

Ashley, Richard K. (1976) "Noticing Pre-Paradigmatic Progress," in *In Search of Global Patterns*, edited by James N. Rosenau, New York: Free Press, 150–57.

———(1987) "Foreign Policy as Political Performance," *International Studies Notes*, 13(2):51–54.

Axelrod, Robert (ed.) (1976) *Structure of Decision*, Princeton, NJ: Princeton University Press.

Bailey, Thomas A. (1948) *The Man in the Street: The Impact of American Public Opinion on Foreign Policy*, New York: Macmillan.

Baker, Russell (1997) "What LBJ Knew," *New York Times*, March 18, A19.

Ball, Desmond (1992) "Strategic Culture in the Asia-Pacific Region," Reference Paper No. 189, The Strategic and Defence Studies Centre, The Research School of Pacific Studies, Australian National University, Canberra, Australia.

Banerjee, Sanjoy (1991) "Reproduction of Perception and Decision in the Early Cold War," in *Artificial Intelligence and International Politics*, edited by Valerie M. Hudson, Boulder, CO: Westview, 310–26.

———(1991) "Reproduction of Subjects in Historical Structures: Attribution, Identity, and Emotion in the Early Cold War," *International Studies Quarterly*, 35(1):19–38.

———(1997) "The Cultural Logic of National Identity Formation: Contending Discourses in Late Colonial India," in *Culture and Foreign Policy*, edited by Valerie M. Hudson, Boulder, CO: Rienner, 27–44.

Barber, James David (1972; 1985) *The Presidential Character: Predicting Performance in the White House*, Englewood Cliffs, NJ: Prentice Hall.

Beal, Richard S., and Ronald Hinckley (1984) "Presidential Decisionmaking and Opinion Polls," *Annals*, 472:72–84.

Beasley, Ryan (1998) "Collective Interpretations: How Problem Representations Aggregate in Foreign Policy Groups," in *Problem Representation in Foreign Policy Decision Making*, edited by Donald A. Sylvan and James F. Voss, Cambridge: Cambridge University Press, 80–115.

Beer, Francis A. (1981) *Peace against War: The Ecology of International Violence*, San Francisco: Freeman.

Benedict, Ruth (1934) *Patterns of Culture*, Boston: Houghton Mifflin.

———(1946) *The Chrysanthemum and the Sword*, Boston: Houghton Mifflin.

———(1949) "Child Rearing in Certain European Countries," *American Journal of Orthopsychiatry*, 19:342–50.

Bennett, W. Lance, and David Paletz (eds.) (1994) *Taken by Storm: The Media, Public Opinion, and US Foreign Policy in the Gulf War*, Chicago: University of Chicago Press.

Billings, R., and C. F. Hermann (1994) "Problem Identification in Sequential Policy Decisionmaking," paper presented at the 35th annual conference of the International Studies Association, Washington, DC, March 28–April 1.

Binnendijk, Hans (ed.) (1987) *National Negotiating Styles*, Washington, DC: Foreign Service Institute.

Bleiker, Roland (1993) "Neorealist Claims in Light of Ancient Chinese Philosophy: The Cultural Dimension of International Theory," *Millennium*, 22(3):401–22.

Bobrow, Davis B., Steve Chan, and John A. Kringen (1979) *Understanding Foreign Policy Decisions: The Chinese Case*, New York: Free Press.

Bonham, G. Matthew, Victor M. Sergeev, and Pavel B. Parshin (1997) "The Limited Test-Ban Agreement: Emergence of New Knowledge Structures in International Negotiation," *International Studies Quarterly*, 41(2):215–40.

Booth, Ken (1979) *Strategy and Ethnocentrism*, London: Croom Helm.

Boynton, G. R. (1991) "The Expertise of the Senate Foreign Relations Committee," in *Artificial Intelligence and International Politics*, edited by Valerie M. Hudson, Boulder, CO: Westview, 291–309.

Boynton, G. R. (1996) *The Art of Campaign Advertising*, Chatham, NJ: Chatham House Publishing.

Brecher, Michael (1972) *The Foreign Policy System of Israel: Setting, Images, Process*, London: Oxford University Press.

Brecher, Michael, and Jonathan Wilkenfeld (1997) *A Study of Crisis*, Ann Arbor: University of Michigan Press.

Bremer, Stuart A. (1993) "Democracy and Militarized Interstate Conflict, 1816–1965," *International Interactions*, 18:231–49.

Breslauer, George W., and P. Tetlock (eds.) (1991) *Learning in US and Soviet Foreign Policy*, Boulder, CO: Westview.

Breuning, Marijke (1992) "National Role Conceptions and Foreign Assistance Policy Behavior: toward a Cognitive Model," doctoral dissertation, Ohio State University.

———(1997) "Culture, History, Role: Belgian and Dutch Axioms and Foreign Assistance Policy," in *Culture and Foreign Policy*, edited by Valerie M. Hudson, Boulder, CO: Rienner, 99–124.

———(1998) "Configuring Issue Areas: Belgian and Dutch Representations of the Role of Foreign Assistance in Foreign Policy," in *Problem Representation in Foreign Policy Decision Making*, edited by Donald A. Sylvan and James F. Voss, Cambridge: Cambridge University Press, 303–32.

Broderson, A. (1961) "National Character: An Old Problem Revisited," in *International Politics and Foreign Policy*, edited by James N. Rosenau, Glencoe, IL: Free Press of Glencoe, 300–8.

Brody, Richard (1991) *Assessing the President: The Media, Elite Opinion, and Public Support*, Stanford, CA: Stanford University Press.

Bruner, Jerome, and Postman, Leo (1949) "On the Perceptions of Incongruity: A Paradigm," in *Perception and Personality*, edited by Jerome Bruner and David Krech, Durham, NC: Duke University Press.

Bueno de Mesquita, Bruce, and David Lalman (1992) *War and Reason: Domestic and International Imperatives*, New Haven, CT: Yale University Press.

Bueno de Mesquita, Bruce, Alastair Smith, Randolph M. Siverson, James D. Morrow (2003) *The Logic of Political Survival*, Cambridge, MA: MIT Press.

Callahan, P., L. Brady, and M. G. Hermann (eds.) (1982) *Describing Foreign Policy Behavior*, Beverly Hills, CA: Sage.

Campbell, A., P. E. Converse, W. E. Miller, and D. E. Stokes (1964) *The American Voter*, New York: Wiley.

Cantril, H. (1967) *The Human Dimension: Experiences in Policy Research*, New Brunswick, NJ: Rutgers University Press.

Caporaso, J. A., C. F. Hermann, and C. W. Kegley (1987) "The Comparative Study of Foreign Policy: Perspectives on the Future," *International Studies Notes*, 13(2):32–46.

Carbonell, Jaime G. (1978) "POLITICS: Automated Ideological Reasoning," *Cognitive Science*, 2:27–51.

Carey, Benedict (2005) "At Ground Zero, Vision by Committee," *New York Times*, July 3, Sec 4:1,3.

Carlnaes, Walter (1992) "The Agency-Structure Problem in Foreign Policy Analysis," *International Studies Quarterly*, 36:245–70.

Carman, John, and Mark Juergensmeyer (1990) *A Bibliographic Guide to the Comparative Study of Ethics*, New York: Cambridge University Press.

Caspary, W. R. (1970) "The Mood Theory: A Study of Public Opinion and Foreign Policy," *American Political Science Review*, 64:536–47.

Chafetz, Glenn, Hillel Abramson, and Suzette Grillot (1997) "Cultural and National Role Conceptions: Belarussian and Ukrainian Compliance with the Nuclear Nonproliferation Regime," in *Culture and Foreign Policy*, edited by Valerie M. Hudson, Boulder, CO: Westview, 169–200.

Chan, Stephen (1993) "Cultural and Linguistic Reductionisms and a New Historical Sociology for International Relations," *Millennium*, 22(3):423–42.

Checkel, Jeffrey T. (1993) "Ideas, Institutions, and the Gorbachev Foreign Policy Revolution," *World Politics*, 45(2):271–300.

————(1998) "The Constructivist Turn in International Relations Theory," *World Politics*, 50(2):324–48.

Chidester, David (1987) *Patterns of Action: Religion and Ethics in a Comparative Perspective*, Belmont, CA: Wadsworth.

Chittick, William O. (1970) *State Department, Press, and Pressure Groups: A Role Analysis*, New York: Wiley Inter-science.

Choucri, Nazli, and Robert C. North (1975) *Nations in Conflict*, San Francisco: Freeman.

Cohen, Raymond (1991) *Negotiating across Cultures*, Washington, DC: United States Institute of Peace Press.

Converse, Philip (1964) "The Nature of Belief Systems in Mass Publics," in *Ideology and Discontent*, edited by D. E. Apter, New York: Free Press.

Costa, P., and R McCrae (1992) "Four Ways the Five Factors Are Basic," *Personality and Individual Differences*, 13:653–65.

Cottam, Martha, and Dorcas E. McCoy (1998) "Image Change and Problem Representation after the Cold War," in *Problem Representation in Foreign Policy Decision Making*, edited by Donald A. Sylvan and James F. Voss, Cambridge: Cambridge University Press, 116–46.

Cottam, Martha L. (1986) *Foreign Policy Decision Making: The Influence of Cognition*, Boulder, CO: Westview.

Cottam, Martha L., and Chih-yu Shih (eds.) (1992) *Contending Dramas: A Cognitive Approach to International Organizations*, New York: Praeger.

Cottam, Richard (1977) *Foreign Policy Motivation: A General Theory and a Case Study*, Pittsburgh, PA: University of Pittsburgh Press.

Crawford, Neta C. (2000) "The Passion of World Politics: Propositions on Emotion and Emotional Relationships," *International Security*, 24(4):116–56.

Cushman, D., and S. King (1985) "National and Organizational Culture in Conflict Resolution," in *Communication, Culture, and Organizational Process*, edited by W. Gudykunst, L. Stewert, and S. Ting-Toomey, Beverly Hills, CA: Sage, 114–33.

Dahl, Robert (ed.) (1973) *Regimes and Oppositions*, New Haven, CT: Yale University Press.

Dallin, Alexander (1969) *Soviet Foreign Policy and Domestic Politics: A Framework for*

Analysis, New York: Russian Institute, School of International Affairs, Columbia University.

d'Andrade, R. G. (1984) "Cultural Meaning Systems," in *Culture Theory: Essays on Mind, Self, and Emotion*, edited by R. Shweder and R. LeVine, Cambridge: Cambridge University Press, 88–119.

de Rivera, Joseph (1968) *The Psychological Dimension of Foreign Policy*, Columbus, Ohio: C. E. Merrill Publishing Co.

Deutsch, K. W., L. J. Edinger, R. C. Macridis, and R. L. Merritt (1967) *France, Germany, and the Western Alliance*, New York: Charles Scribner's Sons.

Dixon, William J. (1993) "Democracy and the Management of International Conflict," *Journal of Conflict Resolution* 37:42–68.

Douglas, Mary, and Aaron Wildavsky (1982) *Risk and Culture: An Essay on the Selection of Technical and Environmental Dangers*, Berkeley: University of California Press.

Drezner, Daniel W. (2000) "Ideas, Bureaucratic Politics, and the Crafting of Foreign Policy," *American Journal of Political Science*, 44:733–49.

Druckman, Daniel, A., A. Benton, F. Ali, and J. S. Bagur (1976) "Cultural Differences in Bargaining Behavior: India, Argentina, and the United States," *Journal of Conflict Resolution*, 20:413–48

East, Maurice A. (1978) "National Attributes and Foreign Policy," in *Why Nations Act*, edited by M. A. East, S. A. Salmore, and C. F. Hermann, Beverly Hills, CA: Sage, 143–60.

East, Maurice A., and Charles F. Hermann (1974) "Do Nation-Types Account for Foreign Policy Behavior?" in *Comparing Foreign Policies*, edited by James N. Rosenau, New York: Wiley, 269–303.

East, Maurice A., Stephen A. Salmore, and Charles F. Hermann (eds.) (1978) *Why Nations Act*, Beverly Hills, CA: Sage.

Eccles, Marriner S. (1951) *Beckoning Frontiers: Public and Personal Recollections*, edited by Sidney Hyman, New York: Knopf.

Ehrenhaus, P. (1983) "Culture and the Attribution Process: Barriers to Effective Communication," in *Intercultural Communication Theory: Current Perspective*, edited by W. B. Gudykunst, Beverly Hills, CA: Sage, 259–70.

Einstein, A., and L. Infeld (1938) *The Evolution of Physics*, New York: Simon & Schuster.

Esherick, J. W., and J. N. Wasserstrom (1990) "Acting Out Democracy: Political Theater in Modern China," *The Journal of Asian Studies*, 49(4):835–65.

Etheredge, Lloyd (1978) *A World of Men: The Private Sources of American Foreign Policy*, Cambridge: MIT Press.

———(1985) *Can Governments Learn? American Foreign Policy and Central American Revolutions*, New York: Pergamon.

———(1992) "On Being More Rational Than the Rationality Assumption: Dramatic Requirements, Nuclear Deterrence, and the Agenda for Learning," in *Political Psychology and Foreign Policy*, edited by Eric G. Singer and Valerie M. Hudson, Boulder, CO: Westview, 59–78.

Evans, Peter, Dietrich Rueschmeyer, and Theda Skocpol (1985) *Bringing the State Back In*, Cambridge: Cambridge University Press.

Evans, Peter B., Harold K. Jacobson, and Robert D. Putnam (1993) *Double-Edged Diplomacy: International Bargaining and Domestic Politics*, Berkeley: University of California Press.

Falkowski, Lawrence S. (ed.) (1979) *Psychological Models in International Politics*, Boulder, CO: Westview.

Farnham, Barbara (2002) "Perceiving the End of Threat: Ronald Reagan and the Gorbachev Revolution," in *Good Judgment in Foreign Policy*, edited by S. A. Renshon and D. W. Larson, Lanham, MD: Rowman & Littlefield, 153–90.

Farrell, R. Barry (ed.) (1966) *Approaches in Comparative and International Politics*, Evanston, IL: Northwestern University Press.

Festinger, Leon, Henry W. Riecken, and Stanley Schachter (1956) *When Prophecy Fails: A Social and Psychological Study of a Modern Group That Predicted the Destruction of the World*, New York: Harper & Row.

Final, Bernard I., and Kristin M. Lord (eds.) (2000) *Power and Conflict in the Age of Transparency*, New York: Palgrave.

Fisher, Glen (1980) *International Negotiation: A Cross-Cultural Perspective*, Yarmouth, ME: Intercultural Press.

Fiske, S. T., and S. E. Taylor (1984) *Social Cognition*, Reading, MA: Addision Wesley.

Freud, Sigmund, and W. C. Bullitt (1967) *Thomas Woodrow Wilson: A Psychological Study*, Boston: Houghton Mifflin.

Fulbrook, Edward (2001) "A Brief History of the Post-Autistic Economics Movement," available at www.paecon.net.

Gaddis, John Lewis (1992/93) "International Relations Theory and the End of the Cold War," *International Security*, 17(3):5–58.

Gaenslen, Fritz (1989) "On the Consequences of Consensual Decision Making: 'Rational Choice' in Comparative Perspective," University of Vermont.

———(1992) "Decision Making Groups," in *Political Psychology and Foreign Policy*, edited by Eric Singer and Valerie M. Hudson, Boulder, CO: Westview, 165–94.

———(1997) "Advancing Cultural Explanations," in *Culture and Foreign Policy*, edited by Valerie M. Hudson, Boulder, CO: Rienner, 265–80.

Galtung, Johan (1971) "A Structural Theory of Imperialism," *Journal of Peace Research*, 8(2):81–117.

Geertz, Clifford (1973) *The Interpretation of Cultures*, New York: Basic.

George, Alexander L. (1969) "The 'Operational Code': A Neglected Approach to the Study of Political Leaders and Decision-Making," *International Studies Quarterly*, 13:190–222.

———(1976) "Bridging the Gap between Theory and Practice," in *In Search of Global Patterns*, edited by James N. Rosenau, New York: Free Press, 114–19.

———(1979) "Case Studies and Theory Development: The Method of Structured Focused Comparison," in *Diplomacy: New Approaches in History, Theory, and Policy*, edited by Paul Gordon Lauren, New York: Free Press, 43–68.

———(1993) *Bridging the Gap between Theory and Practice*, Washington, DC: US Institute for Peace.

———(1994) "The Two Cultures of Academia and Policy-Making: Bridging the Gap," *Political Psychology*, 15(1):143–71.

George, Alexander L, and J. George (1956) *Woodrow Wilson and Colonel House: A Personality Study*, New York: Dover.

George, Alexander L., and R. Smoke (1974) *Deterrence in American Foreign Policy: Theory and Practice*, New York: Columbia University Press.

———(1989) "Deterrence and Foreign Policy," *World Politics*, 41(2):170–82.

Gerner, Deborah J. (1992) "Foreign Policy Analysis: Exhilarating Eclecticism, Intriguing Enigmas," *International Studies Notes*, 18(4).

Gerner, Deborah J., Phillip A. Schrodt, Ronald A. Francisco, and Judith L. Weddle (1994) "Machine Coding of Events Data Using Regional and International Sources," *International Studies Quarterly*, 38(1):91–20.

Gertner, Jon (2003) "The Futile Pursuit of Happiness," *New York Times Magazine*, September 7, 44f.

Gilbert, R. (1993) "Travails of the Chief," *The Sciences*, January/February, 8.

Gilbert, Robert E. (2003) *The Tormented President: Calvin Coolidge, Death, and Clinical Depression*, New York: Praeger.

Glad, Betty (1989) "Personality, Political, and Group Process Variables in Foreign Policy Decision-Making: Jimmy Carter's Handling of the Iranian Hostage Crisis," *International Political Science Review*, 10:35–61.

Golan, Daphne (1994) *Inventing Shaka: Using History in the Construction of Zulu Nationalism*, Boulder, CO: Rienner.

Golden, Tim (2004a) "After Terror, a Secret Rewriting of Military Law," *New York Times*, October 24, A1.

———(2004b) "Administration Officials Split over Stalled Military Tribunals," *New York Times*, October 25, A1.

Gorer, Geoffrey (1943) "Themes in Japanese Culture," *Transactions of the New York Academy of Sciences*, Ser. II, 5:106–24.

———(1948) *The American People*, New York: Norton.

———, and John Rickman (1949) *The People of Great Russia*, London: Groset.

Gottlieb, Gidon (1993) *Nation against State*, New York: CFR Press.

Graber, Doris A. (1968) *Public Opinion, the President, and Foreign Policy: Four Case Studies from the Formative Years*, New York: Holt, Rinehart and Winston.

Gray, Colin (1986) *Nuclear Strategy and National Style*, New York: Hamilton Press.

Green, Ronald M. (1978) *Religious Reason: The Rational and Moral Basis of Religious Belief*, New York: Oxford University Press.

Grove, Andrea K., and Neal A. Carter (1999) "Not All Blarney Is Cast in Stone: International Cultural Conflict in Northern Ireland," *Political Psychology*, 20(4):725–66.

Guetzkow, Harold (ed.) (1963) "A Use of Simulation in the Study of Inter-nation Relations," in *Simulation in International Relations*, edited by Harold Guetzkow et al., Englewood Cliffs, NJ: Prentice Hall.

Gurr, Ted Robert, and Barbara Harff (1994) *Ethnic Conflict in World Politics*, Boulder, CO: Westview.

Haftendorn, Helga, and Christian Tuschoff (eds.) (1993) *America and Europe in an Era of Change*, Boulder, CO: Westview.

Hagan, Joe D. (1987) "Regimes, Political Oppositions, and the Comparative Analysis of Foreign Policy," in *New Directions in the Study of Foreign Policy*, edited by Charles F. Hermann, Charles W. Kegley, and James N. Rosenau, Boston: Allen & Unwin, 339–65.

———(1993) *Political Opposition and Foreign Policy in Comparative Perspective*, Boulder, CO: Westview.

————(1994) "Regimes, Political Systems, and War," paper presented at the 35th annual conference of the International Studies Association, Washington, DC, March 28–April 1.

Halperin, Morton (1974) *Bureaucratic Politics and Foreign Policy*, Washington, DC: Brookings Institution.

Halperin, Morton H., and Arnold Kanter (eds.) (1973) *Readings in American Foreign Policy: A Bureaucratic Perspective*, Boston: Little, Brown.

Hammond, Ross A., and Robert Axelrod, "The Evolution of Ethnocentrism Based on Tags and Localism," forthcoming.

Hellman, D. (1969) *Japanese Foreign Policy and Domestic Politics*, Berkeley: University of California Press.

Herek, G. M., Irving L. Janis, and P. Huth (1987) "Decision Making during International Crises: Is Quality of Process Related to Outcome?" *Journal of Conflict Resolution*, 312:203–26.

————(1989) "Quality of Decision Making during the Cuban Missile Crisis: Major Errors in Welch's Reassessment," *Journal of Conflict Resolution*, 333:446–59.

Hermann, Charles F. (1978) "Decision Structure and Process Influences on Foreign Policy," in *Why Nations Act*, edited by Maurice A. East, S. A. Salmore, and Charles F. Hermann, Beverly Hills, CA: Sage, 69–102.

————(1990) "Changing Course: When Governments Choose to Redirect Foreign Policy," *International Studies Quarterly*, 34(1):3–22.

————(1995) "Epilogue: Reflections on Foreign Policy Theory Building," in *Foreign Policy Analysis: Continuity and Change in Its Second Generation*, edited by Laura Neack et al., Englewood Cliffs, NJ: Prentice Hall, 243–58.

Hermann, Charles F., Charles W. Kegley, Jr., and James N. Rosenau (eds.) (1987) *New Directions in the Study of Foreign Policy*, Boston: Allen & Unwin.

Hermann, Charles F., and Gregory Peacock (1987) "The Evolution and Future of Theoretical Research in the Comparative Study of Foreign Policy," in *New Directions in the Study of Foreign Policy*, edited by C. F. Hermann, C. W. Kegley, and J. N. Rosenau, Boston: Allen & Unwin, 13–32.

Hermann, Margaret G. (1970) "Explaining Foreign Policy Behavior Using the Personal Characteristics of Political Leaders," *International Studies Quarterly*, 24:7–46.

————(1978) "Effects of Personal Characteristics of Leaders on Foreign Policy," in *Why Nations Act*, edited by M. A. East, S. A. Salmore, and Charles. F. Hermann, Beverly Hills, CA: Sage.

————(1979) "Who Becomes a Political Leader? Some Societal and Regime Influences on Selection of a Head of Government," in *Psychological Models in International Politics*, edited by Lawrence Falkowski, Boulder, CO: Westview.

————(1984) "A Study of 53 Heads of Government," in *Foreign Policy Decision Making: Perception, Cognition, and Artificial Intelligence*, edited by Donald A. Sylvan and Steve Chan, New York: Praeger, 53–80.

————(1987) "Foreign Policy Role Orientations and the Quality of Foreign Policy Decisions," in *Role Theory and Foreign Policy Analysis*, edited by Stephen Walker, Durham, NC: Duke University Press, 123–40.

————(2001) "How Decision Unites Shape Foreign Policy: A Theoretical Framework," *International Studies Review*, 3(2):47–82.

————(2003) "Assessing Leadership Style: Trait Analysis," in *The Psychological Assessment of Political Leaders*, edited by Jerrold Post, Ann Arbor: University of Michigan Press, 178–214.

Hermann, Margaret G., and Charles F. Hermann (1989) "Who Makes Foreign Policy Decisions and How: An Empirical Inquiry," *International Studies Quarterly*, 33(4):361–88.

Hermann, Margaret G., Charles F. Hermann, and Joe D. Hagan (1987) "How Decision Units Shape Foreign Policy Behavior," in *New Directions in the Study of Foreign Policy*, edited by Charles F. Hermann, Charles W. Kegley, and James N. Rosenau, Boston: Allen & Unwin, 309–38.

Hermann, Margaret G., and Charles W. Kegley, Jr. (1994) "Rethinking Democracy and International Peace," paper presented at the annual meeting of the American Political Science Association, New York, September 1–4.

————(1995) "Do Decisionmakers Matter in Understanding Why Democracies Don't Fight One Another?" paper presented at the annual meeting of the International Studies Association, Chicago, Illinois, February 21–25.

Hermann, Margaret G., and Thomas Preston (1994) "Presidents and Their Advisers: Leadership Style, Advisory Systems, and Foreign Policymaking," in *The Domestic Sources of American Foreign Policy: Insights and Evidence*, edited by Eugene R. Wittkopf, New York: St. Martin's, 2nd edition, 340–57.

Hermann, Margaret G., Thomas Preston, Bahgat Korany, and Timothy M. Shaw (2001) "Who Leads Matters: The Effects of Powerful Individuals," *International Studies Review*, 3(2):83–132.

Hermann, Margaret G., with Thomas W. Milburn (eds.) (1977) *A Psychological Examination of Political Leaders*, New York: Free Press.

Herrmann, Richard (1985) *Perceptions and Behavior in Soviet Foreign Policy*, Pittsburgh: University of Pittsburgh Press.

————(1986) "The Power of Perceptions in Foreign Policy Decision Making: Do Views of the Soviet Union Determine the Policy Choices of American Leaders?" *American Journal of Political Science*, 30(4):841–75.

————(1988) "The Empirical Challenge of the Cognitive Revolution: A Strategy for Drawing Inferences about Perceptions," *International Studies Quarterly*, 32(2):175–204.

————(1993) "The Construction of Images in International Relations Theory: American, Russian, and Islamic World Views," paper presented at the 34th annual conference of the International Studies Association, Acapulco, Mexico, March 23–27.

Herskovits, M. J. (1955) *Cultural Anthropology*, New York: Knopf.

Hess, R. (1963) "The Socialization of Attitudes toward Political Authority: Some Cross-National Comparisons," *International Social Science Journal*, 15:542–59.

Heuer, Richards (1999) *The Psychology of Intelligence Analysis*, Washington, DC: Government Printing Office.

Hill, Christopher (2003) *The Changing Politics of Foreign Policy*, NY: Palgrave.

Hilsman, Roger (1967) *To Move a Nation*, New York: Doubleday.

————(1987) *The Politics of Policy Making in Defense and Foreign Policy: Conceptual Models and Bureaucratic Politics*, Englewood Cliffs, NJ: Prentice Hall.

Hoffman, S. (1961) "International Systems and International Law," in *The State of War: Essays on the Theory and Practice of International Politics*, New York: Praeger.

Hofstede, Geert (1980) *Culture's Consequences*, Beverly Hills, CA: Sage.

———(1991) *Cultures and Organizations*, London: McGraw-Hill.

Holland, H. (1984) *Managing Diplomacy*, Stanford, CA: Hoover Institution Press.

Holsti, Kal J. (1970) "National Role Conceptions in the Study of Foreign Policy," *International Studies Quarterly*, 14:233–309.

Holsti, Ole (1962) "The Belief System and National Images: A Case Study," *Journal of Conflict Resolution*, 6(3):244–52.

———(1989) "Crisis Decision Making," in *Behavior, Society, and Nuclear War*, Volume I, edited by P. Tetlock, J. Husbands, R. Jervis, P. Stern, and C. Tilly, New York: Oxford University Press, 8–84.

Holsti, Ole, Robert North, and Richard Brody (1968) "Perception and Action in the 1914 Crisis," in *Quantitative International Politics: Insights and Evidence*, edited by J. David Singer, New York: Free Press, 123–58.

Holsti, Ole R. (1977) *The "Operational Code" as an Approach to the Analysis of Belief Systems*, Durham, NC: Duke University Press.

Holsti, Ole R., and James N. Rosenau (1979) "Vietnam, Consensus, and the Belief Systems of American Leaders," *World Politics*, 32:1–56.

Hoyt, P. D., and J. A. Garrison (1997) "Political Manipulation within the Small Group: Foreign Policy Advisers in the Carter Administration," in *Beyond Groupthink: Political Group Dynamics and Foreign Policy-Making*, edited by Paul 't Hart, Eric K. Stern, and Bengt Sundelius, Ann Arbor: University of Michigan Press, 249–74.

Hudson, Valerie M. (1987) "Using a Rule-Based Production System to Estimate Foreign Policy Behavior; Conceptual Issues and Practical Concerns, in *Artificial Intelligence and National Security*, edited by Stephen Cimbala, Lexington, MA: Lexington Books, 109–32.

———(1990) "Birth Order of World Leaders: An Exploratory Analysis of Effects on Personality and Behavior," *Political Psychology*, 11(3):583–602.

———(1991) "Scripting International Power Dramas: A Model of Situational Predisposition," in *Artificial Intelligence and International Politics*, edited by Valerie M. Hudson, Boulder, CO: Westview, 194–220.

———(1994) "Foreign Policy Analysis," in *The Encyclopedia of Policy Studies*, second edition, edited by Stuart Nagel, New York: Marcel Dekker, Inc.

———(1994) "International and Domestic Security: System Deconcentration in the AsiaPacific," paper presented at the 35th annual conference of the International Studies Association, Washington, DC, March 28–April 1.

———(1999) "Cultural Expectations of One's Own and Other Nations' Foreign Policy Action Templates," *Political Psychology*, 20(4):767–802.

———(2002) "Decision Making," in *The Encyclopedia of American Foreign Policy*, Volume 1, edited by Alexander De Conde, Richard Dean Burns, and Fredrik Logevall, New York: Charles Scribner's Sons, 427–37.

———(2002) "Foreign Policy Decision-Making: A Touchstone for International Relations Theory in the Twenty-first Century," in *Foreign Policy Decision-Making (Revisited)*, edited by Richard C. Snyder, H. W. Bruck, and Burton Sapin, New York: Palgrave Macmillan, 1–20.

————(2005) "Foreign Policy Analysis: Actor-Specific Theory and the Ground of International Relations," *Foreign Policy Analysis*, 1(1):1–30.

————(editor and contributor) (1991) *Artificial Intelligence and International Politics*, Boulder, CO: Westview.

————(ed.) (1997) *Culture and Foreign Policy*, Boulder, CO: Rienner.

Hudson, Valerie M., and Andrea M. Den Boer (2004) *Bare Branches: The Security Implications of Asia's Surplus Male Population*, Cambridge, MA: MIT Press.

Hudson, Valerie M., Charles F. Hermann, and Eric G. Singer (1989) "The Situational Imperative," *Cooperation and Conflict*, 24(3/4):117–40.

Hudson, Valerie M., and Martin Sampson (1999) "Culture Is More Than a Static Residual," *Political Psychology*, 20(4):667–75.

Hudson, Valerie M., Philip A. Schrodt, and Ray D. Whitmer (2004) "A New Kind of Social Science: The Path beyond Current (IR) Methodologies May Lie beneath Them," paper presented at the annual International Studies Association conference, Montreal, Quebec, Canada, March.

————(2005) "A New Kind of Social Science: Moving Ahead with Results from Reverse Wolfram Models as Applied to Event Data," paper presented at the annual meeting of the International Studies Association. Hilton Hawaiian Village, Honolulu, Hawaii, February 2.

Hudson, Valerie M., Susan M. Sims, and John C. Thomas (1993) "The Domestic Political Context of Foreign Policy Making: Explicating a Theoretical Construct," in *The Limits of State Autonomy: Societal Groups and Foreign Policy Formulation*, volume sponsored by the Foreign Policy Analysis Section of the International Studies Association, edited by David Skidmore and Valerie M. Hudson, Boulder, CO: Westview, 49–102.

Hudson, Valerie M., with Christopher A. Vore (1995) "Foreign Policy Analysis Yesterday, Today, and Tomorrow," *Mershon International Studies Review*, 39(2):209–38.

Hughes, Barry B. (1978) *The Domestic Context of American Foreign Policy*, San Francisco: Freeman.

Huntington, Samuel (1960) "Strategic Planning and the Political Process," *Foreign Affairs*, 38(2):285–99.

————(1993) *The Clash of Civilizations?: The Debate*, New York: Council on Foreign Relations Press.

————(1996) *The Clash of Civilizations and the Remaking of World Order*, New York: Simon & Schuster.

ICONS (2004) "About ICONS," www.icons.umd.edu.

Inglehart, Ronald (1988) "The Renaissance of Political Culture," *American Political Science Review*, 82(4):1203–30.

Inkeles, Alex, and D. J. Levinson (1968) "National Character: The Study of Modal Personality and 30 Sociocultural Systems," in *Handbook of Social Psychology*, Volume II, edited by G. Lindzey, Cambridge, MA: Addison Wesley, 977–1020.

International Studies Review (2001) special issue on "Leaders, Groups, and Coalitions: Understanding the People and Processes in Foreign Policymaking," edited by Margaret G. Hermann, 3(2) (Summer).

Jakobsen, Peter Viggo (2000) "Focus on the CNN Effect Misses the Point: The Real

Media Impact on Conflict Management Is Invisible and Indirect," *Journal of Peace Research*, 37(2):131–43.

Janis, Irving L. (1982) *Groupthink*, Boston: Houghton Mifflin.

Jervis, Robert (1976) *Perception and Misperception in International Politics*, Princeton, NJ: Princeton University Press.

Jervis, Robert, Richard Ned Lebow, and Janice Gross Stein (eds.) (1985) *Psychology and Deterrence*, Baltimore, MD: Johns Hopkins University Press.

Johnson, L. K. (1977) "Operational Codes and the Prediction of Leadership Behavior: Frank Church at Mid-Career," in *A Psychological Examination of Political Leaders*, edited by Margaret G. Hermann, New York: Free Press.

Kaarbo, Juliet (1993) "Power and Influence in Foreign Policy Decision-Making: The Role of Junior Parties in Coalition Cabinets in Comparative Perspective," paper presented at the annual meeting of the International Studies Association, Acapulco, Mexico, March 23–27.

———(1994) "Junior Party Influence in Coalition Cabinets: Insights from Israeli and German Foreign Policy," paper presented at the annual meeting of the International Studies Association, Washington, DC, March 28–April 1.

Kahn, Herman (1993) "The Confucian Ethic and Economic Growth," in *Development and Underdevelopment: The Political Economy of Inequality*, edited by Mitchell A. Seligson and John T. Passe-Smith, Boulder, CO: Rienner, 169–72.

Kahneman, Daniel (2000) "Experienced Utility and Subjective Happiness, in *Choices, Values and Frames*, edited by Daniel Kahneman and Amos Tversky, Cambridge: Cambridge University Press, 673–92.

Kahneman, Daniel, Paul Slovic, and Amos Tversky (eds.) (1982) *Judgment under Uncertainty: Heuristics and Biases*, Cambridge: Cambridge University Press.

Kaplan, Fred (2005) "How Many Government Agencies Does It Take to Teach Soldiers Arabic?" April 6, http:/slate.msn.com/id/2116330.

Kaplan, Morton (1957) *System and Process in International Politics*, New York: Wiley.

———(1972) "Variants on Six Models of the International System," in *International Politics and Foreign Policy*, edited by James N. Rosenau, Glencoe, IL: Free Press of Glencoe, 291–303.

Kasza, Gregory (2001) "Perestroika: For an Ecumenical Science of Politics," available at www.paecon.net.

Katzenstein, L. C. (1997), "Change, Myth, and the Reunification of China," in *Culture and Foreign Policy*, edited by Valerie M. Hudson, Boulder, CO: Rienner, 45–72.

Katzenstein, Peter (1985) *Small States in World Markets: Industrial Policy in Europe*, Ithaca, NY: Cornell University Press.

Katzenstein, Peter J. (ed.) (1996) *The Culture of National Security: Norms and Identity in World Politics*, New York: Columbia University Press.

Kean, James, and Patrick McGowan (1973) "National Attributes and Foreign Policy Participation: A Path Analysis," in *Sage International Yearbook of Foreign Policy Studies*, Volume 1, edited by Patrick McGowan, Beverly Hills, CA: Sage, 219–52.

Kegley, Charles W. (1980) "The Comparative Study of Foreign Policy: Paradigm Lost?" Institute of International Studies, Essay Series #10, University of South Carolina.

Khong, Yuen Foong (1992) *Analogies at War: Korean, Munich, Dien Bien Phu, and the Vietnam Decisions of 1965*, Princeton, NJ: Princeton University Press.

Klineberg, Otto (1945) "Racial Psychology," in *The Science of Man in the World Crisis*, edited by Ralph Linton, New York: Columbia University Press, 63–77.

Kluckhohn, Clyde (1951) "The Study of Culture," in *The Policy Sciences*, edited by Daniel Lerner and Harold D. Lasswell, Stanford, CA: Stanford University Press.

Korany, Bahgat (ed.) (1986) *How Foreign Policy Decisions Are Made in the Third World*, Boulder, CO: Westview.

Kozak, David C., and James M. Keagle (eds.) (1988) *Bureaucratic Politics and National Security: Theory and Practice*, Boulder, CO: Rienner.

Krasner, Stephen D. (1971), "Are Bureaucracies Important? (Or Allison Wonderland)," *Foreign Policy*, 7:159–79.

Kroeber, A. L., and Clyde Kluckhohn (1952) *Culture: A Critical Review of Concepts and Definitions*, Cambridge, MA: Harvard University Press.

Krogrnan, W. M. (1945) "The Concept of Race," *The Science of Man in the World Crisis*, edited by in Ralph Linton, New York: Columbia University Press, 38–62.

Kruger, Justin, and David Dunning (1999) "Unskilled and Unaware of It: How Difficulties in Recognizing One's Own Incompetence Lead to Inflated Self-Assessment," *Journal of Personality and Social Psychology*, 77(6):1121–34.

Kurtz, L. (1986) *The Politics of Heresy*, Berkeley: University of California Press.

Lamborn, Alan C., and Stephen P. Mumme (1989) *Statecraft, Domestic Politics, and Foreign Policy Making: The El Chamizal Dispute*, Boulder, CO: Westview.

Lampton, David M. (1986) *Paths to Power: Elite Mobility in Contemporary China*, Volume 55, Ann Arbor: University of Michigan Press.

Lane, Ruth (1990) "Concrete Theory: An Emerging Political Method," *American Political Science Review*, 84(3):927–40.

Lapid, Yosef, and Friedrich Kratochwil (eds.) (1996) *The Return of Culture and Identity in IR Theory (Critical Perspectives on World Politics)*, Boulder, CO: Rienner.

Larson, Deborah W. (1985) *Origins of Containment: A Psychological Explanation*, Princeton, NJ: Princeton University Press.

———(1993) "Reagan, Bush, and Gorbachev: Changing Images and Building Trust," paper presented at the annual meeting of the International Studies Association, Acapulco, Mexico, March 23–27.

Lasswell, Harold D. (1930) *Psychology and Politics*, Chicago: University of Chicago Press.

———(1948) *Power and Personality*, New York: Norton.

Leana, C. R. (1975) "A Partial Test of Janis' Groupthink Model: Effects of Group Cohesiveness and Leader Behavior on Defective Decision-Making," *Journal of Management*, 111:5–17.

Lebow, R. N., and J. G. Stein (1990) "Deterrence: The Elusive Dependent Variable," *World Politics*, 42(3):336–69.

Leites, Nathan (1951) *The Operational Code of the Politburo*, New York: McGraw-Hill.

Lenin, Vladimir Ilyich (1916, this edition 1997) *Imperialism: The Highest Stage of Capitalism*, New York: International Publishers.

Leuchtenberg, W. E. (1993) *The Perils of Prosperity: 1914–1932*, Chicago: University of Chicago Press.

Leung, Kwok (1987) "Some Determinants of Reactions to Procedural Models for Conflict Resolution: A Cross-National Study," *Journal of Personality and Social Psychology*, 53:898–908.

LeVine, Robert A. (1973) *Culture, Behavior, and Personality*, Chicago: Aldine Publishing Company.

Levy, Jack (1988) "Domestic Politics and War," *Journal of Interdisciplinary History*, 18(4):653–74.

———(1994) "Learning and Foreign Policy: Sweeping a Conceptual Minefield," *International Organization*, 48(2) (Spring):279–312.

Levy, Jack, and Lily Vakili (1989) "External Scapegoating by Authoritarian Regimes: Argentina in the Falklands/Malvinas Case," paper presented at the annual meeting of the American Political Science Association, Atlanta, August 31–September 3.

Linton, Ralph (1945) *The Cultural Background of Personality*, New York: Appleton-Century-Crofts.

Lippmann, Walter (1955) *Essays in the Public Philosophy*, Boston: Little, Brown.

Lipset, S. M. (1966) "The President, the Polls, and Vietnam," *Transaction*, September/October:19–24.

Little, David, and Sumner B. Twiss (1978) *Comparative Religious Ethics: A New Method*, San Francisco: Harper & Row.

Livingston, Steven (1997) "Beyond the CNN Effect: The Media-Foreign Policy Dynamic," in *Politics and the Press: The News Media and Their Influences*, edited by Pippa Norris, Boulder, CO: Rienner.

Lotz, Hellmut (1997) "Myth and NAFTA: The Use of Core Values in U.S. Politics," in *Culture and Foreign Policy*, edited by Valerie M. Hudson, Boulder, CO: Rienner, 73–98.

Lowery, David, and Lee Sigelman (1982) "Political Culture and State Public Policy: The Missing Link," *Western Political Quarterly*, 35 (September):376–84.

Luker, K. (1984) *Abortion and the Politics of Motherhood*, Berkeley: University of California Press.

Mallery, John (1991) "Semantic Content Analysis," in *Artificial Intelligence and International Politics*, edited by Valerie M. Hudson, Boulder, CO: Westview, 347–85.

Mandlebaum, M., and W. Schneider (1979) "The New Internationalisms," in *Eagle Entangled: US Foreign Policy in a Complex World*, edited by Kenneth A. Oye et al., New York: Wiley.

Maoz, Zeev, and Bruce Russett (1993) "Normative and Structural Causes of the Democratic Peace, 1946–86," *American Political Science Review*, 87:624–38.

March, James G., and Herbert A. Simon (1993) *Organizations*, Cambridge, MA: Blackwell.

Marfleet, B. Gregory (2000) "The Operational Code of John F. Kennedy during the Cuban Missile Crisis: A Comparison of Public and Private Rhetoric," *Political Psychology*, 21(3):545–58.

Mastanduno, Michael, David Lake, and John Ikenberry (1989) "Toward a Realist Theory of State Action," *International Studies Quarterly*, 33(4):457–74.

McCauley, C. (1989) "The Nature of Social Influence in Groupthink: Compliance and Internalization," *Journal of Personality and Social Psychology*, 572:250–60.

McClelland, David C. (1985) *Human Motivation*, Glenview, IL: Scott Foresman.

McClosky, Herbert (1962) "Concerning Strategies for a Science of International Politics," in *Foreign Policy Decision-Making*, edited by Richard C. Snyder, H. W. Bruck, and Burton Sapin, Glencoe, IL: Free Press, 186–205.

McDaniels, T. L., and R. S. Gregory (1991) "A Framework for Structuring Cross-Cultural Research in Risk and Decision-Making," *Journal of Cross-Cultural Psychology*, 22(1):103–28.

McDermott, Rose (2004) *Political Psychology in International Relations*, Ann Arbor: University of Michigan Press.

——(forthcoming) "The Feeling of Rationality: The Meaning of Neuroscience for Political Science," *Perspectives on Politics*.

McGowan, P., and H. B. Shapiro (1973) *The Comparative Study of Foreign Policy: A Survey of Scientific Findings*, Beverly Hills, CA: Sage.

McKeown, B. (1984) "Q Methodology in Political Psychology: Theory and Technique in Psychoanalytic Applications," *Political Psychology* 5:415–35.

Mefford, Dwain (1991) "Steps toward Artificial Intelligence: Rule-Based, Case-Based and Explanation-Based Models of Politics," in *Artificial Intelligence and International Politics*, edited by Valerie M. Hudson, Boulder, CO: Westview, 56–96.

Merelman, R. M. (1969) "The Development of Political Ideology: A Framework for the Analysis of Political Socialization," *American Political Science Review*, 69:21–31.

Merelman, Richard M. (1986) "Revitalizing Political Socialization," in *Political Psychology*, edited by M. G. Hermann, San Francisco: Jossey-Bass, 279–319.

Merritt R. L., and D. A. Zinnes (1991) "Democracies and War," in *On Measuring Democracy*, edited by A. Inkeles, New Brunswick, NJ: Transaction, 207–34.

Millennium, special issue on Culture in International Relations (1993), 22(3) (Winter).

Milner, Helen V. (1997) *Interests, Institutions, and Information: Domestic Politics and International Relations*, Princeton, NJ: Princeton University Press.

Mintz, Alex (2004) "How Do Leaders Make Decisions? A Poliheuristic Perspective," *Journal of Conflict Resolution*, 3–13.

——(ed.) (2003) *Integrating Cognitive and Rational Theories of Foreign Policy Decision Making*, New York: Palgrave Macmillan.

Mintz, Alex, Nehemia Geva, Steven B. Redd, Amy Carnes (1997) "The Effect of Dynamic and Static Choice Sets on Political Decision Making: An Analysis Using the Decision Board Platform," *American Political Science Review*, 91(3): 553–66.

Modelski, George (1981) "Long Cycles, Kondratieffs, and Alternating Innovation," in *The Political Economy of Foreign Policy Behavior*, edited by C. W. Kegley and P. McGowan, Beverly Hills, CA: Sage, 63–83.

Morgan, T. Clifton (1992) "Democracy and War: Reflections on the Literature," *International Interactions*, 18:197–203.

Most, Benjamin A., and Harvey Starr (1986) *Inquiry, Logic, and International Relations*, Columbia: University of South Carolina Press.

Motokawa, Tatsuo (1989) "Sushi Science and Hamburger Science," *Perspectives in Biology and Medicine*, 32(4):489–504.

Mueller, J. E. (1973) *War, Presidents, and Public Opinion*, New York: Wiley.

Munton, Don (1976) "Comparative Foreign Policy: Fads, Fantasies, Orthodoxies, and Perversities," in *In Search of Global Patterns*, edited by James N. Rosenau, New York: Free Press.

NASA (2003) "Columbia Accident Investigation Board Report," Washington, DC: Government Printing Office, August.

Neack, Laura, J., A. Hey, and P. J. Haney (1995) *Foreign Policy Analysis: Continuity and Change in Its Second Generation*, Englewood Cliffs, NJ: Prentice Hall.

Neustadt, Richard E. (1970) *Alliance Politics*, New York: Columbia University Press.

Nisbett, R. E., and D. Cohen (1996) *Culture of Honor: The Psychology of Violence in the South*, Boulder, CO: Westview.

Nisbett, R. E., and T. D. Wilson (1977) "Telling More Than We Can Know: Verbal Reports on Mental Processes," *Psychological Review*, 84:231–59.

Ogata, Sadako (1977) "The Business Community and Japanese Foreign Policy," in *The Foreign Policy of Modern Japan*, edited by R. A. Scalapino, Berkeley: University of California Press, 175–203.

Omestad, Thomas (1994) "Psychobabble at the CIA," *New York Times*, June 12, A28.

Paige, Glenn (1959) *The Korean Decision*, Evanston, IL: Northwestern University Press.

———(1968) *The Korean Decision, June 24–30, 1950*, New York: Free Press.

Pickering, A. (1984) *Constructing Quarks: A Sociological History of Particle Physics*, Edinburgh: Edinburgh University Press.

Posen, Barry (1984) *The Sources of Military Doctrine: France, Britain, and Germany between the World Wars*, Ithaca, NY: Cornell University Press.

Post, Jerrold (1991) "Saddam Hussein of Iraq: A Political Psychology Profile," *Political Psychology*, 12(1): 279–89.

———(ed.) (2003) *The Psychological Assessment of Political Leaders*, Ann Arbor: University of Michigan Press.

Post, Jerrold M. (2003) "Assessing Leaders at a Distance: The Political Personality Profile," in *The Psychological Assessment of Political Leaders, with Profiles of Saddam Hussein and Bill Clinton*, edited by J. M. Post, Ann Arbor: University of Michigan Press, 69–104.

Powlick, Philip J. (1995) "The Sources of Public Opinion for American Foreign Policy Officials," *International Studies Quarterly*, 39:427–52.

Purkitt, Helen E. (1998) "Problem Representations and Political Expertise: Evidence from 'Think Aloud' Protocols of South African Elite," in *Problem Representation in Foreign Policy Decision Making*, edited by Donald A. Sylvan and James F. Voss, Cambridge: Cambridge University Press, 147–86.

Putnam, Robert (1988) "Diplomacy and Domestic Politics: The Logic of Two-Level Games," *International Organization*, 42(3):427–60.

Pye, Lucian (1968) *The Spirit of Chinese Politics: A Psychocultural Study of the Authority Crisis in Political Development*, Cambridge, MA: MIT Press.

———(1986) "Political Psychology in Asia," in *Political Psychology*, edited by Margaret G. Hermann, San Francisco: Jossey-Bass, 467–86.

———(1988) *The Mandarin and the Cadre: China's Political Cultures*, Ann Arbor: Center for Chinese Studies, the University of Michigan.

———(1991) "Political Culture Revisited," *Political Psychology*, 12(3) (September):487–508.

Pye, Lucian W., and Sidney Verba (eds.) (1965) *Political Culture and Political Development*, Princeton, NJ: Princeton University Press.

Ray, James Lee (1993) "Wars between Democracies" Rare or Nonexistent?" *International Interactions*, 18:251–76.

Renshon, Stanley A. (2003) "Psychoanalytic Assessments of Character and Performance in Presidents and Candidates: Some Observations on Theory and Method," in *The Psychological Assessment of Political Leaders*, edited by Jerrold Post, Ann Arbor: University of Michigan Press, 105–36.

Renshon, Stanley Allen (ed.) (1977) *Handbook of Political Socialization: Theory and Research*, New York: Free Press.

Richardson, Neil R., and Charles W. Kegley, Jr. (1980) "Trade Dependence and Foreign Policy Compliance: A Longitudinal Analysis," *International Studies Quarterly*, 24 (June):191–222.

Ripley, Brian (1989) "Kennedy, Johnson, and Groupthink: A Theoretical Reassessment," paper presented at the annual meeting of the American Political Science Association, Atlanta, Georgia, August 31–September 3.

———(1993) "Psychology, Foreign Policy, and International Relations Theory," *Political Psychology*, 14:403–16.

Root-Bernstein, Robert (1989) "How Scientists Really Think," *Perspectives in Biology and Medicine*, 32(4):472–88.

Rosati, J., J. D. Hagan, and Martin Sampson (eds.) (1995) *Foreign Policy Restructuring*, Columbia: University of South Carolina Press.

Rose, Gideon (1998) "Neoclassical Realism and Theories of Foreign Policy," *World Politics*, 51(1) (October):144–72.

Rosecrance, Richard N. (1963) *Action and Reaction in World Politics: International Systems in Perspective*, Boston: Little, Brown.

Rosenau, James N. (1966) "Pre-Theories and Theories of Foreign Policy," in *Approaches in Comparative and International Politics*, edited by R. Barry Farrell, Evanston, IL: Northwestern University Press.

Rummel, Rudolph J. (1972) *The Dimensions of Nations*, Beverly Hills, CA: Sage.

———(1977) *Understanding Conflict and War*, Beverly Hills, CA: Sage.

———(1979) *National Attributes and Behavior*, Beverly Hills, CA: Sage.

Russett, Bruce M. (1993a) *Grasping the Democratic Peace: Principles for a Post-Cold War World*, Princeton, NJ: Princeton University Press.

———(1993b) "Can a Democratic Peace Be Built?" *International Interactions*, 18:277–82.

Salmore, Barbara G., and Stephen A. Salmore (1978) "Political Regimes and Foreign Policy," in *Why Nations Act*, edited by M. A. East et al., Beverly Hills, CA: Sage, 103–22.

Sampson, Martin W. (1987) "Cultural Influences on Foreign Policy," in *New Directions in the Study of Foreign Policy*, edited by Charles F. Hermann, Charles W. Kegley, and James N. Rosenau, Boston: Allen & Unwin, 384–408.

Sampson, Martin W., and Stephen Walker (1987) "Cultural Norms and National Roles: A Comparison of Japan and France," in *Role Theory and Foreign Policy Analysis*, edited by Stephen Walker, Durham, NC: Duke University Press, 105–22.

Sampson, Martin W., and Valerie M. Hudson (eds.) (1999) "Culture and Foreign Policy," special issue of *Political Psychology*, 20(4) (December).

Sapolsky, Robert M. (1997) *Why Zebras Don't Get Ulcers*, New York: Henry Holt.

Schilling, W. R., P. Y. Hammond, and G. H. Snyder (1962) *Strategy, Politics, and Defense Budgets*, New York: Columbia University Press.

Schmemann, Serge (1995) "Negotiators, Arabs and Israeli, Built Friendship from Mistrust," *New York Times*, September 28, A1.

Schrodt, Philip A. (1995) "Event Data in Foreign Policy Analysis," in *Foreign Policy Analysis: Continuity and Change in Its Second Generation*, edited by Laura Neack et al., Englewood Cliffs, NJ: Prentice Hall, 145–66.

Schwartz, Barry (2004a) *The Paradox of Choice: Why More is Less*, New York: Ecco.

———(2004b) "The Paradox of Choice: Why More Is Less," *New York Times*, January 22, A27.

Seeger, Joseph (1992) "Towards a Theory of Foreign Policy Analysis Based on National Role Conceptions: An AI/IR Approach," master's thesis, Brigham Young University.

Semmel, A. K. (1982) "Small Group Dynamics in Foreign Policy-Making," in *Biopolitics, Political Psychology, and International Politics*, edited by G.W. Hopple, New York: St. Martin's, 94–113.

Semmel, A. K., and D. Minix (1979) "Small Group Dynamics and Foreign Policy Decision-Making: An Experimental Approach," in *Psychological Models in International Politics*, edited by L. S. Falkowski, Boulder, CO: Westview, 251–87.

Sen, Amartya (1982) *Choice, Welfare, and Measurement*, Cambridge, MA: MIT Press.

———(1987) *On Ethics and Economics*, New York: Basil Blackwell.

Shapiro, Michael, and Matthew Bonham (1973) "Cognitive Process and Foreign Policy Decision-Making," *International Studies Quarterly*, 17:147–74.

Shih, Chih-yu (1993) *China's Just World: The Morality of Chinese Foreign Policy*, Boulder, CO: Rienner.

Simon, Herbert (1985) "Human Nature in Politics: The Dialogue of Psychology with Political Science," *American Political Science Review*, 79:293–304.

Singer, Eric G., and Valerie M. Hudson (eds.) (1992) *Political Psychology and Foreign Policy*, Boulder, CO: Westview.

Singer, J. D., S. Bremer, and J. Stuckey (1972) "Capability Distribution, Uncertainty, and Major Power War, 1820–1965," in *Peace, War, and Numbers*, edited by B. M. Russett, Beverly Hills, CA: Sage.

Skidmore, David, and Valerie M. Hudson (1993a) "Establishing the Limits of State Autonomy: Contending Approaches to the Study of State-Society Relations and Foreign Policy Formulation," in *The Limits of State Autonomy: Societal Groups and Foreign Policy Formulation*, volume sponsored by the Foreign Policy Analysis Section of the International Studies Association, edited by David Skidmore and Valerie M. Hudson, Boulder, CO: Westview, 1–24.

———(eds.) (1993b) *The Limits of State Autonomy: Societal Groups and Foreign Policy Formulation*, volume sponsored by the Foreign Policy Analysis Section of the International Studies Association, Boulder, CO: Westview.

Skinner, B. F. (1981) "Selection by Consequences," *Science*, 213, 501–4.

Smith, S. (1987) "CFP: A Theoretical Critique," *International Studies Notes*, 13(2):47–48.

Snare, Charles (1992) "Applying Personality Theory to Foreign Policy Behavior: Evaluating Three Methods of Assessment," in *Political Psychology and Foreign Policy*, edited by Eric Singer and Valerie M. Hudson, Boulder, CO: Westview, 103–34.

Snyder, Richard, and Glenn Paige (1958) *The United States Decision to Resist Aggression in Korea: The Application of an Analytical Scheme*, Glencoe, IL: Free Press.

Snyder, Richard C., H. W. Bruck, and Burton Sapin (1954) *Decision-Making as an Approach to the Study of International Politics*, Foreign Policy Analysis Project Series No. 3, Princeton, NJ: Princeton University Press.

———(ed.) (1962) *Foreign Policy Decision-Making: An Approach to the Study of International Politics*, Glencoe, IL: Free Press.

———(eds.) (2002) *Foreign Policy Decision-Making (Revisited)*, New York: Palgrave Macmillan.

Solomon, Richard (1971) *Mao's Revolution and Chinese Political Culture*, Berkeley: University of California Press.

———(1992) "Political Culture and Diplomacy in the Twenty-First Century," in *The Political Culture of Foreign and Area Studies: Essays in Honor of Lucian W. Pye*, edited by R. J. Samuels and M. Weiner, New York: Brassey's.

Sprout, Harold, and Margaret Sprout (1956) *Man-Milieu Relationship Hypotheses in the Context of International Politics*, Princeton, NJ: Princeton University Press.

———(1957) "Environment Factors in the Study of International Politics," *Journal of Conflict Resolution*, 1:309–28.

———(1965) *The Ecological Perspective on Human Affairs with Special Reference to International Politics*, Princeton, NJ: Princeton University Press.

Stern, Eric K. (1997) "Probing the Plausibility of Newgroup Syndrome: Kennedy and the Bay of Pigs," in *Beyond Groupthink: Political Group Dynamics and Foreign Policy-Making*, edited by Paul 't Hart, Eric K. Stern, and Bengt Sundelius, Ann Arbor: University of Michigan Press, 153-90.

Stewart, L. (1977) "Birth Order and Political Leadership," in *A Psychological Examination of Political Leaders*, edited by Margaret G. Hermann, New York: Free Press, 206–36.

Stewart, Philip D., Margaret G. Hermann, and Charles F. Hermann (1989) "Modeling the 1973 Soviet Decision to Support Egypt," *American Political Science Review*, 83(1):35–59.

Stoessinger, John (2001) *Why Nations Go to War*, New York: St. Martin's.

Suedfeld, Peter, and Phillip Tetlock (1977) "Integrative Complexity of Communications in International Crisis," *Journal of Conflict Resolution*, 21:169–84.

Swidler, Ann (1986) "Culture in Action: Symbols and Strategies," *American Sociological Review*, 51:273–86.

Sylvan, David, Stephen Majeski, and Jennifer Milliken (1991) "Theoretical Categories and Data Construction in Computational Models of Foreign Policy," in *Artificial Intelligence and International Politics*, edited by Valerie M. Hudson, Boulder, CO: Westview, 327–46.

Sylvan, Donald A., and Deborah M. Haddad (1998) "Reasoning and Problem Representation in Foreign Policy: Groups, Individuals, and Stories," in *Problem Representation in Foreign Policy Decision Making*, edited by Donald A. Sylvan and James F. Voss, Cambridge: Cambridge University Press, 187–212.

Sylvan, Donald A., and James F. Voss (eds.) (1998) *Problem Representation in Foreign Policy Decision Making*, Cambridge: Cambridge University Press.

't Hart, Paul (1990) *Groupthink in Government*, Amsterdam: Swets and Zeitlinger.

't Hart, Paul, Eric K. Stern, and Bengt Sundelius (eds.) (1997) *Beyond Groupthink: Political Group Dynamics and Foreign Policy-Making*, Ann Arbor: University of Michigan Press.

Taber, Charles S. (1997) "Cognitive Process Tracing through Computational Experiments," *The Political Psychologist*, 2(1):12–16.

Tanaka, Akihiko (1984) "China, China Watching, and CHINA_WATCHER," in *Foreign Policy Decision Making: Perception, Cognition, and Artificial Intelligence*, edited by Donald A. Sylvan and Steve Chan, New York: Praeger, 281–310.

Terhune, Kenneth W. (1970) "From National Character to National Behavior: A Reformulation," *Conflict Resolution*, 14(2):203–63.

Tetlock, Philip E. (1979) "Identifying Victims of Groupthink from Public Statements of Decision Makers," *Journal of Personality and Social Psychology*, 37:1314–24.

Thaler, Richard (2000) "Mental Accounting Matters," in *Choices, Values, and Frames*, edited by Daniel Kahneman and Amos Tversky, Cambridge: Cambridge University Press.

Thompson, Michael, Richard Ellis, and Aaron Wildavsky (1990) *Cultural Theory*, Boulder, CO: Westview.

Thorson, Stuart, and Donald A. Sylvan (1982) "Counterfactuals and the Cuban Missile Crisis," *International Studies Quarterly*, 26(December):539–71.

Triandis, Harry C. (1994) *Culture and Social Behavior*, New York: McGraw-Hill.

Tse, David K., et al. (1988) "Does Culture Matter? A Cross-Cultural Study of Executives' Choice, Decisiveness, and Risk Adjustment in International Marketing," *Journal of Marketing*, 52:81–95.

Tunander, Ola (1989) *Cold Water Politics: The Maritime Strategy and Geopolitics of the Northern Front*, London: Sage.

Uchitelle, Louis (2000) "He Didn't Say It. He Knew It All Along," *New York Times*, April 30, Section 3, 1.

Van Belle, Douglas (1993) "Domestic Imperatives and Rational Models of Foreign Policy Decision Making," in *The Limits of State Autonomy: Societal Groups and Foreign Policy Formulation*, edited by David Skidmore and Valerie M. Hudson, Boulder, CO: Westview, 151–83.

———(2000) *Press Freedom and Global Politics*, Westport, CT: Praeger.

Van Belle, Douglas, Jean-Sebastien Rioux, and David M. Potter (2004) *Media, Bureaucracies, and Foreign Aid: A Comparative Analysis of the United States, the United Kingdom, Canada, France, and Japan*, New York: Palgrave Macmillan.

Vasquez, John (1986) *Evaluating U.S. Foreign Policy*, Boulder, CO: Praeger.

Vasquez, John A. (1997) "The Realist Paradigm and Degenerative Versus Progressive Research Programs: An Appraisal of Neotraditional Research on Waltz's Balancing Proposition," *American Political Science Review*, 91:899–912.

Verba, S., and R. A. Brody (1970) "Participation, Policy Preferences, and the War in Vietnam," *Public Opinion Quarterly*, 34:325–32.

Verba, S., R. A. Brody, E. B. Parker, N. H. Nie, N. W. Polsby, P. Ekman, and G. Black (1967) "Public Opinion and the War in Vietnam," *American Political Science Review*, 61:317–33.

Vertzberger, Yaacov (1990) *The World in Their Minds: Information Processing, Cognition, and Perception in Foreign Policy Decisionmaking*, Stanford, CA: Stanford University Press.

———(1997) "Collective Risk Taking: The Decision-Making Group," in *Beyond*

Groupthink: Political Group Dynamics and Foreign Policy-Making, edited by 't Hart, Paul, Eric K. Stern, and Bengt Sundelius, Ann Arbor: University of Michigan Press, 275–308.

Voss, James, and Ellen Dorsey (1992) "Perception and International Relations: An Overview," in *Political Psychology and Foreign Policy*, edited by Eric Singer and Valerie M. Hudson, Boulder, CO: Westview, 3–30.

Voss, James, et al. (1991) "From Representation to Decision: An Analysis of Problem Solving in International Relations," in *Complex Problem Solving: Principle and Mechanisms*, edited by R. Sternberg and P. Frensch, Hillsdale, NJ: Erlbaum, 119–58.

Voss, J. C., C. R. Wolfe, J. Lawrence, and R. Engle (1991) "From Representation to Decision: An Analysis of Problem Solving in International Relations," in *Complex Problem Solving: Principles and Mechanisms* edited by R. Sternberg and P. Frensch, Hillsdale, NJ: Erlbaum, 119–58.

Walker, Stephen (1987) "The Correspondence between Foreign Policy Rhetoric and Behavior: Insights from Role Theory and Exchange Theory," in *Role Theory and Foreign Policy Analysis*, edited by Stephen Walker, Durham, NC: Duke University Press, 81–93.

Walker, Stephen G. (1977) "The Interface between Beliefs and Behavior: Henry A. Kissinger's Operational Code and the Vietnam War," *Journal of Conflict Resolution*, 21: 129–68.

———(ed.) (1987) *Role Theory and Foreign Policy Analysis*, Durham, NC: Duke University Press.

Walt, Stephen (1992) "Revolution and War," *World Politics*, 44:3 (April):321–68.

Waltz, Kenneth (1979) *Theory of International Politics*, Reading, MA: Addison Wesley.

Waltz, Kenneth N. (1986) "Reflections on *Theory of International Politics*: A Response to My Critics," in *Neorealism and its Critics*, edited by Robert Keohane, New York: Columbia University Press, 322–46.

———(2000) "Structural Realism after the Cold War," *International Security*, 25(1) (Summer):5–41.

Weber, Max (1930) *The Protestant Ethic and the Spirit of Capitalism* (trans. by Talcott Parsons), New York: Charles Scribner's Sons.

———(1951a) *The Religion of China* (trans. by H. Gerth), Glencoe, IL: Free Press.

———(1951b) *The Religion of India* (trans. by H. Gerth), Glencoe, IL: Free Press.

———(1963) *Sociology of Religion* (trans. by E. Fischoff), Boston: Beacon.

———(1964) *The Theory of Social and Economic Organizations* (trans. by A. M. Henderson and Talcott Parsons, edited by Talcott Parsons), New York: Free Press.

Weiner, David L. (2002) *Power Freaks*, Amherst, NY: Prometheus.

Weintraub, Walter (2003) "Verbal Behavior and Personality Assessment," in *The Psychological Assessment of Political Leaders*, edited by Jerrold Post, Ann Arbor: University of Michigan Press, 137–52.

Wendt, Alexander (1999) *Social Theory of International Politics*, Cambridge: Cambridge University Press.

Whorf, B. L. (1956) *Language, Thought, and Reality* (ed. J. B. Carroll), New York: Wiley.

Wiarda, Howard J. (1990) *Foreign Policy without Illusion: How Foreign Policy Making*

Works and Fails to Work in the United States, New York: Scott Foresman/Little, Brown.

Wight, Colin (1999) "They Shoot Dead Horses Don't They? Locating Agency in the Agent-Structure Problematique," *European Journal of International Relations*, 5(1) (March):109–42.

Wildavsky, Aaron (1987) "Choosing Preferences by Constructing Institutions: A Cultural Theory of Preference Formation," *American Political Science Review*, 81(1):3–21.

Wilkenfeld, Jonathan, et al. (1980) *Foreign Policy Behavior: The Interstate Behavior Analysis Model*, Beverly Hills, CA: Sage.

Wilkening, K. F. (1999) "Culture and Japanese Citizen Influence on the Transboundary Air Pollution Issue in Northeast Asia," *Political Psychology*, 20(4) (December):701–24.

Winter, David G. (1973) *The Power Motive*, New York: Free Press.

————(1990) Measuring Personality at a Distance: Development of an Integrated System for Scoring Motives in Running Text," in *Perspectives in Personality: Approaches to Understanding Lives*, edited by A .J. Stewart, J. M. Healy Jr., and D. J. Ozer, London: Jessica Kingsley Publishers.

————(2003) "Measuring the Motives of Political Actors," in *The Psychological Assessment of Political Leaders*, edited by Jerrold Post, Ann Arbor: University of Michigan Press, 153–77.

Winter, David G., Margaret G. Hermann, Walter Weintraub, and Stephen G. Walker (1991) "The Personalities of Bush and Gorbachev Measured at a Distance: Procedures, Portraits, and Policy," *Political Psychology*, 12(2):215–45.

Wish, Naomi (1980) "Foreign Policy Makers and Their National Role Conceptions," *International Studies Quarterly*, 24:532–43.

Wittkopf, Eugene (1994) *The Domestic Sources of American Foreign Policy: Insights and Evidence*, New York: St. Martin's.

Wittkopf, Eugene, with Michael A. Maggiotto (1981) "American Public Attitudes toward Foreign Policy," *International Studies Quarterly*, 25 (December):601–31.

Wuthnow, R. (1987) *Meaning and Moral Order: Explorations in Cultural Analysis*, Berkeley: University of California Press

Yankelovich, D. (1979) "Farewell to 'President Knows Best,'" *Foreign Affairs*, 57:670–93.

Young, Michael D. (2004) "ProfilerPlus Handbook," unpublished manuscript; see also www.socialscienceautomation.com.

Young, Michael D., and Mark Schafer (1998) "Is There Method in Our Madness? Ways of Assessing Cognition in International Relations," *Mershon International Studies Review*, 42:63–96.

Zimbardo P. G., and M. R. Leippe (1991) *The Psychology of Attitude Change and Social Influence*, New York: McGraw-Hill.

Zisk, Kimberly (1993) *Engaging the Enemy: Organization Theory and Soviet Military Innovation*, Princeton, NJ: Princeton University Press.

Zurovchak, J. F. (1997) "Cultural Influences on Foreign Policy Decisionmaking: Czech and Slovak Foreign Policy Organizations," in *Culture and Foreign Policy*, edited by Valerie M. Hudson, Boulder, CO: Rienner, 99–124.

Index

Abu Ghraib, 94
accountability, 7, 8
actor-specific theory, 6, 8, 11, 31, 32, 186, 191
Adams, Gerry, 122–23
affect, 20
agency/agents, 6, 8, 9, 194; agent-structure debate, 8, 10–14
Air Force, 78
Albright, Madeleine, 67
Allison, Graham, 19, 82, 89
Almond-Lippman consensus, 25
ambiguity. *See* situation
analogy/analogies, 18
anamnesis, 55–56
anarchy, 27, 153, 162
Andriole, Stephen, 170–73
Anglo-Irish Agreement, 122–23
Apple, 77
Army, 78, 79–80
attributes. *See* national attributes

Ball, Desmond, 118
Banerjee, Sanjoy, 114–15
Barber, James David, 54, 192
Bay of Pigs, 71–75, 140, 193
Beasley, Ryan, 72, 92
behavioralism, 20, 28
beliefs/belief systems, 13, 23, 51. *See also* individual, cognition

biases. *See* cognition
Bissell, Richard, 71
bounded rationality, 24, 41
Boynton, G. R., 18, 113
Brecher, Michael, 21, 22, 169–71, 172
Breslauer, George, 18
Breuning, Marijke, 105, 116
Bruck, H. W., 7
Bueno de Mesquita, Bruce, 125
Bundy, McGeorge, 71
bureaucratic politics/bureaucracy, 19–20, 27, 65, 75, 89–101, 186; action channels within, 90–91; coalitions within, 89, 93–94; compromise and, 89, 93; interagency committees and, 67, 79, 89; political games within, 89, 91–93, 95; resultants from, 89, 91; stakeholders within, 90; subversion through, 95–95
Burton, Dan, 90
Bush, George H. W., 48
Bush, George W., 63, 127, 137

Cabinda, 151–52
CACIS (Computer-Aided Conflict Information System), 29
Carter, Neal, 122
CASCON (Computer-Aided System for Handling Information on Local Conflicts), 29

Castro, Fidel, 73
CFP. *See* comparative foreign policy
Checkel, Jeffrey, 12, 13
China Hands, 83, 139
Choucri, Nazli, 147–48
CIA (Central Intelligence Agency), 37,
    55, 56, 59, 72, 77, 78, 79, 90
Clancy, Tom, 78
Clinton, Bill, 63, 112
cognition/cognitive processes and con-
    straints, 24, 40; attributions, 44, 51,
    53; biases, 40; cognitive dissonance,
    53; components of, 40; evaluation of
    evidence, 43–45; experts/expertise,
    39, 72, 92; heuristics/heuristic fallac-
    ies, 40, 41–45; memory, 41–42;
    mental models, 41, 51; pattern rec-
    ognition, 42, 63, 188; scripts/sche-
    mas, 24, 42, 50, 51; stereotypes, 40.
    See also beliefs, individual, percep-
    tion
cognitive maps/mapping, 24, 61–62, 63
Cold War, 10, 13, 15, 30, 31, 37, 103,
    136, 138, 152
Columbia/Columbia Accident Investi-
    gation Board (CAIB), 84–89
comparative foreign policy (CFP), 20–
    22, 23, 27, 28–30, 59
comparative politics, 28
Comprehensive Test Ban Treaty, 137
constructivism/constructivists, 9, 10–14
contingency plans/planning. *See* small
    group dynamics.
content analysis, 56–63, 114, 178; the-
    matic, 57; word count, 57. *See also*
    ProfilerPlus
Coolidge, Calvin, 55
COPDAB (Conflict and Peace Data
    Bank), 21
Cottam, Martha, 23, 63
Cottam, Richard, 23
CREON (Comparative Research on the
    Events of Nations), 21, 23, 59, 175,
    178–84, 187, 190
crisis. *See* situation
Cronkite, Walter, 141

Cuban Missile Crisis, 19, 38, 72, 82–83,
    92, 140, 144, 166, 193
culture and foreign policy, 7, 24, 32, 68,
    73, 103–23, 126, 183, 186; compar-
    ative strategic culture, 116; defini-
    tions of, 106–7; dramaturgical
    school (*see* role theory); heroic his-
    tory and, 105, 121; national charac-
    ter, 104, 107; national identity and,
    105, 117; organization of meaning,
    108–9, 111–15, 117; political cul-
    ture, 112; templates of strategy, 108,
    110–11; value preferences, 108,
    109–10

Dahl, Robert, 24, 126
DARPA (Defense Advanced Research
    Projects Agency), 20–21, 173
DDIR (Data Development for Interna-
    tional Relations), 21
decisionmaking, 8, 27, 31; group,
    17–20; and Richard Snyder et al., 15;
    theoretical intersection in, 7
decisions, foreign policy: characteriza-
    tion of, 4–5
democratic peace theory, 26, 125, 149
Department of Defense (DoD)/Penta-
    gon 76, 78, 79, 81, 88
de Rivera, Joseph, 22
Derrida, Jacques, 115
deterrence, 23, 37
discourse analysis, 32, 105, 106, 122
DNI (Directorate of National Intellli-
    gence), 77, 79, 80, 84
domestic political factors and foreign
    policy, 24–27, 32, 125–41, 186;
    actor characteristics, 129–31; and
    foreign policy, 135–41; influence of
    institutions on, 126; media and
    ("CNN effect"), 127, 133; proximity
    of actors, 128–29; rally 'round the
    flag and, 137; regime strategy and,
    131–35; regime type and, 126. *See
    also* regime
DON (Dimensions of Nations) Project,
    21
Douglas, Mary, 109, 111

dramaturgical school. *See* role theory
Dulles, Allen, 71
Dulles, John Foster, 57
Durkheim, Emile, 108

Eagleton, Thomas, 54
East, Maurice, 154
Eisenhower, Dwight, 55, 71, 139, 141
emotions. *See* individual
Etheredge, Lloyd, 62, 119
events data, 5, 20–21, 29, 173, 187;
  machine coding of, 21
EWAMS (Early Warning and Monitoring
  System), 29, 173
ExCom, 72, 92. *See also* Cuban Missile
  Crisis
expertise. *See* cognition

fallacies. *See* "heuristics" under cognition
Farnham, Barbara, 13
FBI (Federal Bureau of Investigation),
  77, 81, 90
FDA (Food and Drug Administration),
  90
FEMA (Federal Emergency Management
  Agency), 84
filters. *See* cognition, perception
Foreign Policy Analysis (FPA): evaluation and, 192; explanandum of, 4,
  20 (*see also* foreign policy behavior);
  explanans of, 5–6; future directions
  of, 185–94; general characteristics of,
  6; as ground of International Relations, 3, 6; historical overview of,
  14–33; and International Relations
  theory, 7–14
foreign policy behavior, 20, 143, 175,
  187
framing. *See* situation
Freud, Sigmund, 54
fundamental attribution error. *See*
  "attributions" under cognition

Gaenslen, Fritz, 118
Galtung, Johan, 161
Garrison, Jean, 75

Geertz, Clifford, 108–9
generalizations, cross-national, 15, 16,
  17; aggregate statistical analysis and,
  16, 20, 26
genotypes of nations, 15, 168–69
George, Alexander, 6, 22, 23, 54, 117,
  118, 191
Gilbert, Daniel, 46
Glad, Betty, 23
Gorbachev, Mikhail, 13, 31
Gore, Al, 114
Great Man approach, 37. *See also* individual
groups. *See* small group dynamics, organizations, bureaucratic politics
groupthink, 18, 67–75, 101, 193. *See*
  also small group dynamics
Grove, Andrea, 122
Guetzkow, Harold, 21

Haddad, Deborah, 74
Hagan, Joe, 25, 129
Halperin, Morton, 19–20, 76, 79, 94
Harding, Warren G., 55
Hegel, Friedrich, 11
Hermann, Charles F., 18, 66–67,
  178–79
Hermann, Margaret G., 23, 39, 58, 59–
  61, 62, 63, 118, 178, 191
Herrmann, Richard, 23
Heuer, Richards, 24, 41, 43
heuristics/heuristic fallacie. *See* cogni-
  tion
Hofstede, Geert, 109, 117
Holsti, Kal, 24, 116
Holsti, Ole, 23, 25, 57
Hoover, Herbert, 55
Hopple, Gerald, 170–73
Hoyt, Paul, 75
Hudson, Valerie, 119, 120, 174–77
Hume, John, 122–23
Huntington, Samuel, 103–4
Hussein, Saddam, 47, 58, 68, 90, 105,
  136, 145, 149

IBA (Interstate Behavior Analysis) Project, 21, 170–73

ICONS Project, 54
ideation/ideational, 7, 10
identity, national. *See* culture
image theory, 23, 63
imperialism, 159–62
implementation. *See* organizations
individual/individual level of analysis,
    22–24; age and, 49; attitudes, 32;
    character, 53; conceptual complexity,
    52; disease and pain, 48; drug use,
    48, 56; emotion, 32, 38, 45–47, 52,
    67, 74; ideology, 56; interest of a
    leader, 38; memory, 32, 50–53, 183;
    mental illness, 47, 56; methodolo-
    gies to assess, 54–63; personality, 52,
    56, 57, 60, 66; training of a leader,
    39; traits, 52, 55, 58, 60; values, 51,
    56. *See also* beliefs, motives, styles,
    cognition, perception
information processing. *See* cognition
INS (Inter-nation Simulation), 21
interagency committees. *See* bureau-
    cratic politics
integration, theoretical, 7, 16, 27, 33,
    165–84, 189;
goals of, 165–66; obstacles to, 166–67;
    rule-based production systems and,
    173–77
international political economy (IPE),
    26
International Relations, 30, 104, 107,
    109, 111, 125, 190; ground of, 3, 6;
    relationship to Foreign Policy Analy-
    sis, 7–14, 143

Janis, Irving, 18, 67–75, 190, 192–93
Jervis, Robert, 23
Johnson, Lyndon B., 55, 57, 105, 127,
    137–41

Kahneman, Daniel, 24, 41
Kaplan, Fred, 81–82
Kaplan, Morton, 26, 154–56
Katzenstein, Lawrence, 119
Katzenstein, Peter, 26
KEDS (Kansas Events Data System), 21
Kegley, Charles, 26, 28

Kennedy, John F., 38, 48, 53, 55, 57,
    71–75, 82, 92, 140
Kennedy, Robert, 71, 72
Khamenei, Ali, 63
Khong, Yuen Foong, 18
Khruschev, Nikita, 72
Kim Jong Il, 38
Korean War, 18

Larson, Deborah Welch, 23
Lasswell, Harold, 22
lateral pressure, 147–48
leaders. *See* individual
Lebow, Richard Ned, 23
Leites, Nathan, 22, 117
Lenin, Vladimir Ilyich, 159–62
Linton, Ralph, 110
long cycles. *See* systems
Lotz, Hellmut, 113–14

Majeski, Stephen, 113
March, James, 82
Marines, 78
Marx, Karl, 11, 158–62
Marxism-Leninism, 158–62
material/materialism, 7, 10
McCarthy, Joseph, 83, 139, 140, 141
McCone, John, 83, 166
McDermott, Rose, 45
McNamara, Robert, 92
Mead, Margaret, 108
memory. *See* individual
Mendel, Gregor, 15, 168
methodology/methodological issues,
    17, 27–30, 32, 173, 188–89; at-a-
    distance methodologies for leaders,
    54–63
Microsoft, 77
Milliken, Jennifer, 113
Milner, Helen, 125, 126, 129
Mintz, Alex, 54
misperception. *See* perception
Mitterand, François, 58
models, mental. *See* cognition
Modelski, George, 157–58
Morris, Edmund, 14

motives/motivations, 23, 52–53, 54, 56. *See* also individual

NAFTA (North American Free Trade Agreement), 114
NASA, 76, 84–89
national attributes, 26, 144–53; demographics, 147–49; economic capabilities, 150–53; geography, 146–47; military capabilities, 149–50; natural resources, 145–46; political system, 149; size, 144–45
National Counterterrorism Center, 90
national role conception (NRC), 24, 32, 116, 118. *See also* role theory
National Science Foundation, 21
Navy, 77, 78, 82, 132
negotiation(s), 37, 50, 56, 115–16
neoliberalism, 10
neorealism, 10–14, 30, 153
neuroscience, 32, 46, 184, 188
Nixon, Richard, 38, 48, 53, 55, 57, 71, 137, 139, 141
North, Robert, 147–48
NSA (National Security Agency), 81
NSC (National Security Council), 89, 127

operational code, 22, 23, 63, 118
opinion: mass, 25–26, 28; elite, 25–26
organizations/organizational process and behavior, 15, 19–20, 75–89; budget, 19, 76, 78–79, 84; and complexity, 80; essence, 19, 76–78; implementation of policy, 19, 65, 82, 183; inertia, 19, 81; innovation, 19; mission, 19; morale, 19, 76, 79; organizational culture, 77, 89; SOP (standard operating procedures), 19, 82–83, 84, 88, 89; specialization of function, 76; survival, 19; turf, 19, 76, 78, 84, 89. *See also* bureaucratic politics
orientations, foreign policy. *See* Hermann, Margaret G.

Paige, Glenn, 17
parsimony/parsimonious, 10, 28–29, 188
Parsons, Talcott, 108
pattern recognition. *See* cognition
Pentagon. *See* Department of Defense
perception, 16, 23, 40, 41. *See also* cognition, individual
Perot, Ross, 114
personal characteristics. *See* individual
political science, 27, 109
Post, Jerrold, 47, 54, 55–56, 68, 191
prediction, 29, 166, 167, 191
ProfilerPlus, 62–63. *See also* content analysis
prospect theory, 50
psychobiography, 54–56, 57
psychology, 27, 28, 39. *See also* individual
psychomilieu, 16
Putnam, Robert, 7, 25, 28, 128
Pye, Lucian 104

Q-sort, 62, 172

rational choice theory/rational choice, 30, 32, 45, 111, 121, 125. *See also* unified rational actor, rational choice
rationality. *See* rational choice, unified rational actor, bounded rationality, cognition
Reagan, Ronald 13, 14, 55, 127
realism/Realpolitik, 10–14, 121, 192
regime/regime types: fragmentation thereof, 25, 129; and leader influence, 38, 47; vulnerability, 25, 129. *See also* domestic political factors
Richardson, Neil, 26
risky shift. *See* small group dynamics
role theory, 24; dramaturgical school, 110, 118, 143. *See also* national role conception
Roosevelt, Franklin Delano, 55, 77, 138
Rose, Gideon, 11
Rosenau, James, 14, 15–16, 20, 25, 26, 28, 30, 167–69
Rossa, Paul, 170–73

rule-based production systems. *See* integration
Rusk, Dean, 71

Sampson, Martin, 116
Sapin, Burton, 7
schemas. *See* cognition
Schlesinger, Arthur, 71, 72
Schrodt, Philip, 42
Schwartz, Barry, 46
scientism, 20, 28–29
scripts. *See* cognition
sensory information. *See* cognition
Shafer, Mark, 63
Shih, Chih-Yu, 119
Shiller, Robert, 46
Simon, Herbert, 24, 41, 82
situation: ambiguity within, 38, 67; context for decisionmaking, 49–50; crisis, 38, 49–50, 66, 67; definition of, 8; framing of, 32, 91–92; uncertainty within, 22, 38, 67
situational predisposition, 174–77. *See also* rule-based production systems
Slovic, Paul, 24, 41
small group dynamics, 17–19, 39, 66–75; contingency planning by, 72, 81, 122; dehumanization of outgroups by, 70; insincere agreement within, 70, 72; risky shift, 70; structure, 66. *See also* groupthink
Snyder, Richard, 7, 8, 14, 17
social constructions, 7, 10–14. *See also* constructivism
Sprout, Harold and Margaret, 15, 16, 22, 26
Stasser, Garold, 74
state: as a metaphysical abstraction, 4, 5, 7, 9, 15
State Department, 76, 77, 83, 94
Stewart, Philip, 178
Stein, Janice Gross, 23
stereotypes. *See* cognition
Stern, Eric, 74
Stoessinger, John, 137–38, 141
stress, 22, 48, 70. *See also* situation
structures/structuralism, 12

style: decision, 23, 56; interpersonal, 23, 56; leadership, 39, 56, 118. *See also* individual, cognition
Sylvan, David, 113
Sylvan, Donald, 18, 74
substitutability of foreign policy, 8
Sundelius, Bengt, 74
Swidler, Ann, 110
systems/system-level analysis, 12, 13, 26, 31, 153–62; long cycles, 157–58; system change, 156–62; system rules, 154

Taft, William Howard, 55
Tetlock, Philip, 18
't Hart, Paul, 68, 74
theory: actor-general, 16, 27, 31, 32, 120, 186; grand, 15, 30; mid-range, 16, 30, 31. *See also* actor-specific theory, integration
think-aloud protocols, 61, 184
Treasury, 77
Triandis, Harry, 109
Truman, Harry, 55, 138
Tunander, Ola, 115
two-level game, 7, 25, 28, 32, 128
Tversky, Amos, 24, 41

uncertainty. *See* situation
unitary rational actor, 3, 19, 75, 76. *See also* bounded rationality, rational choice, rationality
values. *See* individual

Van Belle, Douglas, 132
Vasquez, John, 11, 193
Verbal Behavior Analysis (VBA), 63. *See also* content analysis, ProfilerPlus
Verbs In Context System (VICS), 63, 118. *See also* content analysis, ProfilerPlus
Vietnam War, 18–20, 25, 39, 79, 83, 105, 127, 137–41
Villard, Henry, 94
Vertzberger, Yaacov, 75, 112, 118
Voss, James, 18

Walker, Stephen, 24, 63, 116, 117
Walt, Stephen, 23
Waltz, Kenneth, 10–14, 27, 125
war, 26
Weber, Max, 19, 108, 110
Weintraub, Walter, 63
WEIS (World Event/Interaction Survey), 21, 172, 187
Whorfian hypothesis, 109
Wight, Colin, 11, 12
Wildavsky, Aaron, 109, 111

Wilkenfeld, Jonathan, 169–73
Wilkening, Kenneth, 117, 121
Wilson, Woodrow, 48, 54, 55
Winter, David, 53

XAIDS (Crisis Management Executive Decision Aids), 29

Young, Michael, 62–63

Zelikow, Philip, 89
Zurovchak, John, 116–17

About the Author

Valerie M. Hudson is professor of political science at Brigham Young University. She received her doctorate in political science from the Ohio State University in 1983, and taught previously at Northwestern University and Rutgers University. Hudson served as director of graduate studies in the David M. Kennedy Center for International and Area Studies for eight years. Her research foci include national security affairs, foreign policy analysis, and gender in international relations. Hudson has previously served as the president of the Foreign Policy Analysis section of the International Studies Association. She is the author of numerous articles and volumes; her latest book is *Bare Branches: Security Implications of Asia's Surplus Male Population,* co-authored with Andrea Den Boer. This book won the Otis Dudley Duncan Award as well as the American Association of Publishers' Award for the Best Book in Political Science in 2004. Hudson is also the recipient of several teaching and research honors, including the Karl G. Maeser Excellence in Teaching Award, and has received National Science Foundation support for a research project with Philip A. Schrodt on new social science methodologies.

Breinigsville, PA USA
22 April 2010
236617BV00002B/2/P